NATIONAL GEOGRAPHIC LEARNING | CENGAGE Learning

D1919594

Life

ELEMENTARY STUDENT'S BOOK

John Hughes
Paul Dummett
Helen Stephenson

Contents Split Edition A

Listening	Reading	Critical thinking	Speaking	Writing
an explorer talking about a photographer an interview with an explorer people at a conference	an article about a family of explorers an article about world population	the writer's purpose	asking questions friends and family facts about countries	text type: a personal description writing skill: *and*, *but*
someone talking about a family's plastic possessions an interview with Andy Torbet	an article about four apartments in Seoul an article about a global product	close reading	your objects and possessions a room in your home where things are from	a description of a room in your home text type: adverts writing skill: describing objects with adjectives
someone talking about a 24-hour restaurant in Norway an interview with a student living in London an interview with Beverley Goodman	an article about no-car zones an article about languages spoken around the world	relevance	your life exchanging information about a photographer favourite numbers and their relevance	text type: a description of a place writing skill: capital letters
three people talking about their free-time activities an interview with Norbert Rosing	an article about identical twins an article about a nature photographer an article about extreme sports an advert for volunteer work	fact or opinion	likes and dislikes daily life your abilities	text type: short emails writing skill: reference words
someone talking about a noodle chef in Chinatown people describing famous dishes from their countries a conversation at a market	an article about food markets around the world an article about the Svalbard Global Seed Vault	summarising	famous dishes from different countries planning a special meal buying food at a market summarising an article	text type: instructions writing skill: punctuation
someone talking about a street musician an interview with two people at a museum people asking for money in different situations	an article about currency an article about treasure an article about the history of money	relevance	someone's past life important years in your life a survey about money	a description of someone's life text type: thank you messages writing skill: formal and informal expressions

Contents Split Edition B

Listening	Reading	Critical thinking	Speaking	Writing
someone talking about the Mayflower a programme about journeys in history a programme about animal migration	an article about a flight from the past an article about space travel	fact or opinion	a journey you made your opinion a general knowledge quiz	a general knowledge quiz text type: a travel blog writing skill: *so, because*
someone describing the Dinagyang festival a conversation about masks at a festival	an article about a fashion photographer an article about tattoos a text about emoticons	close reading	people's appearance what people are wearing	text type: texts and online messages writing skill: textspeak
someone talking about an outdoor cinema two people at a film festival an interview with Adrian Seymour two people discussing a Broadway show	an article about the *All roads film festival* an article about a wildlife filmmaker an article about nature in art	the writer's preferences	deciding which films to see your future plans explaining preferences	text type: reviews and comments writing skill: giving your opinion with sense verbs
someone talking about the human brain an interview with someone about technology a news report about a memory champion someone phoning his office	a survey about outdated technology jigsaw reading about memory an article about new inventions	the main argument and supporting information	experience with technology something you have learned	the main argument text type: a telephone message writing skill: imperatives
someone talking about their holiday a podcast from a travel programme two friends discussing a trip to South America	a quiz from a travel magazine a tourist information leaflet a travel article	arguments for and against	advice for a tourist rules what's important in a hotel	a description of a tourist destination text type: a feedback form writing skill: closed and open questions
a documentary about a photographer an interview about film director James Cameron and the Mariana Trench	maps showing climate change an article about unexplored places on Earth an article about a new planet an article about Earth Day	structuring an argument	your future places on Earth life on another planet	text type: a poster writing skill: important words and information

Video in Split Editions A and B

Life around the world

Unit 1 World party

How big is seven billion?

Unit 7 Women in space

The story of the first female astronauts.

Unit 10 Memory and language learning

Compare ways of learning languages.

Unit 12 Volcanoes

The science and history of Earth's most amazing places.

Unit 3 Cowley Road

See the people and places on an English road.

Unit 9 Camera traps

How a director films the secret lives of animals.

Unit 4 In my free time

Interviews with real people about their passions.

Unit 5 Gelato University

Learn how to make ice cream in Italy.

Unit 8 Festivals and special events

Visit some of the world's most colourful festivals.

Unit 6 Bactrian teasure

Discover the history of an ancient civilisation.

Unit 11 Mecca and the Hajj

Follow people who take religious holidays.

Unit 2 Coober Pedy's opals

Go under a town in Australia for opals.

Split Editions A and B

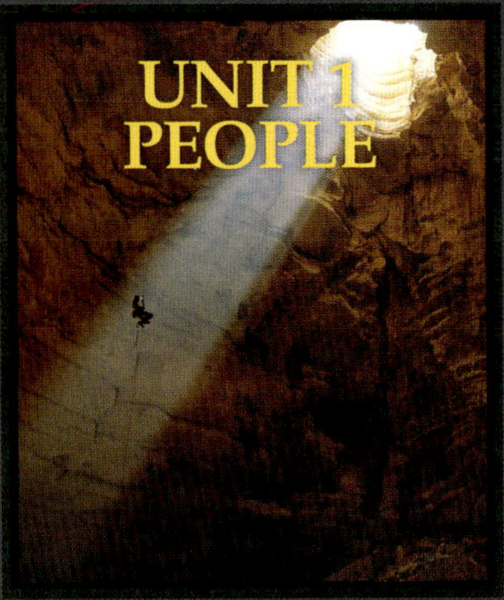

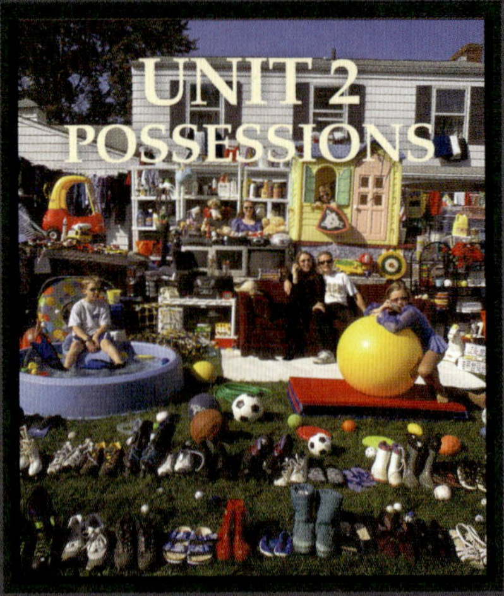

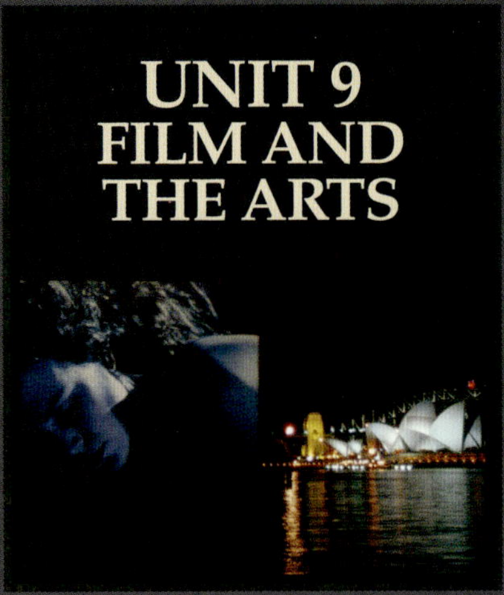

Unit 7 Journeys

The journey of Mayflower II
Photo by B. Anthony Stewart

FEATURES

1 Look at the photo and the caption. What transport can you see? Is this the first Mayflower ship or the second?

2 **2.1** Listen to a description of the first Mayflower. How many people travelled across the Atlantic Ocean in 1620? How many times did the Mayflower sail across the Atlantic Ocean?

3 Choose the correct travel verbs to complete the text about the Mayflower II in the photo.

> The Mayflower II is a copy of the seventeenth century ship, the Mayflower. The ship [1] *sailed / flew* from England to the USA in 1957. It [2] *arrived in / left* England on 20th April with thirty-four crew. The journey was similar to the first Mayflower. The weather was good, but later, there were bad storms at sea. It [3] *arrived in / left* the USA on 12th June and hundreds of people [4] *travelled / drove* by sea and air to meet the ship. Nowadays, you can see the Mayflower II in Plymouth Harbour, Massachusetts in the USA.

4 Work in pairs. Ask and answer the questions. Use these verbs.

> cycle drive fly sail take (public transport)
> travel by (car/train/ship, etc.)

1 How do you normally travel to work (or school)?
2 What's your favourite way to travel? Why?
3 What's your favourite journey? Why?

reading a journey from the past • grammar past simple: negatives • listening journeys in history • grammar past simple: questions and short answers • speaking a journey in the past

7a Flight of the Silver Queen

Reading

1 Look at the photo and map of a journey. Where was the flight from and to?

2 The article about the journey is in the wrong order. Number the paragraphs 1 to 4.

3 Read the article again. Are these sentences true (T) or false (F)?

1 The journey was in 1920.
2 All the aeroplanes landed in Cape Town.
3 The first part of the journey was from England to Italy.
4 Van Ryneveld and Brand stopped between Italy and Cairo.
5 They didn't have any problems with the plane's engine.
6 They left Bulawayo in the *Silver Queen*.
7 The journey took 44 days.
8 They received £10,000 from the newspaper.

4 Discuss these questions as a class.

1 Why do you think these pilots went on these journeys?
2 Was it for money or was it for something else?
3 Would you like to go on a similar journey?

Grammar past simple: negatives

5 Look at these two sentences from the article. Answer the questions.

Four aeroplanes didn't finish the journey.
The newspaper didn't give them £10,000.

1 What is the auxiliary verb in past simple negative sentences?
2 Does the negative auxiliary verb change for *I/you/we/they* and *he/she/it*?
3 What form of the verb is after the negative auxiliary?

Flight of the SILVER QUEEN

A ☐
It was a long and dangerous journey. Van Ryneveld and Quintin Brand flew in a plane called the *Silver Queen*. They travelled from England to Italy. Then, a few days later, they took off again for Egypt. They didn't stop over the Mediterranean Sea and landed the next day in Cairo.

B ☐
Eventually, 44 days later, they landed in Cape Town and won. However, the newspaper didn't give them £10,000, but only £5,000. This was because they didn't use the same plane for the whole journey. But it was still an incredible journey.

C ☐
In 1920, a British newspaper offered £10,000 to fly from England to South Africa. Five aeroplanes entered the competition, but four aeroplanes didn't finish the journey. The pilots Pierre Van Ryneveld and Quintin Brand finally landed in Cape Town and won the race.

D ☐
Through Africa, they had a lot of mechanical problems with the plane and its engine. The worst problem was in Bulawayo. The *Silver Queen* couldn't take off so in the end they changed their plane for a different one.

take off (v) /ˈteɪkˌɒf/ to leave the ground (for aeroplanes)
land (v) /lænd/ to return to the ground (for aeroplanes)

> **PAST SIMPLE: NEGATIVES**
>
> I/you/he/she/it/we/they **didn't** fly.
> (not: *They ~~didn't flew~~.*)
>
> For further information and practice, see page 83.

6 Work in pairs. Make true sentences about the 1920s with the words in this table. Use the affirmative or negative form of the past simple.

In the 1920s, people		travel pay play use	into space by train by credit card with cash games computer games maps satellite navigation
	didn't		

Example:
In the 1920s, people didn't travel into space.
In the 1920s, people travelled by train.

7 Write down three things you didn't do ten years ago, but you do now. Tell your partner.

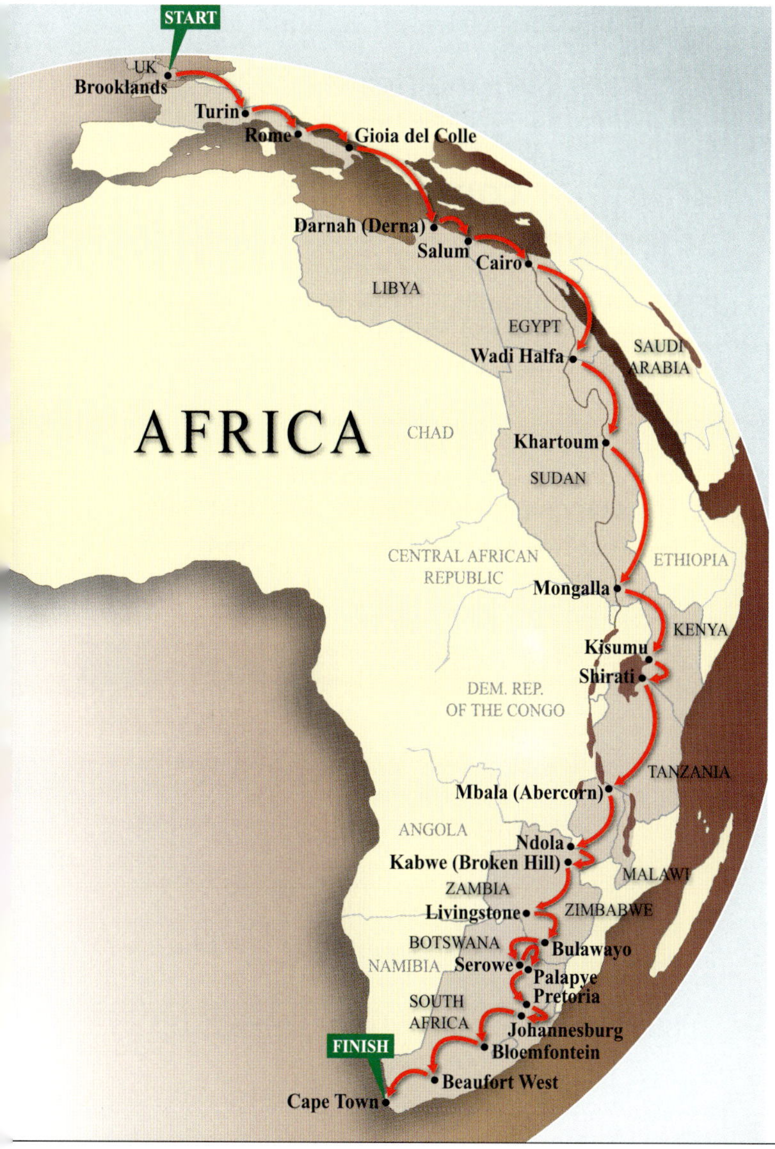

Listening

8 2.2 Listen to part of a radio programme called *Journeys in history*. Number these topics in the order they discuss them (1–3).

a the reasons why they travelled
b where the *Silver Queen* travelled
c who the pilots were

9 2.2 Listen again and choose the correct options to complete the sentences.

1 Pierre Van Ryneveld and Quintin Brand *had / didn't have* maps for Europe, Egypt and South Africa.
2 They *had / didn't have* maps for other parts of Africa.
3 Van Ryneveld and Brand *went / didn't go* for the money.
4 They *wanted / didn't want* to be the first.

Grammar past simple: questions and short answers

10 Look at the two questions from the radio programme. What is the auxiliary verb in past simple questions?

Did Pierre Van Ryneveld and Quintin Brand have maps?
Why did they go on this journey?

> **PAST SIMPLE: QUESTIONS AND SHORT ANSWERS**
>
> ***Yes/No* questions and short answers**
> Did they go to London?
> Yes, they did. / No, they didn't.
> ***Wh-* questions**
> When did they do? Why did they go?
>
> For further information and practice, see page 83.

11 Work in pairs. In 1999, three modern pilots went on a similar journey to Van Ryneveld and Brand.

Student A: Turn to page 81.
Student B: Turn to page 82.

Speaking

12 Think about a journey you made in the past. Answer these questions.

- Where did you go?
- Why did you go?
- How did you travel there?
- Did you have any problems?
- How long did the journey take?

13 Work in pairs. Tell your partner about your journey.

7b Animal migrations

Vocabulary journey adjectives

1 Read the text. What kind of journeys does it describe?

Every year, animals around the world go on long and difficult journeys. Sea animals swim across oceans and birds fly north and south with the seasons. And there are the land animals such as the Wildebeest (below). They go on a slow and dangerous journey every year from the Serengeti into Kenya for food and water.

migration (n) /ˈmaɪɡreɪʃn/ when an animal travels from one place to another at different times of the year

2 These adjectives describe travel and journeys. Find the opposite adjectives in the text.

easy fast safe short

3 Work in pairs. Describe these journeys to and from your home with adjectives from Exercises 1 and 2.

1 My journey to work is …
2 The journey home at night is …
3 The bus to the city centre is very …

Listening

4 2.3 Look at the three animals on page 13 and listen to a biologist describing their migration. Match the animals (1–3) with the distances (a–c).

1 saiga
2 loggerhead turtle
3 tree frog

a 30 metres
b 35 kilometres per day
c 14,000 kilometres in fifteen years

male (n/adj) /meɪl/ [male symbol]
female (n/adj) /ˈfiːmeɪl/ [female symbol]
calf (n) /kɑːf/ a baby saiga
lay eggs /leɪ egz/ when a female animal produces eggs

5 2.3 Listen again. Answer the questions.

1 Where does the saiga live?
2 What does the female saiga have in the spring?
3 Where does the loggerhead turtle leave as a baby?
4 Where does the female lay her eggs?
5 Where does the tree frog lay its eggs?

Grammar comparative adjectives

6 We use comparative adjectives to compare two things. Look at the comparative adjectives in these sentences from the listening. Answer the questions.

Many turtles swim longer distances than other sea animals.
The journey is more difficult for a female saiga.

1 What two letters do you add to short adjectives?
2 What word comes before long adjectives?

COMPARATIVE ADJECTIVES

One-syllable adjectives: *It's a warm country.* → *It's warmer than other countries.*
Adjectives ending in one vowel + one consonant: *It's a big animal.* → It's bi**gg**er than a saiga.
Two-syllable adjectives ending -*y*: *It's an easy journey.* → *It's an easier journey.*
Two (or more) syllable adjectives: *It's a **difficult** job.* → *It's **more difficult** than other jobs.*

There are some irregular adjectives: *good* → *better, bad* → *worse*

For further information and practice, see page 83.

1 saiga

2 loggerhead turtle

3 tree frog

7 Complete the table with comparative adjectives.

Adjective	Comparative adjective
big	1 ....
cold	2 ....
hot	3 ....
dangerous	4 ....
cheap	5 ....
expensive	6 ....
long	7 ....
interesting	8 ....
easy	9 ....
high	10 ....

Word focus *than*

8 When we compare two things, we often use *than* after the comparative adjective (e.g. *Africa is hotter than Europe.*). Make similar sentences about these pairs with a comparative adjective + *than*.

1 Australia / Antarctica
2 a car / a bicycle
3 rock-climbing / surfing
4 travel by air / by sea
5 an elephant / a lion
6 a holiday in the city / camping in the countryside
7 Paris / New York
8 train journeys / plane journeys

9 Pronunciation stressed and weak syllables /ə/

2.4 Listen to the stressed and weak syllables in these sentences. Then listen again and repeat.

1 Africa is hotter than Europe. (/ə/ /ə/)
2 Australia isn't colder than Antarctica. (/ə/ /ə/)

Speaking

10 Look at these possible answers from Exercise 8. Which sentence is a fact and which is opinion? Which other sentences are opinions? Say them again with these phrases.

Antarctica is colder than Australia.
Rock-climbing is more dangerous than surfing.

I think ...
In my opinion ...

11 Write sentences with your opinion. Compare two:

- places or cities
- sports or free-time activities
- types of travel
- types of holiday
- places in the city
- types of transport
- famous people

12 Work in pairs. Take turns to read out your opinions. Do you agree with your partner?

I think London is more expensive than Dubai.
I agree! / I don't agree!

7c The longest journey in space

Reading

1 Do you think it's important to travel in space? Why? / Why not?

2 Look at the photos and read the caption on page 15. What is the name of the spacecraft? What did it take photos of?

3 Read the article. Answer the questions.

1 How many Voyager spacecrafts did NASA send into the solar system?
2 Which planets did Voyager 1 visit?
3 Which planets did Voyager 2 visit?
4 Where are the Voyager spacecrafts now?

4 Read the article again. Replace the underlined words in the sentences (1–7) with these words.

Florida Jupiter's Neptune outside the solar system Saturn Uranus Voyager 2

1 NASA sent Voyager 1 and 2 from here.
2 It had a mechanical problem with the camera.
3 This planet is famous for its rings.
4 Scientists learned a lot about its weather.
5 Voyager 2 went to this planet last.
6 This planet is very cold and has lots of ice.
7 Voyager 1 and 2 are on a journey there now.

Critical thinking fact or opinion

5 Look at the first two sentences in paragraph 1 of the article. Which sentence is a fact? Which sentence includes the writer's opinion?

6 Find more sentences in paragraphs 2, 3 and 4 with the writer's opinion.

Grammar superlative adjectives

7 Look at these two sentences. Which sentence compares two things? Which sentence compares more than two things in a group?

a Saturn is smaller than Jupiter.
b Jupiter is the largest planet in the solar system.

> **SUPERLATIVE ADJECTIVES**
>
> It's the largest planet.
> It's the most dangerous place.
>
> For further information and practice, see page 84.

8 Underline the superlative form of these adjectives in the article. Which of the adjectives are irregular? What word comes before the superlative adjective?

good famous cold far amazing

9 Complete the quiz about the planets in our solar system with the superlative form of the adjectives. Then answer the questions. Check your answers on page 81.

1 Which planet is .... (near) to the Sun?
2 Which planet is .... (easy) to see in the sky?
3 Which planet is .... (far) from the Earth?
4 Which planet is the .... (good) for human life?
5 Which planet is the .... (hot)?

Writing and speaking

10 Work in groups. Follow the instructions.

1 Write another general knowledge quiz on different subjects. Write five quiz questions with superlatives.
2 Compete with another group. Ask and answer your questions. Which team got the most correct answers?

Voyager 1 photographed these planets and moons on its journey through our solar system.

The LONGEST JOURNEY IN SPACE

On 20th August and 5th September in 1977, two spacecrafts took off from Florida, USA. Voyager 1 and Voyager 2 started a long and difficult journey to the end of the solar system. They flew past new places in our solar system and sent photos of planets and moons to NASA (National Aeronautics and Space Administration).

Voyager 1's journey

Voyager 1 arrived at Jupiter, the largest planet in the solar system. At a distance of 349,000 kilometres from Earth, scientists received the best photographs of the planet from Voyager 1 and they discovered a lot about the planet's weather from them. They studied the clouds, lightning and strong winds of three hundred kilometres per hour. Jupiter also has a moon with volcanoes. Voyager 1's next stop was Saturn. Saturn is smaller than Jupiter and it's most famous for its rings. From Voyager 1's photographs, scientists discovered the rings are mostly water and ice.

Voyager 2's journey

Voyager 2 also visited Jupiter and Saturn after Voyager 1, but then it continued to Uranus. Uranus is the coldest planet in the solar system. There is a lot of ice on the surface. During its journey round Uranus, there were mechanical problems with Voyager 2's camera. Eventually, scientists fixed it and Voyager 2 travelled to Neptune. Neptune is the furthest planet from the sun (4.5 billion kilometres) and it was the last planet on Voyager 2's journey.

The journey continues

The two Voyagers finished their official journeys in 1989, but they continued travelling. Now they are at the end of our solar system and scientists think the two spacecrafts can travel until 2025. So Voyager 1 and 2 are on their most amazing journey: into space outside our solar system.

7d How was your trip?

Vocabulary *journey, travel* or *trip*?

1 Look at the sentences (1–3). Then match the nouns *journey*, *travel* and *trip* to the definitions (a–c).

1 My **journey** through the Gobi desert was amazing! It took three months.
2 **Travel** is good for you because you learn about different places.
3 I had a short business **trip** to Berlin for two days.

a the activity of going from one place to another place
b when you travel a long distance from one place to another
c when you travel somewhere for short time and return to the same place

2 How often do you go on a trip? Why do you go (e.g. for work)?

3 Look at the pictures from a work trip. Which of these words can you use to describe each part of the trip?

comfortable   delicious   really useful   tiring   terrible   very interesting

A

B

C

D

E

F

WORDBUILDING *really/very* + adjective

You can make some adjectives stronger with *really* and *very*. For example:
The journey was tiring. → *The journey was* ***very*** *tiring /* ***really*** *tiring.*

For further information and practice, see Workbook page 101.

Real life asking about a trip

4 2.5 Doctor Egan is a biologist. Listen to two conversations he has about his trip. For each conversation, answer these questions.

1 Is Doctor Egan still on the trip or is he back in his own country?
2 What parts of the trip does the other person ask about?
3 What is Doctor Egan's answer? What adjectives does he use?

5 2.5 Listen again and complete the questions from the conversations.

ASKING ABOUT A TRIP

1 .... your flight?
2 .... comfortable?
3 .... try the local food?
What 4 .... the weather .... ?
Why? What 5 .... ?

6 **Pronunciation** intonation in questions

2.6 Listen to the questions in Exercise 4. Notice the intonation. Then listen again and repeat with the same intonation.

7 Work in pairs. Student A went on the trip in the pictures in Exercise 3. Act out this conversation.

Student A: Answer Student B's questions about the trip.

Student B: Ask Student A questions about his/her trip.

8 Change roles and have another conversation about a trip. Use the pictures on page 81.

7e The digital nomad

Vocabulary online writing

1 Discuss these questions as a class.

1 Do you read blogs? Which are your favourite blogs?
2 Do you write a blog? What is it about?

2 Read about Andrew Evans. Why is his blog called 'Digital Nomad'? What does he write about?

Travel Home | Top 10 | Destinations A-Z | Trip Ideas |

Digital Nomad
TRAVEL DISPATCHES FROM ANDREW EVANS

Andrew Evans is a blogger for *National Geographic's* website. He's called 'The Digital Nomad' because he travels all the time and he's always online. Every day he blogs about his journeys. He writes posts from different countries and uploads videos of amazing places. Readers can also leave Andrew a comment on his articles.

His homepage is http://digitalnomad.nationalgeographic.com/

3 Match the highlighted words in Exercise 2 with the definitions.

1 a group of pages with information on a subject
2 writes an online diary
3 connected to and using the Internet
4 the first page of a website
5 person who writes for a blog or blogs
6 adds sound, video or pictures to a website or blog
7 a reply or opinion from a reader
8 articles on a blog

Writing a travel blog

4 Read a post about a bus journey on a travel blog. Answer the questions.

1 Where is he?
2 How many days is the journey?
3 What can he see?
4 What happened to the bus?
5 Why did he feel sorry for the bus driver?
6 Why did he walk to the border?

5 Writing skill *so, because*

a Look at *so* and *because* in the third paragraph of the blog in Exercise 4. Which word is about a) the reason for something? b) the result of or response for something?

b Complete the sentences with *so* or *because*.

1 We stopped at a restaurant .... I was hungry.
2 The train was late .... we waited for it.
3 We put on sun cream .... the weather was very hot.
4 It started raining .... we bought an umbrella.
5 I wanted a comfortable bed .... I booked an expensive hotel.
6 We hired a car .... there were no trains or buses.

6 Write a short travel blog about a journey or place you visited. Think about these questions. Use *so* and *because*.

- Where were you?
- When was it?
- Who was there?
- What happened?

7 Work in pairs. Exchange blogs. Use these questions to check your partner's blog.

- Did he/she answer the questions in Exercise 6?
- Did he/she use *so* and *because*?

Today was the final day of my bus journey from Lhasa to Kodari at the border with Nepal. It's the highest road in the world. It's also a very long journey. You travel for three days through the Himalayas and you can see the north side of Everest.

This afternoon, we were only ten kilometres from Kodari and suddenly the bus stopped. The driver got out and looked at the engine. For the next three hours, he tried to fix it, but it didn't start.

Finally, a lot of the passengers got out and started to walk to the border. I felt sorry for the bus driver because he looked a bit sad. However, I also wanted a good hotel and a hot meal so I also left the bus and walked to Kodari.

7f Women in space

Sally Ride, an astronaut with NASA

Before you watch

1 Look at the photo of Sally Ride and read the caption. Discuss the questions.

1 What is her job?
2 Would you like to do this job? Why? / Why not?

2 Work in pairs. Read the sentences and choose the option you think is correct.

1 Sally Ride was the first *woman in space / American woman in space*.
2 She spent six *days / months* in space.
3 She *travelled / never travelled* into space again.
4 After Sally's journey, *other women / no other women* went into space.

While you watch

3 Watch the video and check your answers in Exercise 2.

4 Watch the video again. Match the years (1–8) with the events (a–h).

1 1958	3 1983	5 1984	7 1995
2 1969	4 1963	6 1992	8 2005

a the first Russian woman in space
b Sally Ride's second journey into space
c the first female pilot of a space shuttle
d the first man on the Moon
e Eileen's Collins' third flight
f the first American women in space
g NASA began
h the first African-American woman in space

5 Watch the video again. Choose the correct answers (a–c) for each question. Some questions have more than one answer.

1 What does the phrase 'space was a man's world' mean?
  a All the US astronauts were men.
  b Only men worked for NASA.
  c American women didn't want to go to space.
2 How many women were in the group of candidates to be the first female astronaut.
  a two b six c ten
3 What did Sally do in space?
  a She helped to launch two satellites.
  b She did scientific experiments.
  c She flew the Challenger space shuttle.
4 What did she do after she returned from space?
  a She left NASA.
  b She gave talks across the USA.
  c She trained other female astronauts.
5 What was Mae Jamison's job before she became an astronaut?
  a She was a doctor of Physics.
  b She was a physician.
  c She didn't have a job.
6 At the end of the video we hear: 'Young women – as well as young men – now dream of becoming astronauts and a journey into space.' Why is this?
  a Because of the space shuttle.
  b Because of Sally Ride's journey.
  c Because of female astronauts.

After you watch

6 Role play an interview with Sally Ride

Work in pairs.

Student A: You are Sally Ride. Answer a journalist's questions about your journey into space. Use the information in the video and prepare notes about:

- what you did before you were an astronaut
- the first flight on the Challenger space shuttle
- what you did in space
- what you did after you returned
- why you think your journey was important for other people

Student B: You are a journalist. Interview Sally Ride about her journey into space. Use the information in the video and prepare questions about:

- what she did before she was an astronaut
- the first flight on the Challenger space shuttle
- what she did in space
- what she did after she returned
- why she thinks her journey was important for other people

When you finish, change roles and repeat the conversation.

7 Work in pairs. We can call Sally Ride a role-model for young women. This is someone we admire and try to copy. Think of a role-model in your life or for other people. Think about these questions. Then tell your partner about your role-model.

1 Who is this person?
2 Is it someone in your family? In sport? On TV?
3 Why is he/she a role-model?

experiment (n) /ɪk'sperɪmənt/ scientific tests
launch (v) /lɔːntʃ/ to send a rocket or space vehicle from the ground into the air or into space
pilot (n) /'paɪlət/ person who controls and flies an aeroplane or space vehicle

UNIT 7 REVIEW

Grammar

1 Complete the text with the past simple form of the verbs.

Marco Polo [1] .... (begin) his famous journey to China when he was seventeen years old. He [2] .... (travel) from Venice through to Persia, to Afghanistan and along the Silk Road to Cambulac (now Beijing). The journey [3] .... (take) three years. Polo [4] .... (not return) to Venice for seventeen years because he [5] .... (stay) in China and he [6] .... (work) for the Khan (or Emperor).

Marco Polo returned to Venice in 1295 and he [7] .... (not travel) to Asia again. But his book about the journeys in Asia called *Miracles of the World* [8] .... (become) famous across Europe. People [9] .... (not believe) everything in the book, but they loved the stories. Before Marco Polo died in 1324 he [10] .... (say) everything in the book was true.

2 Write questions about Marco Polo.

1 When / Marco Polo / his journey to China?
When did Marco Polo begin his journey to China?
2 Where / he / from?
3 How long / the journey / ?
4 How long / he / in China?
5 After 1295 / he / to Asia again?

3 Work in pairs. Take turns to ask and answer the questions in Exercise 2.

4 Read the information. Then write two comparative sentences using the adjectives.

1 The summer temperature in Qatar is 40°C. It's 20°C in Berlin. (hot / cold)
Qatar is hotter than Berlin. Berlin is colder than Qatar.
2 A Porsche can travel at 300 kph. A Mini can travel at 225 kph. (fast / slow)
3 This house costs $1,000,000. This apartment costs $250,000. (cheap / expensive)
4 London has a population of eight million. Madrid has a population of three million. (big / small)
5 The Nile River is 6,650 km long. The Amazon River is 6,712 km long. (long / short)

5 Read another sentence and compare it with the information in Exercise 4. Complete the superlative sentence.

1 The summer temperature in London is 18°C. London is *the coldest* city.
2 A Bugatti Veyron can travel at 430 kph. It's .... car
3 This castle costs $10 million. It's .... home.
4 Delhi has a population of 12 million. It's .... capital city.
5 The Mississippi River is 3,733 km. It's .... river.

I CAN	
talk about the past with the past simple tense	☐
ask questions about the past	☐
compare people and things	☐

Vocabulary

6 Write one type of transport you can:

1 ride 2 fly 3 sail 4 drive

7 Choose the correct options. In one sentence, both answers are correct.

1 We went on a long *travel / journey* across the mountains.
2 How was your business *trip / journey*?
3 I always *take / go* the bus to work.
4 My friend is a travel writer. He *writes / blogs* about his journeys.

I CAN	
talk about transport and travel	☐

Real life

8 Complete the questions with these words.

flight hotel meal weather

1 How was the .... ? Delicious!
2 How was the .... ? It rained every day.
3 How was the .... ?
Very comfortable and right in the city centre.
4 How was the .... ?
Tiring. We waited at the airport for six hours!

I CAN	
ask about a trip	☐
talk about a trip	☐

Speaking

9 Work in pairs. How much can you remember about these journeys from Unit 7?

The Mayflower The Flight of the Silver Queen
The Journeys of Voyager 1 and 2

Unit 8 Appearance

The Dinagyang Festival in the Philippines
Photo by Mario Babiera

FEATURES

1 Look at the photo and read the caption. Where is the festival? Which adjectives describe it?

boring colourful crowded exciting fun
loud popular quiet relaxing noisy

2 2.7 Listen to a visitor at the Dinagyang Festival. Are these sentences true (T), false (F) or don't know (DK)?

1 The Dinagyang Festival is always on the fourth Sunday in January.
2 The festival is in different cities in the Philippines.
3 Tourists also wear colourful clothes and make-up.
4 The music wasn't quiet.
5 The visitor didn't eat any of the local food.

3 Discuss these questions. Use the adjectives in Exercise 1.

1 What is an important day or festival in your town or city? When is it?
2 Do people change their appearance (e.g. wear special clothes)?
3 What do people do on the day? Do they eat special food?

... is a popular festival in my country.

There's music and dancing in the city centre.

8a The faces of festivals

Listening

1 Look at the children in masks in the photo. Do you have similar masks in your country? When do people wear them?

2 2.8 Listen to a conversation about the photo. Number the children in the photo in the order they discuss them.

3 2.8 Listen again. Answer the questions.

1 Why was the woman in Spain?
2 Who were in the masks?
3 What season is the festival?
4 Why do people travel there?
5 Does the woman think the masks are beautiful or ugly?
6 What does the man think is 'fantastic'?
7 Are they brothers and sister?
8 Why is the girl similar to the man's daughter?

4 What do you think about the masks? Do you think they are ugly or beautiful?

Grammar *have got / has got*

5 Look at the sentences (a–e) from the conversation in Exercise 2 about appearance. Choose the correct option to complete the rules (1–2).

a Why have they got these masks?
b I think they're a bit ugly.
c He's got a fantastic white face.
d He hasn't got any eyebrows.
e Maybe he's tall.

1 We use *be* / *have got* before an adjective.
2 We use *be* / *have got* before a noun or an adjective + noun.

> ***HAVE GOT / HAS GOT***
>
> We often use *have got / has got* to talk about:
> - **appearance** I've got blue eyes.
> - **possessions** He hasn't got a car.
> - **family** Have you got children?
>
> For further information and practice, see page 84.

6 2.9 Complete the description of a different festival with the correct form of *be* or *have got*. Then listen and check.

FACE AT A FESTIVAL

This Polga tribesman [1] .... a dancer at a festival in Papua New Guinea. All the men [2] .... tall and handsome and they [3] .... colourful clothes with red hats over their short, dark hair. They [4] .... white faces and black lines around their brown eyes, on their eyebrows and on their cheeks. The man in the photo [5] .... red on his lips and nose, and he [6] .... black on his chin and a string of seashells around his neck.

Vocabulary face and appearance

7 Look at the highlighted words in the text in Exercise 6. Point at these parts of the face on the photo or on your own face.

8 Find one more word in the text for each category in the table.

General appearance	Height
beautiful (usually women) .... (usually men) ugly	short / ....
Hair	**Eyes**
long / .... straight / curly .... / fair / blonde	blue green ....

9 Pronunciation groups of consonants

2.10 Many English words have groups of consonants with no vowel sounds between them. Listen to the groups of consonant sounds in these words and repeat them.

lips eyebrows ugly mask cheeks
straight blonde

10 Work in pairs. Make true sentences about the three children in masks in Exercise 1.

He She They	is / are 've got / 's got haven't got / hasn't got	handsome big heads brown hair a white face red cheeks a red ribbon one eyebrow beautiful	a hat red lips ugly blue eyes

11 Write a short description of your appearance. Use words from this page and *be* and *have got*. Then read your description to your partner. Does your partner think it's an accurate description?

Speaking

12 Work in pairs. Play this game. Then change roles and play the game again.

Student A: Choose a person in the class. Answer Student B's questions.
Student B: Ask Student A questions and guess the person.

Has he got ...?

Yes, he has. / No, he hasn't.

Is she ...?

Yes, she is. / No, she isn't.

8b Global fashion

Reading

1 How often do you buy new clothes? Which of these is most important for you: the price, the size, the colour or the brand?

2 Read an article about photographer Gillian Turner-Niles. Answer the questions.

1 What type of photographer is she?
2 Where does she normally work?
3 Where is she at the moment?

3 Read the article again. Choose the correct answer (a or b) for these questions.

1 Where can you see her photographs?
 a in shops b in magazines
2 Who does she work for?
 a a clothing company b different companies
3 What does the writer think about fashion across the world?
 a It's the same. b It's different.
4 Does Gillian agree with this opinion?
 a Yes, in some places. b No, she doesn't.

GLOBAL FASHION

Gillian Turner-Niles is a fashion photographer. She lives in New York and works in the fashion capitals of the world. You can see her photographs on the pages of fashion magazines across the world. Her clients include Gucci, Dior, Ferragamo, even the sports clothing company Nike. But today she's talking to me by phone from the middle of Sudan. So, what is she doing there?

'I'm taking photographs, of course!' She explains, 'I'm not taking photographs for *Vogue* or anyone else. It's like a holiday. In my business, it's easy to forget there's another world out there. And I like looking at clothes in a different way when I travel.'

But in this world of global fashion, people all over the world wear the same clothes. The businessman's suit in Beijing is like the businessman's suit in Berlin. And jeans and T-shirts are almost a type of uniform these days.

'Yes, I think that's true in the big international cities,' Gillian says. 'But I'm visiting regions in the world with their own traditional clothes and their own fashions. That's especially true in this part of Africa.'

suit (n) /suːt/ clothes (jacket and trousers/skirt) made from the same material, often for work.
uniform (n) /ˈjuːnɪfɔːm/ the same clothes for a group of people (e.g. in the army or in school)

Word focus *like*

4 Look at the sentences with the verb *like* from the article. In which sentence does *like* mean 'similar to'? Find another sentence in the article with this meaning of *like*.

1 It's like a holiday.
2 I like looking at clothes.

5 Work in pairs. Discuss these questions.

1 Do you like fashion? Is it important to you?
2 Do you wear clothes like your friends, or like famous people in magazines?

Grammar present continuous

6 Look at these two sentences from the article (a–b). Answer the questions (1–2).

a She lives in New York and works in the fashion capitals of the world.
b Today she's talking to me by phone from the middle of Sudan.

1 Which sentence describes an action now or around the time of speaking?
2 Which sentence describes a permanent state or routine? What tense is the verb?

PRESENT CONTINUOUS

I'm (am) working.
You/we/they're (are) working.
He/she/it's (is) working.

I'm not (am not) working.
You/we/they aren't (are not) working.
He/she/it isn't (is not) working.

Are you/they/we working?
What is he/she/it doing?
Where are you/they/we working?

For further information and practice, see page 85.

7 Find examples of the present continuous form in the article in Exercise 2.

8 2.11 Complete the telephone conversation between Gillian and her colleague Sam. Use the present continuous form. Then listen and check.

S = Sam, G = Gillian
S: Hello?
G: Hi Sam. I [1] .... (call) from Tokyo.
S: Sorry, who [2] .... (speak)?
G: Sam. It's me. Gillian.
S: Oh sorry, Gillian. It's a really bad line. Give me the number of your hotel and I can call you back.
G: No, I [3] .... (not stay) in Tokyo. I [4] .... (wait) for my flight at the airport.
S: Where [5] .... (you / go) now?
G: To Vietnam. Ho Chi Minh City.
S: Oh I see. [6] .... (you / travel) on your own?
G: No, Jess is with me. We [7] .... (work) on a project together. It's about fashion in Asia.
S: Great. Can you email me some of your photographs?
G: Sure, but my email [8] .... (not / work) at the moment.
S: OK, send them tomorrow … Bye.

9 Choose the correct form to complete these sentences about Gillian.

1 At the moment, she *travels* / *is travelling* in Asia.
2 At home, she *doesn't go* / *isn't going* to the gym before work.
3 Now *she visits* / *she's visiting* different parts of the world.
4 She *likes* / *is liking* clothes and fashions.
5 Currently she *takes*/ *is taking* photos for a project on fashion in Asia.
6 She *doesn't take* / *isn't taking* a holiday very often.
7 *Does she have* / *Is she having* a house in New York?
8 Where *does she take* / *is she taking* photos now?

Vocabulary clothes

10 Match these words with the clothes (1–10).

belt dress skirt hat jumper shirt shoes socks tie trousers

Speaking

11 Work in pairs. Take turns and describe what clothes:

- you are wearing today
- your partner is wearing today
- your teacher is wearing today

I'm wearing a red T-shirt.

8c In fashion or for life?

Reading

1 Discuss the questions as a class.

1 What is currently in fashion (popular at the moment) in your country?
2 Look at these categories. What is now out of fashion (i.e. it was popular, but it isn't now)?

clothes music on the Internet technology on TV or video

2 Look at the photos of the two men. Who has got tattoos because they are in fashion? Who has got tattoos because they are traditional in his country?

3 Read the article. Which paragraph (1–4) talks about:

a tattoos in Polynesian culture?
b why modern societies have tattoos?
c tattoos in ancient cultures?
d tattoos in the USA?

Critical thinking close reading

4 Read the article again. According to the information in the article, are these sentences true (T), false (F) or don't know (DK)?

1 Some famous people have got tattoos.
2 In the USA, more women go to tattoo shops than men.
3 Before five thousand years ago, nobody had a tattoo.
4 Different ancient cultures had tattoos.
5 There weren't tattoos in ancient China.
6 In Polynesia, people don't have tattoos anymore.
7 Chris Rainier says tattoos are a type of fashion.
8 The writer doesn't like tattoos.

> ▶ **WORDBUILDING phrasal verbs**
>
> A phrasal verb is a verb with a particle. English has many phrasal verbs. For example: *Every morning I put on my coat and go to work.*
>
> For further information and practice, see Workbook page 109.

Vocabulary parts of the body

5 Underline parts of the body in the article. Then label these pictures.

1 ....
2 ....
3 ....
4 ....
5 ....
6 ....
7 ....
8 ....
9 ....
10 ....

Speaking

6 Discuss the questions in pairs.

1 In your country, are tattoos in fashion? Out of fashion? Traditional? Not part of the culture?
2 Do you like tattoos on other people? Why? / Why not?

TATTOOS *in* fashion *and* for life

In many countries, tattoos are in fashion. On TV you can often see a famous actor with a picture on her arm or foot, or your favourite musician with a word on his hand. Many sports personalities have got them on their necks and backs. In the USA, tattoos are very popular. Forty per cent of Americans aged between twenty-six and forty have got a tattoo and sixty per cent of customers in US tattoo shops are women. These people are often professional people like doctors, teachers and lawyers.

However, tattoos are not modern. In fact, they are very old in human history. For example, archaeologists found a human in ice from five thousand years ago. He had fifty-seven tattoos on his back, ankles, legs, knees and feet. They were used for many different reasons too. In ancient Egypt, people put on tattoos because they were 'beautiful'. But in ancient Rome, tattoos were negative and put on criminals and prisoners. In India, tattoos were religious.

In the sixteenth and seventeenth century, European sailors arrived in the islands of Polynesia. They saw tattoos for the first time. The people on the islands had tattoos on their shoulders, chest, backs and legs. Often the tattoos were of animals or natural features like a river or a mountain. The European sailors liked them and made their own tattoos. And so the idea travelled to Europe. Tattoos in Polynesia are still important today. They show information about a person's history, their island or their job.

So is there a connection between traditional tattoos and fashionable tattoos? And can you call tattoos a fashion? Chris Rainier of *National Geographic* is an expert in tattoos and his book *Ancient Marks* has photos of tattoos from all over the world. He thinks people in modern societies often have tattoos because they are a connection with the traditional world. And anyway, tattoos aren't a fashion like clothes or a haircut because you can't put them on and take them off again like a jacket or a hat. They are permanent and for life.

Polynesian man with tattoos

8d The photos of Reinier Gerritsen

Real life talking about pictures and photos

1 Do you like looking at paintings and photos? Who is your favourite artist or photographer?

2 Look at the photo. Discuss the questions.

1 Where are these people? How do they feel?
2 Do you think it is an interesting photograph? Why? / Why not?

3 2.12 The photo is by Reinier Gerritsen. Listen to someone talking about him and his photography. Answer the questions.

1 Why does the person like his photos?
2 Where are the people in this photo?
3 The speaker talks about the people in the photo. Who does she talk about first, second, third, fourth and fifth?

4 2.12 Listen again and match the sentence beginnings (1–10) with the endings (a–j).

1 His photos are	a people in their everyday life.
2 They often show	b very interesting.
3 This one is	c the man and woman are talking.
4 On the right	d is watching her.
5 The woman in the middle	e a bit sad.
6 In front of her the woman with blonde	f is reading her book.
7 Then the other blonde woman on the left	g I don't normally look at people very closely.
8 She looks	h hair is listening to music.
9 Look at the other woman	i at the back.
10 I like it because	j on the New York subway.

▶ TALKING ABOUT PICTURES AND PHOTOS

Introduce the photo
This photo shows …, I can see …

Location
On the left/right, in the middle, at the front/back

The people (appearance and actions)
She looks sad. He is reading.

Your opinion
I think …, I like it because …

5 Pronunciation silent letters

2.13 Listen to these words from the Listening. Which letter is silent? Then listen again and repeat.

interesting sometimes everyday
listening blonde closely

6 Work in pairs. Look at another photo by Reinier Gerritsen on page 82.

7 Choose a picture or photo you like. Show it to your partner and talk about it.

8e How R U? ☺ tks

Speaking and reading

1 Read the text about emoticons on the right. Then discuss the questions.

1 How are emoticons different in the eastern hemisphere and the western hemisphere?
2 Do you use emoticons in your texts and online messages?
3 Which emoticons do you use in the article? Which other emoticons do you often use?

CULTURE

EASTERN HEMISPHERE		WESTERN HEMISPHERE
(^_^)	happy	:-)
(;_;)	sad	:-(
(*o*)	surprised	:o
(^_~)	winking	;-)
(^o^)	laughing	:D

The whole world uses emoticons in their texts and online messages. But emoticons around the world are not the same. In eastern hemisphere countries, the eyes are very important in emoticons. But with western emoticons, the mouth is more important and you turn your head to the left to read them.

Writing texts and online messages

2 Read messages between two people. How does each person feel?

1 How R U?

2 Gr8 :-) Shopping 4 clothes. u wan 2 come?

3 Sry. Got English exam. :(

4 :0 Didn't know it's 2day. Call me after

5 Thx C U l8r

3 Writing skill textspeak

a The messages in Exercise 2 use 'textspeak'. Compare the messages with the full version in normal English below.

A: How are you?
B: I'm great. I'm shopping for clothes. Do you want to come?
A: Sorry, but I've got an English exam today.
B: I didn't know it's today. Can you call me afterwards?
A: Thanks. See you later.

b Textspeak makes English shorter. Find examples in Exercise 2 of the following:

1 The writer uses numbers with the same sound as a word.
2 The writer uses a letter with the same sound as a word.
3 The writer leaves out some words (e.g. pronouns, auxiliary verbs).
4 The writer leaves out letters when the word is obvious.
5 The writer use imperatives not polite forms.

c Write this textspeak conversation using full sentences.

A: [1] R U in town?
B: [2] Am l8ter 2day.
A: [3] Wan2 meet?
B: [4] OK. @ 3?

d Write these full sentences using textspeak.

1 Thanks for the message.
2 Please meet me at the station.
3 Sorry I'm late.
4 See you on Monday at six.

4 Work in pairs. Arrange to meet this week. Write a text message to your partner. Swap your messages and write a reply. Continue writing and agree on the day, the time and the place.

8f Festivals and special events

An elephant at a festival in Jaipur, India

Before you watch

1 Work in pairs. Look at the photo and read the caption. Discuss the questions.

1 Where is this elephant? Why are there colours on its face?
2 Do you have animals at festivals in your country? Tell the class.

2 Match these words to the pictures (1–7).

mask costume jewellery trumpet
fireworks clown gloves

1

2

3

4

5
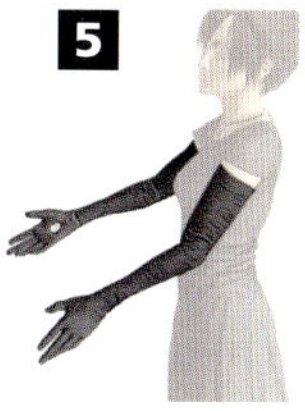
6

7

3 Answer these questions about the objects in Exercise 2.

1 Which can you see in your country?
2 When do you see them (e.g. at festivals, at special events)?

While you watch

4 Watch the video. There are five photos in the video and each one shows a festival or a special event. Tick the words you can see in each photo.

1 Fire Festival: make-up ☐ costume ☐ fireworks ☐
2 Rodeo: make-up ☐ jewellery ☐ clown ☐
3 Wedding: mask ☐ trumpet ☐ fireworks ☐
4 Elephant festival: make-up ☐ gloves ☐ mask ☐
5 Carnival: mask ☐ gloves ☐ jewellery ☐

5 Watch the video again. Answer these questions.

Photo 1
1 Which country is the Beltane Fire Festival in?
2 Does the narrator like the woman's costume?

Photo 2
3 Where is the clown from?
4 Is he making the audience laugh or is he listening to his national anthem?

Photo 3
5 Where is the wedding?
6 What kind of music are the musicians playing?

Photo 4
7 Where is this photo?
8 What colours can you see on the elephant?

Photo 5
9 Which Italian city is the woman in?
10 How often is the carnival?

6 Look at these sentences from the video. Are the underlined words very positive or very negative? Practise reading the sentences. Stress the underlined words.

She's wearing an amazing costume!
You can see some fantastic fireworks.
Those gloves are wonderful!
The colours are incredible.

7 **Fluency practice describing the photos**

Work in pairs.

Play the video again with NO SOUND. Take turns to be the narrator. Describe each photo when it is on the screen. Talk about:

- where it is
- what you can see
- what you like about it

After you watch

8 Read this email. Which event in Exercise 4 is the person writing about?

Hi!
We're having a great time in Scotland! Last night, we went to a festival. There were lots of people and they were wearing interesting costumes and white make-up. One woman had a white dress and an amazing tall hat. Everyone carried fire so it was an incredible event. I've attached a photograph for you to look at.
Bye for now!

9 Choose another festival or event in the video. Imagine you went to it. Write an email to a friend and describe it.

10 Swap your email with a partner. Can you guess which festival or event they described?

UNIT 8 REVIEW

Grammar

1 Complete the sentences with the correct form of *have got*.

1 Penelope .... blue eyes. (+)
2 I .... a moustache. (–)
3 The two sisters .... the same dress. (+)
4 He .... a hat. (–)
5 Maciej and Ania .... long hair. (–)
6 The dancer .... a white face with black lines. (+)
7 .... you .... make-up on your face?
8 .... she .... brown hair or blonde hair?

2 Complete the sentences with the present simple or present continuous form of the verbs.

1 At the moment, they .... (work) in Japan.
2 He .... (always / start) work at nine.
3 What .... (you / do) now?
4 Currently, she .... (write) a book about fashion.
5 We .... (live) in Los Angeles.
6 .... (you / like) this dress?
7 Why .... (you / wear) those shoes this evening? They're ugly!
8 A: Where are Jan and Piotr? They're late.
B: They .... (drive) here now.

I CAN	
use *have got / has got* to talk about appearance	☐
talk about actions now or at the time of speaking	☐

Vocabulary

3 Delete the incorrect word in each group.

1 APPEARANCE
beautiful ~~forehead~~ ugly handsome
2 HEIGHT
short tall ugly medium-height
3 HAIR
straight tall fair long
4 CLOTHES
trousers hat T-shirt lips
5 FACE
neck eyebrows nose chin
6 PUT ON YOUR BODY
tattoo make-up chest clothes

4 Which clothes do you put on these parts of the body? Match 1–5 with a–e.

1 hands	a hat
2 feet	b socks
3 legs	c tie
4 head	d trousers
5 neck	e gloves

5 Write some sentences about the people in this photo. Use words from Exercise 3.

New York City

They're ... They've got ... They're wearing ...

I CAN	
talk about clothes and appearance	☐
talk about the face and parts of the body	☐

Real life

6 Choose the correct option to complete these sentences about the photo in Exercise 5.

1 This photograph *shows / takes* a group of women in New York City.
2 The woman *on the right / in the middle* is looking at the photographer.
3 She *looks / has got* happy.
4 Everyone is wearing a black and white *jumper / T-shirt*.
5 The women have got pink and turquoise *hair / make-up*.
6 Some women are wearing black *hats / belts*.
7 I *like / am liking* the photo because they are having fun.
8 The photo is *interesting / interested*.

I CAN	
describe a picture or photo	☐

7 Work in pairs. Look at photos of people in a newspaper, magazine or on the Internet. Describe the photos.

Speaking

8 Work in pairs. Describe a member of your family. Talk about his/her appearance. Are you like him or her? Why? / Why not?

Unit 9 Film and the arts

Sydney Harbour, Australia
Photo by Annie Griffiths

FEATURES

1 Look at the photo. What is the woman doing? Why do you think she is in Sydney Harbour?

2 2.14 Listen to someone talking about the photo. Choose the correct ending (a or b) to complete the sentences. In one sentence, both endings are possible.

1 The woman is ______ .
  a on an advertisement   b in a film
2 The outdoor cinema screen is ______ .
  a on the side of a building
  b above the water
3 The audience watch their favourite actors ______ .
  a on the beach   b in their cars

3 Complete these sentences for you. Then tell your partner.

- I go to the cinema … (once a week? once a month?)
- I usually watch films on … (TV? DVD? the Internet?)
- I like watching films … (with friends? on my own? with a big audience?)
- The last film I saw at the cinema was … (title?)

SEE OR WATCH?
You **see** films (at the cinema).
You **watch** films (on TV, on DVD, etc.).

TALK ABOUT ▶ A FILM FESTIVAL ▶ YOUR FUTURE PLANS ▶ PAINTINGS YOU PREFER ▶ ARRANGEMENTS
WRITE ▶ REVIEWS AND COMMENTS

9a All roads film festival

Vocabulary types of film

1 Match these types of films with the pictures (a–g).

action film   animation   comedy
documentary   horror film
romantic comedy   science-fiction film

2 Discuss these questions as a class.

1 Can you think of one film for each type in Exercise 1?
2 Which types of films do you like? Which do you never watch?

Reading

3 Read the first paragraph of the article. What types of films can you watch at the *All roads film festival*?

all roads film project

NATIONAL GEOGRAPHIC

Every year, *National Geographic* has a film festival in the USA. It isn't like the Oscars and Bollywood because you don't see lots of famous film stars. The *All roads film festival* has films by directors and actors from many different countries and cultures. You can see many types of films including comedies, documentaries and animation. Here are some of the films this year.

My Wedding and Other Secrets

This is a romantic comedy about a Chinese family in New Zealand. Their daughter loves a local man and the problems begin.

The Tundra Book

This is a documentary by the director Aleksei Vakrushev. It's about the life of the Chukchi people in eastern Russia.

Grandma

Grandma is a short film by the Lebanese director, Merva Faddoul. It's about a teenage girl called Sarah who has a normal life with her sister and grandma. Then, one day, the family's life changes forever.

4 Read the whole of the article. Are these statements true (T) or false (F)?

1 The *All roads film festival* is every year.
2 You can see lots of famous people there.
3 It shows one type of film.
4 This year you can see a film about Russia.
5 *My Wedding and Other Secrets* is a comedy in China.
6 *Grandma* is a story about an old woman.

5 Which of these films at the festival would you like to see? Why?

Listening

6 2.15 Two friends are at the *All roads film festival*. Listen to their conversation and answer the questions.

1 Which film does Beata talk about?
2 Where does Charles invite Beata?
3 Does she answer yes or no?

7 2.15 Listen again and write in the missing verbs.

C = Charles, B = Beata
C: Hey! Beata. Stop!
B: Hi Charles. Sorry, but I'm going to 1 ________ a ticket for the next film. It starts in five minutes. It's called *My Wedding and Other Secrets*. Are you going to 2 ________ it too?
C: No, I'm not, but what are you 3 ________ afterwards? Didier, Monica and I are going to 4 ________ dinner at a Japanese restaurant. Do you want to come?
B: Sorry, but I'm not going to 5 ________ out late tonight. I'm tired.
C: Sure.
B: Oh, I must go. Bye.
C: Bye. See you later.

Grammar *going to* (for plans)

8 Look at the conversation in Exercise 7. Underline four examples of *going to* and one example of the present continuous. Then answer the questions.

1 Do the underlined verbs talk about the present or the future?
2 How do you form the negative and question form of *going to*?

GOING TO (FOR PLANS)

I'm he's/she's/it's you're/we're/they're	*going to* + verb

I'm not/She isn't/They aren't going to have dinner.
What are you going to see?
Are you going to see the film? Yes, I am. / No, I'm not.

going to go* = *going to (*present continuous*)
When we say *going to go* we usually use the present continuous form of *go*: *I'm going to go home.* = *I'm going home.*

For further information and practice, see page 85.

9 Make sentences with *going to* or the present continuous form.

1 we / see a film at the new cinema
2 I / not watch / this DVD
3 you / buy the tickets online or at the cinema?
4 what time / they / go / the cinema?
5 I / not sit / at the front of the cinema
6 where / you / sit?
7 they / meet us after the film?
8 I / never / watch a film by that director again!

10 **Pronunciation** /tə/

2.16 Listen to the sentences in Exercise 9. Notice the weak vowel sound in *to* is /tə/. Listen again and repeat.

Speaking

11 Imagine you are going to a film festival. Choose three films you want to watch and plan your day.

In cinema 1	In cinema 2	In cinema 3
2–3.30 **Animal migrations** – a wildlife documentary	2–3.40 **Summer Love** – a romantic comedy from Canada	2–4 **The Moon at Midnight** – a Hollywood action film with fast cars
3.55–5.25 **Life on Mars** – a Hollywood science-fiction film	4.10–5.30 **Animation festival** – short animation films by young filmmakers	4.15–5.35 **Historical Horror** – a documentary about the history of horror films
5.40–7.15 **The Boy from Mumbai** – music, dance and colour from Bollywood	5.45–6.45 **Everest** – a powerful documentary about the mountain and climbers	5.45–8.15 **Macbeth** – a new film version of Shakespeare's famous play

12 Work in groups. You are going to the festival with the people in your group. Discuss and plan the films you are going to see.

What are you going to see at two o'clock?

The Moon at Midnight *because I love action films. Are you going?*

No, I'm not. We're going to watch Summer Love.

9b People in film and the arts

Vocabulary art and entertainment

1 Work in pairs. Imagine you have a free evening. Number these activities (1–6) in your order of preference (1 = first choice).

- watch a film on the TV at home
- see a film at a cinema
- go to a theatre and see a play
- go to an art gallery and look at the paintings
- listen to live music at a concert hall
- read a novel at home

2 Complete the table with these words.

art and paintings
artist or painter   in a book
at a cinema   at a concert hall
director, actors, actresses (x2)
music   a play or a musical

What?	Where?	Who?
film		
	at the theatre	
	in an art gallery	
novel		writer
		musicians

3 Look at the different types of people in Exercise 2. Talk about some of your favourite directors, actors, artists, writers and musicians. Why do you like them?

WORDBUILDING suffixes (2)

We make nouns from verbs + suffix to describe people's jobs and occupations:
act – actor, direct – director, paint – painter, write – writer.

For further information and practice, see Workbook page 117.

Reading

4 Look at the photo of Adrian Seymour. Then choose the correct words (a, b or c) to complete the gaps in the article (1–8).

Making films in the wild

Doctor Adrian Seymour is a film [1] .... But in his films, the animals are the [2] .... and the scenery is some of the most beautiful and remote parts of the world. Adrian [3] .... wildlife films and documentaries about his expeditions for television channels.

As a child, he wanted to live in the jungle and he kept lots of plants in his bedroom. He loved [4] .... TV programmes about the natural world with famous [5] .... like the underwater expert, Jacques Cousteau.

Before he [6] .... a film-maker, he studied biology and zoology at university and went on scientific expeditions. Later, he made his first film in 2006 and learned how to use a film [7] ....

Nowadays, he films [8] .... in jungles, mountains and rainforests all over the world.

1 a actor b director c artist
2 a actors b directors c writers
3 a does b has c makes
4 a watching b seeing c going to
5 a directors b explorers c painters
6 a started b made c became
7 a video b camera c cinema
8 a action films b comedies c documentaries

Listening

5 2.17 Listen to an interview with Adrian. Number the topics (a–c) in the order he talks about them.

a planning a film
b the subject of his next film
c the number of people in the film crew

6 2.17 Listen again. Answer the questions with *Yes*, *No* or *Doesn't say*.

1 Does Adrian plan his journeys?
2 Does he use more than one camera?
3 Is there always a director and camera person on a film?
4 Is Adrian going to film in the winter?
5 Is he going to take a year to make the film?
6 Is his next film for the cinema?
7 Is the film about an explorer from the nineteenth century?
8 Is it going to be a long film?
9 Does he plan to have a holiday?

7 Discuss these questions as a class.

1 Would you like a similar job to Adrian?
2 Do you ever make films or videos (e.g. of your friends and family)?

Grammar infinitive of purpose

8 Look at the two parts of the sentence from the interview with Adrian. Answer the questions.

1: *I'm going to Malaysia* | 2: *to make a film.*

1 Which part of the sentence describes the speaker's plan?
2 Which part of the sentence describes why the speaker does something?

INFINITIVE OF PURPOSE

You use the infinitive of purpose to say why you are going to do something:
*I'm going to a café **to meet some friends.***
*I'm going to London **to see a musical.***

For further information and practice, see page 86.

9 Work in pairs. Match 1–4 with a–d and make sentences starting with *I'm going to …*

1 buy this book about Martin Scorsese
2 art school
3 play this computer game again
4 the theatre

a to read about his life
b to reach level five
c to see a play by Shakespeare
d to study painting

10 Think about your plans. Tell your partner where you are going, when you are going and why you are going. Use the time expressions and some of the places.

the cinema	tomorrow
the theatre	on Friday
a concert	at the weekend
an art gallery	next week
a museum	next month
another place?	

I'm going to the cinema at the weekend to see Johnny Depp's new film.

Speaking

11 Work in pairs. Write down three of your future plans. Take turns to tell each other your plans. Ask your partner for the reason or more details.

I'm going to London tomorrow.

Why are you going?

To meet some friends.

9c Nature in art

Vocabulary nature

1 Look at the five pieces of art about nature (1–5). Answer the questions.

1 Are they modern or traditional?
2 Do you know which country or period in history they are from?
3 What can you see in each one? Use these words.

birds butterflies flowers fruit grass trees
kangaroos leaves mountains rocks sea sky

2 Do you have paintings or photos in your home? What kinds of pictures are they? What do they show (e.g. people, animals, places)?

Reading

3 Read about the five artists on page 39. Match each artist with their work (1–5) in Exercise 1.

4 Read the article again. Tick the true sentences for each artist, according to the information in the article.

	Stanislaw Witkiewicz	Ginger Riley Munduwalawala	Andō Hiroshige	Damien Hirst	Vincent Van Gogh
1 This artist paints and uses nature in art.	✓	✓	✓	✓	✓
2 This artist is living now.					
3 This artist painted the same subject eleven times.					
4 Nowadays, one of his paintings costs millions.					
5 People can't agree about this artist.					
6 He didn't have money when he died.					
7 This artist's paintings are similar to much older types of paintings.					
8 This artist has a lot money.					

Critical thinking the writer's preferences

5 Compare the verbs *like* and *prefer* in this sentence about the first artist. Does *prefer* mean like or like one thing more than another?

Many people like Stanislaw Witkiewicz's paintings of people's faces, but I prefer his paintings of landscapes.

6 Read about the other four artists. Answer the questions.

1 Which of the four artists does the writer like?
2 Which of their paintings does she prefer?

Speaking

7 Work in pairs. Discuss the art in Exercise 2.

- Say which art you prefer in each of these pairs and say why: 1 or 2? 2 or 3? 3 or 4? 4 or 5? 5 or 1?
- Which one do you like the most? Why?

Which do you prefer?

I prefer this one because …

This is my favourite painting because …

2

3

4

Nature in art

You can see paintings of nature everywhere in the world. Many artists paint and use nature in their work, but the results are very different. Art critic, Liz Searle-Barnes looks at five of them.

Stanislaw Witkiewicz Stanislaw Witkiewicz was born in 1885 in Zakopane. He died in 1939 but you can see his paintings in art galleries in Poland. Many people like Witkiewicz's paintings of people's faces, but I prefer his paintings of nature and landscapes. He painted this one in 1907. It shows the Hinczow Lakes in the Tatra mountains in southern Poland. There are the green fields and the white rocks and I like this painting because the water in the lake is so blue. I want to swim in it.

Ginger Riley Munduwalawala In the past, Aboriginal people painted pictures of nature and animals on rocks. In parts of Australia, their Rock Art is 30,000 years old. Nowadays, modern aboriginal artists also paint nature. For example, this colourful painting by Ginger Riley Munduwalawala (1937–2002) shows hills, rivers, birds and kanagroos.

Andō Hiroshige Japanese art is famous for landscape paintings. You can often see the sea and sky, and the mountains and trees. Andō Hiroshige worked in the nineteenth century and he's one of Japan's most famous artists. He printed and sold thousands of beautiful prints in his lifetime. However, he was poor when he died.

Damien Hirst Damien Hirst is the richest artist in England. He is a painter, but he is more famous for art with different animals (living and dead) including a cow, a sheep and a shark. In one room of a gallery, he put lots of fruit and real butterflies live there. They fly round the heads of the visitors. For some people he is a genius, but other people disagree. Personally, I like his work, but I prefer his early paintings.

Vincent Van Gogh Van Gogh made eleven paintings of sunflowers. They were also Van Gogh's favourite paintings because he loved the colour yellow. I prefer his other paintings, but many people love his sunflower paintings. They are everywhere. You see them on cards, postcards and T-shirts. Van Gogh died with no money, but in 1987 someone bought the last sunflower painting for $49 million.

art critic (n) /ˈɑːt ˌkrɪtɪk/ a person who studies and writes about art
landscape (n) /ˈlændskeɪp/ a painting of an area outside (with trees, rivers, mountains, etc.)

5

9d Making arrangements

Listening

1 Look at the photo of some theatres in Broadway, New York. Answer the questions.

1 Is there a theatre district in your town or city? What kinds of shows are there (e.g. plays, musicals, dance)?
2 What was the last show you saw? What was it about?

2 2.18 Two friends are talking about seeing a show at a Broadway theatre. Listen to their phone conversations and answer the questions.

Conversation 1
1 Which show in the photo are they talking about?
2 When is the show?
3 Why isn't Adriana free?

Conversation 2
4 Can Adriana finish work early?
5 What time does the show start?
6 What time are they going to meet?

Real life inviting and making arrangements

3 2.18 Complete the expressions for inviting and making arrangements with these words. Then listen again and check.

free great like 'd love meet
see 'm sorry time want

INVITING AND MAKING ARRANGEMENTS

Inviting
Would you [1] .... to come?
Are you [2] .... ?
Do you [3] .... to go?

Respond to the invitation
Thanks. I [4] .... to.
I [5] .... , but I'm working late tonight.
That's [6] ....

Making arrangements
What [7] .... does it start?
Let's [8] .... at seven.
[9] .... you at seven.

4 Pronunciation showing enthusiasm

2.19 Listen to these phrases for responding to invitations. Underline the word with the most stress. Then listen again and repeat.

1 I'd love to!
2 I'd really like to!
3 That's great!
4 That sounds fantastic!

5 Grammar present continuous for future reference

Look at the sentences from the Listening in the grammar box. What is the tense? Are they talking about the present or the future?

PRESENT CONTINUOUS FOR FUTURE REFERENCE

I'm going to the theatre tonight.
I'm sorry, but I'm working late tonight.

For further information, see pages 85 and 86.

6 Work in pairs. Practise these telephone conversations.

Student A: You've got tickets for the musical *Jersey Boys* tomorrow night. It starts at 8 p.m. Telephone Student B and invite him/her.

Student B: Answer the phone. You are at work. Listen to Student A's invitation and say yes. Arrange to meet.

Then change roles and practise the same conversation for the musical *Wicked*. It starts at 8.30 p.m.

9e It looks amazing!

Writing reviews and comments

1 People often write reviews and comments on websites. Do you ever read them? Which ones?

2 Match these extracts from reviews and comments (1–5) with these categories.

an art exhibition a film music perfume a restaurant

1 I loved their first album so I was excited about their second. Some of the tracks are good, but it sounds very slow. Overall, it's a bit disappointing.

2 After the show, we had a meal at this new place in the centre. The starters were very good. I had the tomato soup and it tasted great. Unfortunately, the main course wasn't so good, but in general I liked it.

3 There's one room in the gallery with paintings by the artist Picasso when he was very young. They look amazing! You can't believe he was only twenty when he painted them.

4 I felt scared at the beginning because it starts in the middle of the night. There are two people in a car and they break down. So they go to a house and a strange man opens the door. But after that it's very funny. I laughed for two hours.

5 I bought this because it has the name of my favourite actress on it, but it smells awful!

3 Which reviews in Exercise 2 are positive? Which are negative?

4 Writing skills giving your opinion with sense verbs

a Sense verbs are *look, feel, sound, taste, smell*. We often use sense verbs + adjectives in reviews because they give our opinion about something. Underline five sense verbs + adjectives in the reviews in Exercise 2.

b Work in pairs. Which sense verbs could you use to write about these items? You can choose more than one for each item.

a musical at the theatre a very long book
a fitness centre a new building
a new type of sports car some men's aftershave
clothes in a shop a new type of chocolate
a computer game

c Which of these adjectives can you use with the verbs *look, feel, sound, taste, smell*? You can use the adjectives more than once.

angry beautiful bored delicious loud
interesting nice soft terrible tired

5 Choose two of the topics in Exercise 4b. Write a short review or comment for a website about them. Use sense verbs and adjectives.

6 Work in pairs. Exchange reviews. Use these questions to check your partner's reviews.

- Are the reviews positive or negative?
- Did he/she use sense verbs and adjectives?
- Are you now interested in the item in the review?

9f Camera traps

A 'camera trap' took this photograph of an African Leopard

Before you watch

1 Look at the photo. Why do you think this animal is difficult to photograph?

2 Read the text about a camera trap. It took the photo of the leopard. Answer the questions.

1 How does it take a photo?
2 Why do wildlife conservationists use camera traps?
3 Why do camera traps take photos with no animals?
4 Where do you need to put the camera?

A camera trap is a special type of camera. When something moves in front of it, it takes a photograph. Wildlife conservationists use this technology because animals come near the camera. They can get a lot of information about the animals during the day and also at night. Sometimes, camera traps take photos of animals you rarely see.

There are also disadvantages with a camera trap. When a plant moves in the wind, it sometimes takes photos with no animals. It's also difficult to put the camera in the right place. You need to put them where animals spend time and usually this isn't easy.

wildlife conservationist (n) /'waɪldˌlaɪf ˌkɒnsə'veɪʃnɪst/ person who protects animals in natural areas
wild (animals) (adj) /'waɪld/ animals in natural areas

3 You are going to watch a video about the filmmaker Adrian Seymour. Answer the questions.

1 What can you remember about him?
2 Why do you think he uses camera traps?

While you watch

4 Watch the video with NO SOUND. Number Adrian's actions in the order he does them (1–9).

a He's getting up.
b He's going to bed.
c He's walking through the rainforest.
d He's putting a camera trap in a tree.
e He's taking a camera trap off a tree.
f He's looking for animals in the photos.
g He's having a bath.
h He's watching an animal on his computer.
i He's climbing up a tree.

5 Watch the video again WITH SOUND. Choose the correct answer for the questions.

1 Where is the rainforest?
  a in Guatemala
  b in Costa Rica
  c in Honduras
2 Where do a lot of the animals live?
  a in rivers
  b in trees
  c under the ground
3 How many camera traps does he put in the trees?
  a six
  b sixteen
  c sixty
4 How long does Adrian wait before he looks at his camera traps?
  a four hours
  b four days
  c four weeks
5 When Adrian looks at the first photos, what does he think?
  a He thinks the cameras don't work.
  b He doesn't think there are any animals.
  c He doesn't know what the problem is.
6 He sees a kinkajou in the pictures. Which three facts are true about kinkajous?
  a They come out at night.
  b They live in rainforests.
  c They also live in the desert.
  d They eat meat and fruit.

After you watch

6 Role play an interview with Adrian Seymour

Work in pairs.

Student A: You are Adrian Seymour. A journalist is going to interview you about your filmmaking in Honduras. Think about what you are going to say.

Student B: You are a journalist. You are writing an article about Adrian Seymour. Prepare some questions about Adrian's filmmaking and his work with camera traps in Honduras.

When you finish, change roles and repeat the interview.

UNIT 9 REVIEW

Grammar

1 Complete the sentences with the *going to* form of these verbs.

buy   not drive   have   meet   play (x2)
watch   not write

1 We .... a film on TV this evening.
2 Matt and Raul .... tennis.
3 I .... friends for dinner.
4 They .... here because there's a problem with their car.
5 .... you .... a holiday this year?
6 Rachel .... the tickets online before we leave.
7 The author .... another book ever again.
8 .... she .... her guitar at the concert?

2 Make five sentences with *going to* and the infinitive of purpose.

I'm going to	the theatre a concert hall an art gallery a café the shops	to have to see to listen to to look at to buy	a drink. a musical. music. clothes. paintings.

3 Read these present continuous sentences. Do they talk about the present (P) or the future (F)?

1 I'm making a documentary about butterflies at the moment.
2 I'm sorry, but I'm working late tonight.
3 Why are they waiting outside the cinema?
4 Where are you going after work?
5 They aren't leaving tomorrow.
6 Chen and Jens aren't coming to this meeting so let's start.

I CAN	
talk about future plans with *be going to*	☐
talk about the purpose and reason for a plan or action	☐
use the present continuous for future arrangements	☐

Vocabulary

4 Match these types of film with the comments (1–6).

action film   animation   comedy
documentary   horror   science fiction

1 It's a story in space with aliens.
2 It was very funny and I laughed for hours afterwards.
3 It's all about polar bears and how they live.
4 I couldn't watch the film. It was very scary!
5 There are fast cars and the hero always wins.
6 In the past, they drew all the pictures on paper. Nowadays, they make them with computers.

5 Complete the missing word in these sentences.

1 Actors work in TV, films and in the t.......... .
2 You look at paintings in an a.......... g.......... .
3 J K Rowling writes n.......... about a boy called Harry Potter.
4 I play the guitar with a group of m.......... .
5 Steven Spielberg is a famous film d.......... .
6 We listened to the music in a c.......... h.......... .

6 Complete the table with these words.

birds   butterflies   flowers   grass   kangaroos
mountains   sea   sky   trees

landscape	plants	animals

I CAN	
talk about types of films	☐
talk about art and entertainment	☐
talk about nature	☐

Real life

7 Number the lines of the conversation in the correct order (1–8).

1 Would you like to come to the cinema?
Sorry, but I'm working late.
When are you going?
OK. I'd love to come at nine.
The film is also on at nine.
Great. Let's meet outside the cinema at quarter to nine.
At six.
8 Right. See you there. Bye.

I CAN	
invite someone	☐
make an arrangement	☐

8 Work in pairs. Role play a telephone conversation. Arrange to meet next week. Then change partners and make another arrangement for a different day next week.

Speaking

9 Work in groups. Tell the others about your favourite musician, writer, actor or actress and artist. Say why you like them.

Unit 10 Science

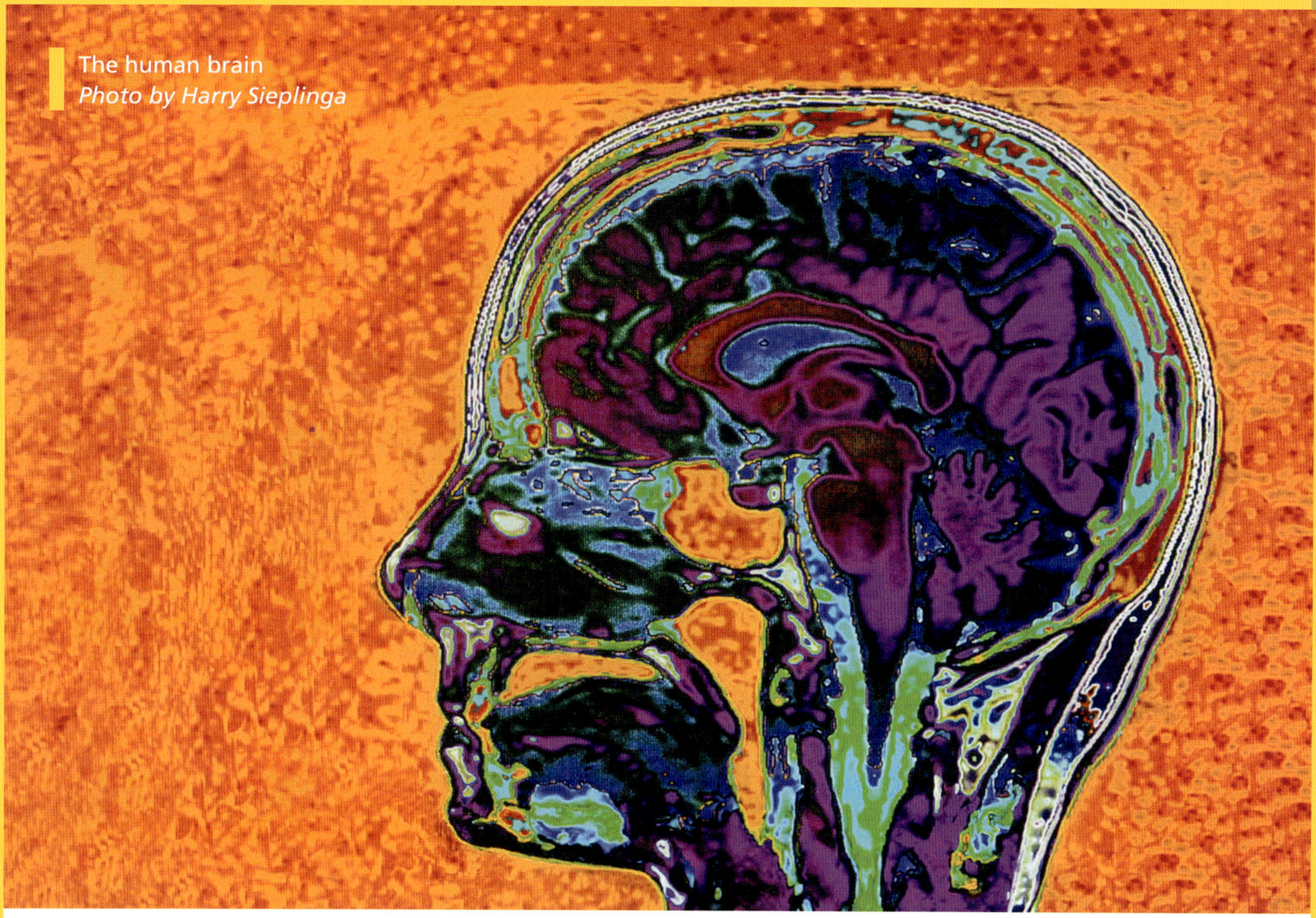

The human brain
Photo by Harry Sieplinga

FEATURES

1 Look at the photo of a human brain. Which is more intelligent: a human brain or a computer? Give reasons for your answer.

2 Look at the list. Which is true for a human brain (B)? Which is true for a computer (C)? Some sentences are true for both.

1 It needs energy. *B, C*
2 It uses chemicals.
3 It stores information.
4 It's usually easy to fix.
5 We don't know everything about it.
6 It can shut down.

3 **2.20** Listen to a neuroscientist (a scientist who studies the brain). She is comparing a brain to a computer. Check your answers in Exercise 2.

4 Neuroscience is the science of the brain. Match these other subjects with the type of science (a–f).

1	astronomy	a	heat, light, energy
2	zoology	b	new machines
3	physics	c	planets and outer space
4	chemistry	d	living things
5	biology	e	chemicals
6	technology	f	animals

5 Which sciences did you study at school? Which do you like reading about in magazines or watching on TV? Why?

TALK ABOUT ▶ EXPERIENCE WITH TECHNOLOGY ▶ SOMETHING YOU HAVE LEARNED ▶ PROBLEMS WITH TECHNOLOGY
WRITE ▶ MAIN ARGUMENTS AND SUPPORTING SENTENCES ▶ A TELEPHONE MESSAGE

10a Technology has changed our lives

Vocabulary everyday technology

1 Look at the photo in the article. What is the boy doing? Do you ever use one of these? Why? / Why not?

2 Look at these pairs of words. Which do you use most? Which do you never use?

email / letter   music download / CD
search engine / library
book / ebook   map / sat nav (GPS)
online video / DVD   podcast / radio
text message / postcard

3 Think about people in these age groups: *teenagers, young adults, middle-aged people, sixties* and *over sixties*. Discuss these questions.

1 Which do they use the most in Exercise 2?
2 How important is technology for these people?

Reading and listening

4 Read the article. Are these sentences true (T) or false (F)?

1 On average, there are four computers in British houses.
2 Over half the British population think their life is better with technology.
3 Lots of people in Britain use public telephones.
4 Young people still write letters by hand.

5 Ask everyone in the class these questions. What are the results for your class?

1 How many computers have you got in your house?
2 Is your life better with technology? Why?

6 2.21 Listen to part of the survey from Exercise 4. The researcher interviews someone under the age of thirty. Tick the six activities (1–15) in the article that she asks about.

Technology HAS changed our lives

a public telephone

People in Britain love technology. In a new survey of people in the country, researchers found:

- there are four computers in the average British household.
- six out of ten people say their life is better with technology.

The researchers also say that new technology has changed our world forever. Modern communication is a good example of this. For example, have you ever telephoned from a public telephone? Have you ever written a letter by hand? Many people haven't done these things or they don't do them anymore. In particular, the survey found that young people have never done the following activities because of modern technology:

1 Telephoned a cinema for the times of the films.
2 Booked a holiday at a travel agent.
3 Used a public telephone.
4 Bought tickets for a concert over the phone.
5 Printed photos.
6 Bought a CD.
7 Written a letter by hand.
8 Used an address or telephone book.
9 Looked at a map before a car journey.
10 Faxed a document.
11 Paid by cheque.
12 Watched programmes at the time they are on TV.
13 Put an advert in a newspaper.
14 Sent a letter in an envelope.
15 Bought flowers from a shop in the high street.

7 2.21 Listen again. Choose the correct ending (a, b or c) for the sentences. Sometimes two endings are correct.

1 He always books holidays ....
  a at the travel agent
  b online
  c by phone
2 He bought his father a CD because he ....
  a doesn't have much money
  b had a birthday
  c can't download music
3 A sat nav is ....
  a good for his job
  b fast
  c not expensive
4 He pays with ....
  a credit card
  b cash
  c online banking
5 He watches programmes on ....
  a TV
  b DVD
  c YouTube
6 He sends ....
  a texts
  b postcards
  c emails

Grammar present perfect

8 Look at this question and answer from the interview. Answer the questions.

A: Have you ever booked a holiday at a travel agent?
B: Yes, I have, but it was a long time ago.

1 Are they talking about an experience in the past or present?
2 Do we know exactly when the action happened?

PRESENT PERFECT

Use the present perfect to talk about experiences in the past. We don't say exactly when it happened.

	have	past participle
I/you/we/ they	have (haven't)	booked a ticket. telephoned the cinema.
He/she/it	has (hasn't)	

Questions (with *ever*)
With the present perfect, we often use *ever* in questions and *never* in negative answers:
Have you ever downloaded music?
Yes, I have. / No, I haven't. I've never downloaded music.

For further information and practice, see page 86.

9 Look at the grammar box. Then complete the extracts from the survey interview with the present perfect form of the verbs or *have/haven't*.

A: Have you ever bought a CD?
B: Actually, yes, I [1] .... (buy) a CD. Normally I download music, but last week I bought a CD for my father.

A: And before a car journey, have you ever used a map?
B: Yes, I [2] .... Well, I did in the past, but now I use a sat nav, you know, a GPS, because I drive a lot for my job.

A: Have you ever paid for something by cheque?
B: No, because I [3] .... (never / have) a cheque book.

A: So you never watch TV programmes online?
B: Oh, I see what you mean. Well, I [4] .... (watch) videos on YouTube.

A: OK. And finally, [5] .... (you / ever / send) a letter in an envelope?
B: I'm not sure. Let me think. No, I [6] .... because I send emails or texts.

10 **Pronunciation *'ve/'s***

2.22 Listen to eight sentences. Do you hear the full form or the contracted form?

1	have	've	5	have	've
2	has	's	6	has	's
3	have not	haven't	7	have not	haven't
4	has not	hasn't	8	has not	hasn't

Speaking

11 Work in pairs. Ask each other *Have you ever …?* questions about the fifteen activities in the article.

Have you ever telephoned a cinema for the times of the films?
Yes, I have.
Have you ever booked a holiday at a travel agent?
No, I haven't. I've never …

12 Think of other technology words. Ask your partner what technology he/she has used. Then work with another pair. Tell them what your partner has done or hasn't done.

He's read an ebook.
She's never downloaded a podcast.

speaking and reading your memory • vocabulary memory and learning • listening a news report • grammar present perfect and past simple • speaking talking about learning

10b How well can you remember?

This violinist reads the music and then she memorises every note afterwards.

Speaking and reading

1 Have you got a good memory? Which of these are easy for you to remember? What techniques do you use to remember them?

- people's names and faces
- directions and addresses
- telephone numbers
- dates and facts in history
- food on shopping lists
- new words in English

2 Work in groups of three. Each person reads a short paragraph, then memorises the important information and write notes in this table.

Student A: Turn to page 82.

Student B: Turn to page 81.

Student C: Turn to page 82.

	Student A	Student B	Student C
What was the topic of the article?			
What techniques did it describe?			

3 In your group, tell each other about the information in your article. When you listen to the other students, write notes in the table.

4 Afterwards, read the three articles again and compare your notes. Discuss these questions.

1 How much information did you remember?
2 How much information did the other students remember?
3 Which memory techniques in the articles do you use?

Vocabulary memory and learning

5 Look at these groups of verbs. Two words have a similar meaning. Cross out the word with an opposite or different meaning.

1 study learn teach
2 know understand test
3 remember forget memorise
4 train relax practise

WORDBUILDING synonyms and antonyms

Synonyms are words with similar meanings: learn – study
Antonyms are words with opposite meanings: learn ≠ teach

For further information and practice, see Workbook page 125.

6 Work in pairs. Ask and answer these questions.

1 How often do you study English at home?
2 How many new words in English do you learn a week?
3 How do you memorise new words (e.g. in sentences, with pictures, writing them down)?
4 Do you ever test yourself? How?

Listening

7 Look at the photos and the headline. Answer the questions.

1 Who is the man in the first photo?
2 What has he won? Has he ever won it before?

NEWS

Nelson Dellis wins USA Memory Championship again!

Nelson Dellis and 'Memory athletes' at the USA Memory Championship

8 2.23 Listen to a news report about Nelson Dellis. Number these topics in the order the reporter mentions them.

a the USA Memory Championships
b what Nelson can remember
c Nelson's memory techniques

9 2.23 Listen again. Answer the questions.

1 How many new names and faces can Nelson memorise?
2 How many different numbers can he hear and repeat?
3 Which years did he win the USA Memory Championship?
4 Which sporting event are Memory Championships similar to?
5 What did he study in 2010?
6 How much did he practise?
7 Who does he teach his techniques to?

Grammar present perfect and past simple

10 Compare the verbs in these two sentences from the news report.

Nelson **has won** the USA Memory Championship twice. He **won** the competition in 2011 and again in 2012.

1 What are the two tenses?
2 Which tense do we use when we know the exact time?
3 Which tense do we use when we don't say or know the exact time?

PRESENT PERFECT AND PAST SIMPLE

We use the present perfect when we talk about something in the past, but we don't say (or know) exactly when it happened:
He's studied memory techniques.

We use the past simple when we talk about something in the past and we say exactly when it happened (with a time expression):
*He won a memory competition **last year**.*

For further information and practice, see pages 86 and 87.

11 Work in pairs. We often start a conversation with a question in the present perfect and then continue with past simple questions.

Have you ever studied in another country?

Yes, I've studied in Mexico.

When did you study there?

I studied in Mexico in 1993.

Write four similar conversations. Make questions with the words and write answers.

1 Have / take / an English exam? When / take it?
2 Have / study / science? Where / study?
3 Have / teach / a subject? What / teach?
4 Have / learn / a musical instrument? What / learn?

Speaking

12 Ask your partner more questions about something they have learned.

Have you ever learned ...?

When did you ...?

What did you ...?

Where did you ...?

10c Why haven't scientists invented it?

Vocabulary science and invention

1 Look at these scientific inventions. Categorise them into groups a, b or c. Tell the class your answers and say why.

a I need it every day.
b I sometimes need it.
c I never need it.

an ipod or MP3 player
a wheel a vacuum cleaner
electricity a knife fire
sticky tape the Internet

Reading

2 Look at the pictures of new inventions (A–D) on page 51. Match them with the section titles (1–4) in the article.

3 Read the article about four types of scientific invention. Answer the questions.

1 Which two haven't scientists invented?
2 Which two have scientists invented, but we don't have them in our everyday life?

4 Match these words from the article (1–5) with the definitions (a–e).

1 invent
2 discover
3 test
4 break down
5 prototype

a the first one (e.g. a machine) before you make lots of them
b to make a machine which people have never made before
c to find information for the first time
d to stop working
e to find out if an invention works

5 Read the article again. Are the sentences true (T) or false (F)?

1 The invisibility coat and the car used cameras.
2 The car was 100% invisible.
3 Flying cars are very popular.
4 The writer doesn't want lots of traffic in the sky.
5 Teleporting doesn't use transport.
6 Scientists can't move atoms across distances.
7 Robots for the home cost a lot of money.
8 The new robot can do everyday jobs.

6 Which invention from the article would you most like to have? Why?

Critical thinking the main argument and supporting information

7 In this article, the writer uses a main argument and supporting information. Look at these sentences from the paragraph about invisible objects.

Main argument: Many scientists have tried to invent invisible objects, but they haven't done it yet.
Supporting information: But as you can see in this photo, the wheels aren't invisible.

Now read these sentences from the article. Which are the main argument (M) and which are supporting information (S)?

1 With all the cars on the road and the problems of traffic, why haven't flying cars become popular?
2 One reason is because cars are very heavy so they are difficult to fly.
3 Cities have roads for cars, but they don't have runways.
4 Teleporting is a very fast way to travel, but scientists haven't discovered how to do it.
5 A human being is made of trillions of atoms, so it's very difficult and scientists don't have the answer at the moment.
6 Scientists have invented robots, so why don't we all have them?
7 Probably because the technology is very expensive and the robots often break down.

Writing

8 Work in groups. Discuss one of these questions and write down two or three reasons. Then write a paragraph with the main argument (the question) and two or three supporting sentences.

1 There are lots of people on Earth, so why haven't we built cities under the ocean?
2 There are about 7,000 different languages on Earth, so why haven't we invented one language for everyone?
3 We have lifts in tall buildings, so why haven't we invented a lift into space?

WHY HAVEN'T SCIENTISTS invented it yet?

Scientists have discovered and invented many things: computers, space travel, mobile communication. But there are a lot more things they haven't invented or we don't use in our everyday life. Are they all impossible or can we have them one day?

invisible (n) /ɪnˈvɪzəbl/ you can't see an object
runway (n) /ˈrʌnweɪ/ road for an aeroplane to take off and land (at an airport)
atom (n) /ˈætəm/ the smallest part of a chemical element
servant (n) /ˈsɜːvənt/ a person who works in another person's home

1 Invisible objects

Many scientists have tried to invent invisible objects, but they haven't done it. One scientist at Tokyo University tested cameras on a coat. The cameras filmed objects behind the coat and showed them on the front of the coat. Unfortunately, the coat wasn't very comfortable! The car manufacturer Mercedes also tried these cameras with a car. They put the camera on one side of the car and showed the images on the other side. But as you can see in this photo, the wheels aren't invisible.

2 Flying car

With all the cars on the road and the problems of traffic, why haven't flying cars become popular? One reason is because cars are very heavy so they are difficult to fly. There are other problems as well. Cities have roads for cars, but they don't have runways. And we have so many problems on our normal roads, do we really want the same problems in the sky?

3 Teleporting

Teleporting is moving objects and people from one place to another without transportation or walking. Teleporting is a very fast way to travel, but scientists haven't discovered how to do it. Solid objects are made of atoms and with teleporting you have to move each atom one by one. A human being is made of trillions of atoms, so it's very difficult and scientists don't have the answer at the moment.

4 Robot servants

Actually, scientists have invented robots, so why don't we all have them? Probably because the technology is very expensive and the robots often break down. But many companies in Japan have made prototype robots for houses. They wash clothes, switch on the TV, turn off the lights and change the music. Many scientists think we can all have a robot servant in our home in about ten years.

A

B

C

D

10d Problems with technology

Listening

1 Look at the photo and discuss the questions.

1 How does the man feel? What do you think has happened?
2 Has your mobile phone or internet connection ever stopped working? How did you feel?

2 2.24 Richard works for Omarox Engineering. He answers a telephone call from Omar. Listen and answer the questions.

1 Where is Omar?
2 What time is it?
3 What isn't working?
4 What is the name of the hotel?
5 What is the number?
6 Where has Richard put the designs?

Real life checking and clarifying

3 2.24 Look at these expressions for checking and clarifying. Then match the responses (a–f) with the expressions. Listen again and check.

▶ CHECKING AND CLARIFYING	
Is that three in the morning?	1 ....
Was that the Encasa Hotel?	2 ....
The number is 603 2169 2266.	3 ....
Is there anything else?	4 ....
Have you called our colleagues?	5 ....
Have you emailed me all the designs?	6 ....

a So that's 603 2169 2266?
b No, in the afternoon.
c Yes, I have.
d Yes, one thing.
e No, the Ancasa Hotel. A for apple.
f No, I haven't.

4 Pronunciation contrastive stress

2.25 Listen and underline the stressed word in the responses. Then listen again and repeat the response.

1 A: Is that three in the morning?
B: No, in the afternoon.
2 A: Was that the Encasa Hotel?
B: No, the Ancasa Hotel.
3 A: Is that E for England?
B: No, it's A for apple.

5 Work in pairs. Practise similar telephone conversations.

Student A

Call 1
- You are working abroad, but your mobile phone isn't working.
- Telephone Student B from the Hotel Innsbruck. Your number is 790 9856 7211.
- Check Student B emailed your PowerPoint presentation for tomorrow's meeting.

Call 2
- Student B is abroad. Answer his/her call.
- Write down information about the hotel (name/number).
- You haven't emailed the video because Student B's email isn't working.

Student B

Call 1
- Student A is abroad. Answer his/her call.
- Write down information about the hotel (name/number).
- Confirm that you have emailed the PowerPoint presentation for tomorrow's meeting.

Call 2
- You are working abroad, but your mobile phone isn't working.
- Telephone Student A from the Embassy Hotel. Your number is 800 7790 0210.
- Check Student A emailed the video for tomorrow's meeting.

10e Please leave a message after the tone

Vocabulary email addresses and websites

1 2.26 Can you say these email addresses and websites? Listen and check your answers.

1 j_jones@hotmail.co.uk

2 www.ancasa.com

3 charityhelp.org/b-2

2 Work in pairs. Take turns to say and write down:

- your email address
- your favourite website

Writing a telephone message

3 2.27 Listen to a voicemail and read the message. There are five mistakes on the message. Correct them.

MESSAGE

Name of caller: Richard Senger

Message for: Doctor Omar Al Harbia

Message: He can't email the designs. Download them from omarox.com/a-1 Call him back on his home number (077 234 3785) or email him at r-sanger@omarox.com

★★★★★ **Urgent** ☑

4 Writing skill imperatives

a When we write messages, we often change the speaker's words and use imperatives. Look at this example.

Can he download them from this website? →

Download them from this website.

b 2.28 Listen to five sentences on voicemails. Write them down as imperatives.

1 *Call Jim back this evening.*
2 ....
3 ....
4 ....
5 ....

5 Prepare a message for a hotel voicemail. Include these details.

- your name
- your number
- your email
- ask a colleague at the hotel to do something

6 Work in pairs. Read your messages in Exercise 5 to each other. Write down the most important information for the colleague at your hotel.

MESSAGE

Name of caller: ________

Message for: ________

Message: ________

★★★★★ **Urgent** ☐

7 Check your partner's phone message. Is it clear? Is everything correct (e.g. the spelling, phone numbers, the email address)?

10f Memory and language learning

Children in a classroom

Before you watch

1 Work in pairs. Look at the photo and read the caption. Answer the questions.

1 What language are they learning?
2 Did you learn another language when you were a child?
3 How old were you when you started learning English?
4 Is it important to learn different languages when you are a child? Why?

While you watch

2 Watch the video. What questions do the people answer?

1 ....?
2 ....?
3 ....?
4 ....?

3 Watch the video again. How do these people answer the questions (1–4)? Write words and phrases for each answer. Don't write full sentences.

4 Work in groups. Compare your answers in Exercise 3 and add more information. Then watch the video again and check.

After you watch

5 Work in pairs. Look back at the answers for each person in Exercise 3. Which answers are also true for you?

6 **Group discussion poster presentation**

Work in groups.

Discuss and plan a list of advice for other people learning English. Talk about these questions.

1 How do you memorise new words in English?
2 How can you learn English outside of the classroom?

Now design a poster of your ideas and advice for learning English. You need large pieces of blank paper. Write your ideas and advice on the poster. You can add pictures and images.

Present your poster to other groups in the class and share your ideas.

	Question 1	Question 2	Question 3	Question 4

UNIT 10 REVIEW

Grammar

1 Write *Have you ever …?* questions with the prompts.

1 see / the Eiffel Tower?
Have you ever seen the Eiffel Tower?
2 ride / a motorbike?
3 learn / a musical instrument?
4 meet / a famous person?
5 make / a film?

2 Match these answers with the questions in Exercise 1.

a Yes, I have. I made a film of my family for a college project.
b Yes, I have. I rode across America on a Harley Davidson last summer.
c No, I haven't, but my friend has met lots of musicians.
d No, I haven't, but I'm going to Paris next year.
e No, I haven't, but I'd like to be able to play the guitar.

3 Work in pairs. Take turns to ask and answer the questions in Exercise 1.

4 Complete the conversation with the present perfect or past simple form of the verbs.

A: [1] ………… (you / ever / visit) Rome?
B: Yes, I have. I was a student at the university.
A: Really? What [2] ………… (you / study)?
B: Art. I also [3] ………… (work) in a museum for three months.
A: When [4] ………… (you / do) that?
B: In 2005.
A: [5] ………… (you / learn) Italian when you were there?
B: No, I didn't, because my parents are Italian so I [6] ………… (speak) Italian all my life.

I CAN	
talk about past experiences with the present perfect	☐
talk about the past with the present perfect and past simple	☐

Vocabulary

5 Replace the old technology words in bold with these modern technology words.

download ~~email~~ GPS podcast search engine text message

1 Have you ever handwritten a **letter**? *email*
2 My son has sent me a **postcard**.
3 Find the town on the **map**.
4 I'm listening to a **radio programme** in English.
5 This **library** gives you lots of different information.
6 Your favourite song is on this **CD**.

6 Choose the correct option to complete the sentences.

1 I *study* / *train* English every day for an hour.
2 Can you *know* / *remember* the past tense of the verb 'go'?
3 I always *memorise* / *forget* this word! What does it mean?
4 We can *practise* / *know* English together by only speaking English.
5 I need to *test* / *learn* myself before the exam.

7 Complete this sentence for you. Then compare with your partner.

This week in my English lessons, I've learned …

I CAN	
talk about everyday technology	☐
talk about learning English	☐

Real life

8 Put the words in the correct order to make questions for checking and clarifying.

1 Amsterdam? / as / in / A / is / that
…………
2 thirteen / that / thirty? / or / was
…………
3 675 6475? / number / the / is
…………
4 there / anything / is / else?
…………
5 have / sent / the / email? / you
…………

I CAN	
check and clarify information	☐

Speaking

9 Work in pairs. Discuss these questions.

1 What was you favourite subject at school?
2 Why did you enjoy it?

Unit 11 Tourism

The desert in Jordan
Photo by Gary Arndt

FEATURES

1 Look at the photo. Why do you think the table is in the desert?

2 2.29 Listen to a man talk about his holiday in Jordan. Why was the table in the desert? What happened?

3 Which holiday did the man in Exercise 2 take?

a camping holiday	backpacking around the world
a sightseeing tour	a package holiday by the beach
hiking in the mountains	

4 Work in groups. Discuss these questions. Which holidays in Exercise 3:

- do you prefer?
- have you done in the past?
- are you going to do in the future?

I prefer package holidays to hiking in the mountains because I like to relax on holiday.

I've never been on a camping holiday.

I'm going backpacking round Ireland next summer.

TALK ABOUT ▶ ADVICE FOR A TOURIST ▶ RULES ▶ MAKING SUGGESTIONS
WRITE ▶ A TOURIST DESTINATION ▶ A FEEDBACK FORM

11a Going on holiday

Reading and vocabulary tourism

1 Work in pairs. Read the quiz below from a tourism magazine. Find words in the quiz to match the definitions (1–7).

1 you buy this ticket to go somewhere and come back *return*
2 you buy this ticket to go somewhere
3 you carry this bag onto the aeroplane
4 to telephone for a hotel room (or reserve it online) before you arrive
5 special objects you buy on holiday
6 to give this bag to the airline and they put it on the plane
7 the activity of looking at famous and interesting places

2 Work in pairs. Answer the quiz and read about your answers. Are you Tourist A, Tourist B or both? Tell the class.

▶ WORDBUILDING word forms (1)

One word often has other forms. For example: *to tour* (verb) – *tourism* (noun) – *tourist* (person) – *tour guide* (noun + noun collocation).

For further information and practice, see Workbook page 133.

Listening

3 Look at the website on page 59. What kind of tourist is it for? What does Jan Lanting talk about in the podcast?

4 2.30 Listen to the podcast. Jan talks about the three places on the website. Number them (1–3) in the order she mentions them.

5 2.30 Listen again. Jan gives advice for different places. Answer the questions.

1 Where are the interviewer and Jan speaking from? What month is it?
2 Which is better: a return train ticket to Thurlestone or renting a car?
3 What clothes do you need at this time of year in England?
4 Why is it a good time to go to Malaysia?
5 Does everyone in Malaysia speak English?
6 In the Malaysian jungle, why is a local guide important?
7 When is a good time to go to the Arctic?
8 How can you travel to the Arctic?

6 Which place would you like to go to? Why?

What kind of TOURIST are you?

Answer the questions for Tourist A and Tourist B.

Tourist A

Do you … (tick)
always buy a return ticket? ☐
check in more than one bag? ☐
book the hotel in advance? ☐
rent a car? ☐
buy souvenirs? ☐
use a tour guide? ☐
like sightseeing? ☐

Tourist B

Do you … (tick)
often buy a single ticket? ☐
only take a carry-on bag? ☐
find a hotel after you arrive? ☐
use public transport? ☐
buy local food at markets? ☐
learn some phrases in the local language? ☐
meet local people? ☐

Did you tick more questions for Tourist A or Tourist B? Turn to page 81.

WWW.INDIETRAVELINFO.COM

Travel information for people who like travelling on their own.

This month, we look at some of the top destinations for independent tourists. Click here to download a podcast of our interview with travel writer Jan Lanting. Listen to her top three suggestions for this time of year.

The jungles of Malaysia

The Arctic Circle

Thurlestone, on the south-west coast of England

Word focus *take*

7 We use the verb *take* with different types of nouns. Match these words to the three types.

a taxi   an umbrella   a lunch break

1 *take* + an object
2 *take* + time when you don't work
3 *take* + type of transport

8 Find four more examples of *take* + noun in the audioscript on page 91.

Grammar *should/shouldn't*

9 Look at the verb *should* in these sentences (a–c) giving advice from the podcast in Exercise 4. Answer the questions.

a Sometimes it rains so you should take a coat.
b You shouldn't go in the winter because it's very cold and very dark.
c Should I go on my own or with a tour?

1 What form is the verb after *should* and *shouldn't*?
2 How do you make a question with *should*? Do you use the auxiliary *do/does*?

SHOULD/SHOULDN'T

I/you/he/she/we/they should rent a car.
I/you/he/she/we/they shouldn't carry a lot of luggage.

Should I buy my ticket at the station?
Yes, you should. / No, you shouldn't.

For further information and practice, see page 87.

10 Work in pairs. Read the sentences (1–6). Then use the words in the table to give advice for each situation.

1 I'm so tired.
2 The sun is shining and the temperature is 40ºC.
3 I can't speak the local language.
4 Public transport is slow to the city centre.
5 This shop is expensive.
6 Venice is a beautiful city.

You	should	take a holiday. go sightseeing. learn some words.
	shouldn't	buy your souvenirs here. take the bus. wear sun cream.

Speaking

11 Work in pairs. Choose a country and prepare advice for a tourist. Include these topics.

- weather
- famous sites
- local food
- transport
- language
- shopping

12 Work with another pair. Take turns to give your advice. You can also ask each other questions.

You should go to the beaches because the weather is hot in this country.

Should I bring sun cream?

11b Planning a holiday

Reading

1 Work in groups. Discuss these questions.

1 When do you normally plan your holiday (e.g. a year before, six months before, the week before)?
2 What do you need to plan for a holiday? What should you do before you leave? Make a list. Afterwards, compare your list with the class.

2 Read the information for tourists and travellers in Australia. Match these sub-headings with the sections of the information leaflet (1–6).

Road travel   Weather   Money and currency
Safety and emergencies   Visas and immigration   Language

Information for tourists and visitors in Australia

1 ....

- You have to get a holiday visa from the Australian Embassy before you leave.
- Tourists and visitors can stay for a maximum of six months.
- You cannot work in Australia without a work visa from the Australian Embassy in your country.

2 ....

- The currency is Australian dollars.
- Most shops, hotels and banks in large cities accept credit cards.
- In smaller towns, you should always have cash with you.

3 ....

- Australia is a multicultural country so there are many different languages.
- Most people speak or understand English.

4 ....

- There are three time zones. Temperature and climate is different from region to region.
- Summers are very hot. Always use lots of sun cream and wear a hat.

5 ....

- In the cities, you should stay with friends and don't carry lots of cash.
- Dial 000 for Police, Fire and Ambulance.

6 ....

- Tourists don't have to get a new driving licence, but after a year, you have to take a new driving test.

hitchhiking (n) /ˈhɪtʃhaɪkɪŋ/ travelling for free in someone's vehicle

3 Read the comments (a–f) from tourists in Australia. Then read the information for tourists leaflet. Tick the comment if they have read the information or put a cross if they haven't.

a I've been a tourist here for seven months now.
b I got a work visa before I left home.
c Can I use US dollars here?
d Is English the only language or do people speak other languages in Australia?
e I've brought sun cream because of the heat.
f I dialled 999, but the police never answered.

Vocabulary in another country

4 Complete the information for visitors to Canada with these words.

climate   currency   hand side
illegal   licence   multicultural
time zones   visa

- For employment in Canada, most people need a work [1] ....
- The Canadian dollar is the national [2] ....
- There are six [3] .... in Canada.
- Canada is a [4] .... country with two official languages (French and English) and 18% of the population have a different first language.
- Canada's [5] .... is very different from season to season. There can be snow in the winter, but in the summer the temperature can be very high.
- Drive on the right [6] .... of the road.
- You have to carry your driving [7] .... when you drive.
- Hitchhiking is [8] .... on motorways in Canada, but you can hitchhike on local roads.

5 How similar is the information about Australia and Canada?

6 Work in groups. Discuss these questions about your country or countries. How many answers do you know? Afterwards, compare your answers with the class.

1 Do tourists need a visa?
2 How many time zones are there?
3 Is the climate different in different areas?
4 Which side of the road do you drive on?
5 Do you always carry your driving licence?
6 Is hitchhiking legal or illegal?

Grammar *have to / don't have to, can/can't*

7 Look at these sentences from the information about Australia in Exercise 2. Match the meaning of the highlighted verbs with the words in the box.

necessary   not necessary   possible
not possible

1 You have to get a holiday visa from the Australian Embassy.
2 Tourists and visitors can stay for a maximum of six months.
3 You cannot work in Australia without a work visa.
4 Tourists don't have to get a new driving licence.

▶ HAVE TO / DON'T HAVE TO, CAN/CAN'T

*You **have to** show your passport to passport control.* (necessary)

*You **don't have to** show a passport for travel in your own country.* (not necessary)

*All passengers **can** take one carry-on bag onto the plane.* (possible)

*You **can't** check in luggage over 50 kilograms.* (not possible)

For further information and practice, see pages 87 and 88.

8 Look at these signs and notices for tourists. Choose the correct verbs.

1 You *have to / can* drive on the left-hand side.
2 Tourists *cannot / don't have to* take photos here.

3 Guests *have to / don't have to* leave their room before 11 a.m. or they pay a fee.
4 Airline passengers with an online boarding card *have to / don't have to* go to the check-in desk.

5 You *can / cannot* smoke in this area.
6 You *can / cannot* use the hotel lift.

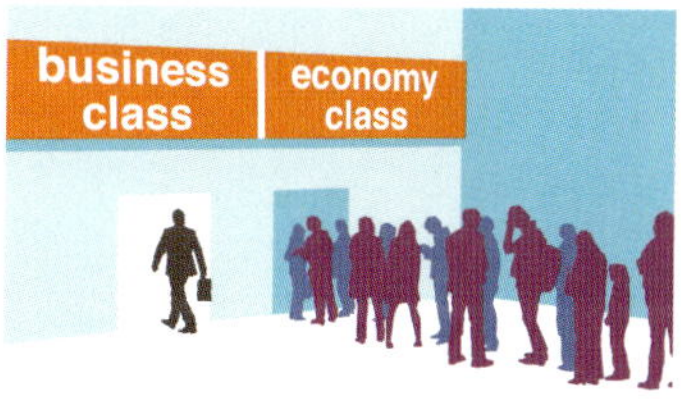

7 Business class passengers *cannot / don't have to* wait.
8 All passengers *have to / can* check in online 24 hours before departure.

9 Pronunciation /hæftə/

2.31 Listen to sentences 1, 3, 4 and 7 with *have to* and *don't have to* from Exercise 8. Notice the pronunciation /hæftə/. Listen again and repeat.

Writing and speaking

10 Work in pairs. Choose one situation below and complete the sentences (1–4).

- visiting another country as a tourist
- studying at your language school
- working for your company

1 You have to …
2 You don't have to …
3 You can …
4 You can't …

11 Work with another pair. Don't say the situation, but read your sentences. The other pair guesses the situation.

11c Should I go there?

Reading

1 Look at the photo on page 63 of tourists on a ship in Antarctica. Why do you think tourists go there? What do you think they can see? Would you like to go? Why? / Why not?

2 Read the article. Which paragraph (1–5) is about:

a why Antarctica is a good holiday destination?
b the writer's problem?
c which holidays the writer likes?
d changes in Antarctica?
e the number of tourists in Antarctica?

3 Work in pairs. Read paragraphs 1 and 2 again. Answer the questions.

1 What does the writer want to do on his next holiday?
2 What types of holiday does he write about?
3 What is his problem? Why?

4 Do you like the same types of holiday as the writer? Do you agree with him about holidays and other tourists? Why? / Why not?

Critical thinking arguments for and against

5 Work in pairs. Read paragraphs 3 to 5 again and make a list of the writer's reasons:

1 for a holiday in Antarctica
2 against a holiday in Antarctica

6 Work with another pair. Compare your lists. Then discuss the question in the last line of the article.

Grammar *everywhere, somewhere, nowhere, anywhere*

7 Look at the sentences from the article. Which highlighted words talk about people or places? An object or event?

There are other tourists everywhere these days.
Nobody lives there.
I'd like to do something exciting.
Is there anywhere in the world without other people?

▶ *EVERYWHERE, SOMEWHERE, NOWHERE, ANYWHERE*

everywhere	somewhere	nowhere	anywhere
everybody	somebody	nobody	anybody
everything	something	nothing	anything

Use *any-* in negative sentences and questions.

For further information and practice, see page 88.

8 Choose the correct words to complete the text from a travel magazine.

You should visit Florence!

Is there [1] *everywhere / anywhere* in the world like the city of Florence in Italy? Of course, there are beautiful cities [2] *everywhere / nowhere* in Italy. But for me, there isn't [3] *anywhere / somewhere* like Florence. [4] *Everything / Nothing* in the city is from the renaissance period including all the buildings, streets and museums. On every street, there's always [5] *anything / something* to see.
If you get lost, ask [6] *somebody / something* for directions. The local people are very friendly!
And after a long day, sit in a café and do [7] *nothing / everything*! Relax and watch [8] *everybody / somebody* else walking past.

Writing

9 Work in pairs. Choose a tourist destination and write a paragraph with the title 'You should visit [name of your destination]!'

10 Put your paragraphs around the classroom. Read about the different holiday destinations. Which would you like to go to? Tell the class about your final choice.

SHOULD I GO THERE?

Travel writer Carlos Gomm is planning his next holiday. But **should he go there?**

I don't like holidays with hotels, beaches and swimming pools, and I'm not interested in sightseeing in old cities. I'd like to do something exciting and nowadays lots of holidays have excitement. There's backpacking over the Andes of South America, or I could go on a safari and see animals in Africa. Maybe I should visit Australia and swim with dolphins along the coast.

But when I choose a holiday, I always have the same problem. I don't want to go somewhere and see lots of other tourists. I want to be the only person there. The problem is there are other tourists everywhere these days. Is there anywhere in the world without other people?

What about Antarctica? It's huge and beautiful. Between 1,000 and 5,000 scientists work there, but nobody lives there. It doesn't have a government and there are no cities so there's no pollution or noisy traffic. It has lots of nature and wildlife. It sounds perfect!

Actually, there are also tourists in Antarctica. Tourism in Antarctica began in the late 1950s. About 500 people a year visited from Chile and Argentina. Nowadays, about 50,000 tourists from all over the world go by ship to the continent every year and the number of cruises is increasing.

So like everywhere else with tourists, Antarctica is changing. You can't stay overnight, but you can visit areas with wildlife. Some people think the numbers of wild animals and birds are decreasing as a result. However, there is also some positive news. Many cruise ships are members of the International Association of Antarctica Tour Operators (IAATO). They teach their passengers about Antarctica and its wildlife. The cruise companies also give money to environmental organisations in the region. These organisations want to help the nature and wildlife of Antarctica so it doesn't change in the future.

So what should I do? Go to Antarctica, go somewhere else or stay at home?

safari (n) /sə'fɑːri/ a type of holiday in Africa to look at animals
environmental organisation (n) /ɪnˌvaɪrən'mentl ˌɔːgənaɪ'zeɪʃn/ a group of people who want to help the natural world

11d A holiday in South America

Listening

1 How do you choose your holiday? Which of these do you use?

- travel books
- a travel website
- videos about places
- advice from family and friends
- a holiday brochure

2 2.32 Two friends are talking about a holiday in South America. Listen to their conversation and answer the questions.

1 Which of the things in Exericse 1 are they looking at?
2 Which countries in South America do they mention?
3 What type of holiday does the other person suggest at the end?

Real life making suggestions

3 2.32 Work in pairs. Listen again and follow the instructions. Then compare answers.

Student A: Match the two halves of the sentences for suggesting.

Student B: Match the two halves of the sentences for responding.

MAKING SUGGESTIONS

Suggesting	
1 You should	a suggestion?
2 How about	travel on your own.
3 Can I make	go on a tour?
4 Why don't you	go on that.
5 You could	visiting the Andes?
Responding	
6 Yes, but	you're right.
7 But the disadvantage is that	good idea.
8 But the advantage is that	there are lots of other people with a bus tour.
9 Maybe	I'm interested in the wildlife.
10 That's a really	you see more with a tour guide.

4 Pronunciation /ʌ/, /ʊ/ or /uː/

a 2.33 Listen to and repeat these vowel sounds: /ʌ/, /ʊ/ and /uː/.

b 2.34 Match these words with the sounds in part a. Then listen, check and repeat.

could cruise bus you should
but love book food

5 Work in pairs. Read about these people and discuss the best type of holiday for each of them.

1 Gary has two weeks' holiday to take. He loves travelling, but he doesn't like crowded cities.
2 Nigella is a student. She has three months in the summer, but she doesn't have much money.
3 Dorothy and Frank are in their sixties. They don't work anymore and they have lots of free time. They never travelled when they were young.

6 Work in pairs. Role play a conversation. Choose one person in Exercise 5.

Student A: You are the person in Exercise 5. Listen to Student B's suggestions and respond.
Student B: Suggest a holiday for Student A.

Then change roles, choose a different person and repeat the role play.

11e Your feedback

Speaking

1 What is most important for you in a hotel? Put this list in order of importance (1 = most important, 8 = not important).

- a good restaurant
- near to the airport and public transport
- comfortable rooms
- internet facilities
- friendly staff
- a fitness gym and swimming pool
- places to meet other people
- near to the beach or the city centre

2 Work in groups. Compare your answers from Exercise 1.

I think a good restaurant is more important than a fitness gym.

I don't agree. Transport is more important.

Writing a feedback form

3 Look at the feedback form for visitors to a hotel. Answer the questions.

1. Do you ever fill in these forms at hotels?
2. Which parts of the hotel does it ask about?
3. How positive or negative was the feedback?

4 Writing skill closed and open questions

a Feedback forms and questionnaires often use a mixture of closed questions and open questions. We answer yes/no to closed questions and give longer answers to open questions. Read these questions from holiday feedback forms. Are they closed (C) or open questions (O)?

1. How was your bus tour? *O*
2. Did the tour guide answer all your questions? *C*
3. Were all our staff polite and helpful?
4. Did you book your holiday online?
5. How easy was our website to use?
6. Did you use the hotel swimming pool and gym?
7. Would you recommend this holiday to your friends?
8. What other suggestions can you make so we can improve our service?

b The feedback form in Exercise 3 uses open and closed questions. How does it ask for more comments after a closed question?

5 Work in pairs. Choose one of the situations below.

- Write a feedback form for passengers at an airport.
- Write a feedback form for customers at a restaurant.
- Write a feedback form for visitors at a sports centre.

6 Swap your feedback form with another pair.

- Imagine you are the passenger, customer or visitor. Write answers on their questionnaire.
- Give the pair feedback on their form. Was it easy to use? Did they write closed or open questions?

KING'S HOTEL

Thank you for your visit to our hotel. We hope you enjoyed your stay. Please spend a few minutes and complete this form. Your feedback and suggestions are very important for us.

How was your room? (Tick)

___ very comfortable ✓ quite comfortable
___ comfortable ___ not very comfortable

How helpful were staff? (Tick)

___ very helpful ___ quite helpful
___ helpful ✓ not very helpful

Comment: *One day I telephoned reception and nobody answered the phone. I rang three times!*

Did you use the fitness gym? Yes / (No)

If 'yes', please comment:

Did you eat in the hotel restaurant? (Yes) / No

If 'yes', please comment: *The waiter wasn't very polite, but fortunately, the food was very good.* ☺

Overall, did you enjoy your stay? Yes / No

Please comment: *Yes and no. Overall, the room and the facilities were very good, but the staff weren't very friendly. They need to be more helpful and polite.*

11f Mecca and the Hajj

Muslim pilgrims walk around the Kaaba in Mecca

Before you watch

1 Work in pairs. Look at the photo and read the caption. Answer the questions.

1 What religion are the pilgrims?
2 Where are they walking?

2 Match the religious people (1–3) to their religious holidays (a–c).

1 Muslims 2 Christians 3 Jews

a Christmas is on the 25th December.
b Hanukkah is a festival of light.
c Eid al-Fitr is a holiday at the end of Ramadan.

3 Which days are holidays in your country? Which of these days are religious holidays?

While you watch

4 Watch the video. Complete the sentences with these words.

Arafat Kaaba Masjid al-Haram Mecca Mina the Hajj

1 .... is a city in Saudi Arabia.
2 .... is a religious journey or 'pilgrimage'.
3 .... is the mosque in the middle of Mecca.
4 .... is a building in the middle of the mosque.
5 .... is a special city for pilgrims on the Hajj.
6 .... is a religious place for Muslims. It is east of Mecca.

5 Watch the video again. Choose the correct answer (a–c) for these questions.

1 Which direction do Muslims pray in?
 a towards Mecca
 b towards Mina
 c towards Arafat
2 How many times in their life should a Muslim visit the Kaaba?
 a at least once
 b twice
 c ten times
3 What do the pilgrims do at the Kaaba?
 a walk around it
 b walk inside it
 c walk under it
4 Where do the pilgrims stay?
 a in Mecca
 b in Mina
 c at Arafat
5 How long do they spend at Arafat?
 a a day
 b a week
 c a month
6 When can the pilgrims return to Mina?
 a when the sun rises
 b at midday
 c when the sun goes down
7 At the end of the journey, what are women pilgrims called?
 a Hajji
 b Hajjah
 c The video doesn't say.

After you watch

6 Complete the text about another religious pilgrimage with these words.

cathedral Christianity pilgrimage pilgrims pray religious

The cathedral at
Santiago de Compostela

Santiago de Compostela is a city in north-western Spain. It's a [1] .... city and, in the centre, there is a famous [2] .... Thousands of people come here to [3] .... Their religion is [4] .... and a lot of them walk on a long journey to the city. The Christian [5] .... start their journey in France or Portugal. There are a lot of different routes to Santiago de Compostela and the [6] .... can last weeks or even months. About 200,000 pilgrims walk there every year.

7 **Group discussion planning a short documentary video**

Work in groups. You are documentary film makers. Discuss and plan a short (2–3 minutes) video documentary about a holiday in your country. It can be a religious holiday or a public holiday. Discuss the following questions:

1 Which holiday is it?
2 When is it?
3 What happens?
4 Which parts do you need to film?

8 Give a short presentation to the class of your plan for the documentary.

pilgrim (n) /ˈpɪlgrɪm/ religious traveller
pilgrimage (n) /ˈpɪlgrɪmɪdʒ/ a religious journey
pray (v) /preɪ/ to speak to God at a religious event or privately

UNIT 11 REVIEW

Grammar

1 Choose the correct option to complete the sentences.

1 This hotel is terrible. We *should / shouldn't* stay here.
2 She doesn't speak the local language. She *should / shouldn't* do a language course before she goes to Italy.
3 You *should / shouldn't* rent a car because it's very expensive.
4 Sometimes the hotels are full so we *should / shouldn't* book a room in advance.

2 Complete the sentences about a tour guide's job with *have to, don't have to, can* or *can't*.

1 I wear nice clothes, but I ______ wear a uniform.
2 The tourists ______ smoke on the tour bus, but they can outside.
3 At lunchtime, I ______ eat with the tourists, but I don't have to.
4 I ______ know everything about the city because the tourists ask a lot of questions.

3 Write four sentences about your job or studies. Use *should, shouldn't, have to, don't have to, can* or *can't*. Then compare your sentences with a partner.

4 Complete the words in the text with *body, thing* or *where*.

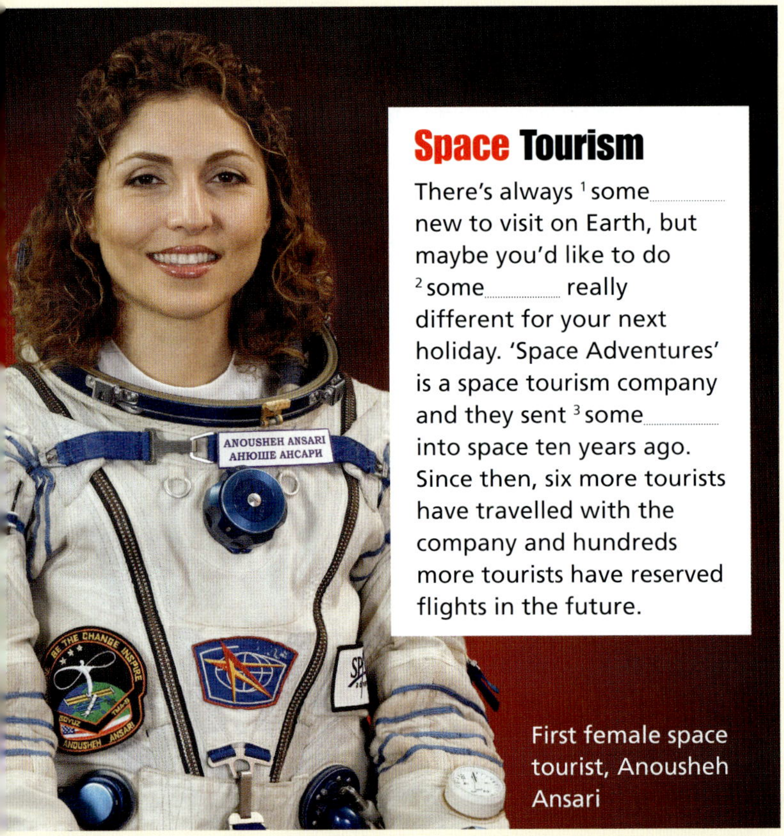

Space Tourism

There's always [1] some______ new to visit on Earth, but maybe you'd like to do [2] some______ really different for your next holiday. 'Space Adventures' is a space tourism company and they sent [3] some______ into space ten years ago. Since then, six more tourists have travelled with the company and hundreds more tourists have reserved flights in the future.

First female space tourist, Anousheh Ansari

I CAN

give advice with *should* or *shouldn't*	☐
talk about necessity and possibility	☐
talk about places, people and things	☐

Vocabulary

5 Complete the categories with these words.

camping hiking return sightseeing
single souvenir tour guide tourist

1 Type of holiday: ______, ______, ______
2 Type of ticket: ______, ______
3 Something you buy on holiday: ______
4 Other people on a holiday: ______, ______

6 Match two words from each box. Then write them in sentences 1–4.

driving hand time work

licence side visa zones

1 My country has three different ______ ______.
2 You have to get a ______ ______ before you get a job in the new country.
3 In most countries, cars drive on the right ______ ______ of the road.
4 You can have a ______ ______ when you pass your test.

I CAN

talk about tourism	☐
talk about visiting another country	☐

Real life

7 Match the suggestions (1–4) with the responses (a–d).

1 How about going on a camping holiday?
2 You should visit the beach.
3 Can I make a suggestion?
4 Why don't you go hiking in the mountains?

a That's a really good idea. I need some exercise.
b Yes, but I don't like bad weather. I prefer sleeping in a hotel.
c Yes, but the disadvantage is that it's very crowded in the summer.
d Sure. What is it?

Speaking

8 Work in pairs. Talk about your last holiday. Consider these questions.

- Where did you go?
- What did you do?
- Who did you go with?
- How was the accommodation?
- Would you recommend this holiday?

Unit 12 The Earth

An Inuit man in the Arctic Circle
Photo by Ira Block

1 Work in pairs. Compare the two photos. How are the places in each one different?

2 2.35 Listen to a documentary about the photographer, Ira Block, and the two photos. Complete the sentences with the missing numbers.

1 The Inuit man lives about .... kilometres from the North Pole.
2 The US state of South Carolina is about .... kilometres from the equator.
3 .... million years ago, the Arctic Circle probably looked like South Carolina.
4 At that time, the temperature at the Arctic was around .... °C.
5 Nowadays, the average temperature in the Arctic Circle is around .... °C.

3 Work in groups. Answer these questions.

1 Is your country nearer to the Arctic Circle, the Antarctic Circle or the Equator?
2 Where is it spring or summer at the moment? In the northern or southern hemisphere?
3 Have you ever travelled across the equator to the other hemisphere? Where did you go?

12a Climate change

Vocabulary measurements

1 Match these abbreviations with their definitions and meaning.

Abbreviation	Meaning	It measures ...
1 %	square metres	temperature
2 °C	kilometres	area
3 km	percentage	distance
4 l	degrees Celsius	weight
5 m²	kilograms	quantity of water (or liquid)
6 kg	litres	an amount out of 100

2 Complete these facts about the Earth with the correct abbreviation from Exercise 1.

Earth Fact File

1 The temperature at the centre of the Earth is about 7,500 ....
2 The North Pole is over 20,000 ...... from the South Pole.
3 70 ...... of the Earth's surface is water.
4 148,940,000,000 ...... of the Earth is land.
5 Objects on the Earth weigh less on the Moon. 100 ...... on the Earth is 16.5 ...... on the Moon.
6 Every day, 914,000,000,000,000 ...... of rain falls on the Earth.

one trillion = one million million (1,000,000,000,000)

3 Which measurement do you look at when you ...

- buy a carton of orange juice?
- watch the weather on TV?
- go on a long journey?
- buy fruit or vegetables from the market?
- pay tax?
- build a new house?

WORDBUILDING word forms (2)

Words about measurements often have more than one form: *long* (adj) – *length* (n), *high* (adj) – *height* (n), *weigh* (v) – *weight* (n)

For further information and practice, see Workbook page 141.

Reading

4 What is the climate in your country (hot, cold, warm)? In recent years, has the climate changed? How?

5 Look at the two maps on page 71 and read the article. Answer these questions for each map.

1 What does the map show?
2 How many years is it for?
3 How does it show the change?

6 Look at the maps again. Are these sentences true (T) or false (F)?

Map 1
1 The temperature in the Arctic Circle has decreased by 4°C.
2 The temperature change in the northern hemisphere is higher than in the southern hemisphere.
3 The temperature in some parts of Antarctica has decreased by 2°C.

Map 2
4 Rainfall has increased in western Australia and it has decreased in eastern Australia.
5 Rainfall has increased in all of Europe.
6 Rainfall has decreased in parts of Africa by 15%.

7 What do the maps show about temperature and rainfall in your country? Is the information similar to your answers in Exercise 4?

CLIMATE CHANGE

Climate scientists have measured the temperature and rainfall on every part of the Earth over many years. They look at the changes and predict the future with the information. The first map shows the temperature over 30 years. In most parts of the world, the temperature has increased by a few degrees and scientists think it will increase in the future.

The second map shows rainfall on the Earth over 30 years. The amount of rain is very different from region to region. Rainfall has increased in some countries and scientists think it will increase in the future. But rainfall has also decreased in other parts and, in these regions, it won't increase. It will decrease.

In conclusion, the changes in climate will continue in the next century. The Earth will feel hotter and rainfall will be higher for some places, but lower for others.

Grammar *will/won't*

8 Look at the two sentences with *will* and *won't (will not)*. Choose the correct option in the rules (1–3). Then underline more examples of *will* in the article in Exercise 5.

*Scientists think it **will** increase in the future.*
*In these regions, it **won't** increase.*

1 We use *will/won't* to talk about the *past / present / future*.
2 We *add / don't add -s* to *will* with the third person form (*he/she/it*).
3 The verb after *will is / isn't* the infinitive form.

▶ *WILL/WON'T*

Use *will* to talk about what we think or know about the future:
I/you/he/she/it/we/they'll (will) feel hotter.
I/you/he/she/it/we/they won't (will not) feel colder.
Will I/you/he/she/it/we/they feel colder?

I (don't) think + will
We often use *will* with *I think*. For example: *I (don't) think it will snow tomorrow.*

For further information and practice, see page 88.

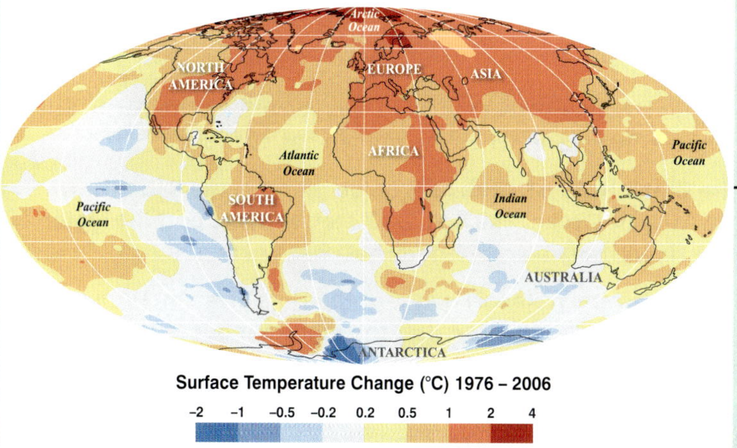

Map 1

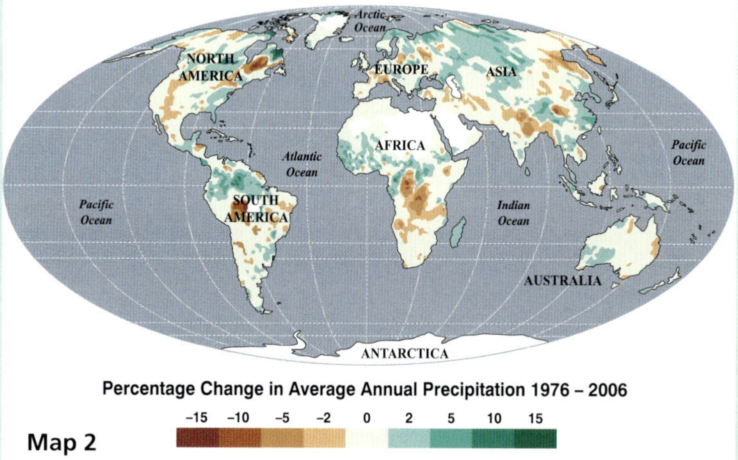

Map 2

9 Reorder the words to make sentences about the future.

1 it / be / hotter in my country / in the future / 'll
2 increase / the temperature in this country / in the future / won't
3 visit / one day / I'll / Antarctica / I think
4 be / more ice / will / in the Arctic Circle / there
5 the percentage of people living in cities / decrease / will
6 English / everyone / speak / will
7 more cars / won't / people / buy
8 I don't think / increase / the number of dry deserts / will

10 Work in pairs. Make the sentences in Exercise 9 into questions. Ask your partner for his/her opinion.

Will it be hotter in your country in the future?

Yes, it will.

11 Pronunciation *'ll*

a 2.36 Listen to six sentences. Do you hear *will* or *'ll*?

1	will	'll	4	will	'll
2	will	'll	5	will	'll
3	will	'll	6	will	'll

b 2.36 Look at the audioscript on page 92. Listen again and repeat.

Writing and speaking

12 Think about your partner's future. Write four sentences about:

- his/her future job
- his/her future travel
- his/her future home
- one other thing in his/her future

13 Tell your partner your sentences. Does your partner think they will come true?

I think you'll become a musician in the future.

I don't think I will. I can't play a musical instrument!

12b Exploring the Earth

Reading and vocabulary land and water

1 Which is your favourite place on Earth? Why? Tell the class.

2 Read the article. Answer the questions.

1 Which unexplored place is water?
2 Which unexplored places are on land?
3 Which place would you like to explore? Why?

3 Complete this table with words from the article.

areas of water	areas of land
sea	desert
o........	i........
l........	f........
r........	m........

4 Work in pairs. Discuss the questions.

1 How many of these geographic places from Exercise 3 are in (or near) your country?
2 Which have you visited?

Grammar definite *the* or no article + names

5 Sometimes we use *the* before names of places on the Earth. Find examples of *the* + these names of places in the article in Exercise 2.

1 a group of islands (or countries)
the Bahamas
2 the name of an ocean
3 a group of mountains
4 the name of a river

6 We can also use no article before some names of places. Find examples of no article + these names of places.

1 the name of a mountain
2 the name of a lake
3 the name of a country
4 the name of a continent

7 Work in groups. Think of one more example from other places on Earth for each category in Exercises 5 and 6. Compare your new lists with the class.

EXPLORING THE EARTH

We think humans have travelled everywhere on the Earth. But here are five places where no human has ever been.

The Black Hole of Andros is on an island in the Bahamas in the Atlantic Ocean. The hole is 47 metres deep, and the water is 36 °C and very black. Nobody has ever swum in it.

Mount Dinpernalason is east of the Himalayan mountains. It's 6,135 metres high so it isn't the highest mountain (Mount Everest is 8,848 metres) but nobody has ever climbed it.

Lake Vostok in Antarctica is 25 million years old and 14,000 square kilometres. Unfortunately, you can't see the lake because it's frozen under a glacier.

The Merume Mountains are at the end of the Mazaruni River in Guyana. The journey by boat is dangerous so nobody has explored many of these mountains.

The Foja Mountains in Papua New Guinea are 8,100 square kilometres of tropical forest. Nobody has ever made a map of the region.

DEFINITE *THE* OR NO ARTICLE + NAMES

Use *the* with the names of:

- deserts, seas, oceans and rivers: *the Gobi desert, the North Sea, The Pacific Ocean, the River Amazon.*
- plural names or groups of places: *The Alps, The United States of America, The Maldives.*

Use no article with the names of continents, countries, lakes or a single mountain: *Europe, Brazil, Lake Como, Mount Kilimanjaro.*

For further information and practice, see page 89.

8 Complete the text with *the* or Ø (no article).

EXPLORING THE DEEPEST PLACE ON THE EARTH

[1] *The* Mariana Trench is in [2] ________ Pacific Ocean. It's east of [3] ________ Mariana Islands and near [4] ________ Japan. It's the deepest place on the Earth. No one has ever travelled to the bottom of the Mariana Trench, until now. The film director James Cameron usually works in Hollywood in [5] ________ United States. Many of his films are famous, including *Titanic* (1997) and *Avatar* (2009). But Cameron is also a *National Geographic* explorer and has made a documentary about [6] ________ Sea of Cortez between California and [7] ________ Mexico. More recently, he has travelled down the Mariana Trench in a one-man submarine with 3D film cameras.

James Cameron

Listening

9 2.37 Listen to a news interview about James Cameron and the Mariana Trench. Number these topics in the order they mention them (1–5).

a the size of the submarine
b the distance and time to reach the bottom of the Mariana Trench
c another explorer
d filming the Mariana Trench
e the cost

10 2.37 Listen to the interview again. Answer the questions.

1 How many kilometres is it to the bottom of the Mariana Trench?
2 How long was his journey to the bottom?
3 How big was the submarine?
4 How could James Cameron see at the bottom of the trench?
5 What does he plan to make?
6 Who is Don Walsh?
7 Where was Don when Cameron went down?
8 How could Cameron afford to explore the Mariana Trench?

Word focus *how*

11 We often ask questions with *How …?* Match these questions from the listening (1–6) with the uses (a–f).

1 How big is it?
2 How well could he see?
3 How old is he?
4 How long did the journey take?
5 How much did James Cameron spend on this?
6 How did he travel there?

a ask about quantity and price
b ask about period of time
c ask about ability
d ask about age
e ask about the way something happens
f ask about size

Speaking

12 Write down the names of three famous places you have visited on Earth. Use these categories.

Category A: a mountain, forest, jungle, desert or island
Category B: an ocean, sea, river or lake
Category C: a city, country or continent

13 Work in pairs. Tell your partner the category (but not the place). You are going to guess your partner's place. Take turns to ask each other questions with *How*.

How far/near is the place from here?

How do you travel there?

12c Looking for a new Earth

Speaking

1 Work in groups. In the future, do you think humans will live in these places? Answer in three ways (A, B or C) and give reasons.

under the ocean   on the Moon
in the sky   near the Sun

A Yes, definitely!
B Possibly, but I'm not sure.
C No, never!

2 Do you think we will live anywhere else in the future?

Reading

3 Read the article on page 75. Add the sentences (a–d) to the end of each paragraph.

a As a result they are too hot and gassy or too cold and icy for human life.
b With current space technology, humans will take 766,000 years to travel there.
c And what will a new Earth look like?
d So if water isn't on the surface of the planet, it's sometimes under the rocks.

Vocabulary the Earth and other planets

4 Match these pairs of words from the article to the correct definition (a or b).

1 astronomers / explorers
  a someone who travels to and studies new places
  b someone who studies new places in space
2 planet / star
  a large round of object of burning gas in space (e.g. the sun)
  b large round object in space made of rock and metal or gas
3 to travel / to orbit
  a to go round a planet or star
  b to go on a journey from one place to another
4 surface / rock
  a the outside or top part of something (e.g. the ground on the Earth or a planet)
  b solid part of the Earth or a planet

Critical thinking structuring an argument

5 Writers use the words and phrases (1–5) to structure their arguments. Find these words in the article. Then match them with their purpose (a–e).

1 First of all	a add information
2 More importantly	b introduce bad news
3 Unfortunately	c give a reason
4 However	d introduce your first point
5 That's because	e introduce an opposite idea

Speaking

6 What's your opinion about finding a new Earth? Is it important? Is life on the Earth and life on other planets too different? Complete these sentences, then tell your partner.

In my opinion …
I think …
I don't think …

7 Write a short paragraph about your opinion in Exercise 6. Use some of the words and phrases in Exercise 5 to structure your argument. Begin your paragraph with: *Scientists are looking for a new Earth. In my opinion …*

LOOKING FOR A NEW EARTH

For thousands of years, humans have explored the Earth. Nowadays, we are exploring space. Astronomers are the modern-day explorers. Currently, many astronomers are looking for new planets and new places for humans to live in the future. But where do astronomers start looking?

First of all, astronomers look for a star. That's because our own Earth orbits a star (the Sun). More importantly, it is the correct distance from the Sun for heat and light. So when astronomers have found the star, they look at the planets around it. In recent years, astronomers have found nearly 400 new planets with stars. Unfortunately, many of these planets are either too near to the star or too far away.

However, if the planet is in a good position, astronomers look for three key things: water, air and rock. Water is important because all life needs water. Humans can drink it and they can also grow plants with water. And plants produce air for humans to breathe and food to eat. So all life on other planets will need water and air. Rock on a planet is also important. That's because there is often water under the rocks.

After many years of looking, astronomers have found a planet that is similar to Earth. It's Gliese 581g and it's near a star. The astronomers think it has water and rock and the average temperature is between –31°C and –12°C. That's cold, but not colder than Antarctica or the Arctic Circle, for example. Gliese 581g is bigger than the Earth and a year on Gliese 581g is only 37 Earth days instead of 365. But astronomers do not think these are big differences and some of them think Gliese 581g will be a new Earth. However, Gliese 581g is twenty light years from Earth – a distance of 18 trillion km.

12d Earth Day

Reading

1 Read about Earth Day. Answer the questions.

1 What do people do on Earth Day?
2 When and where was the first Earth Day?
3 Why did people go to it?

Real life making a presentation

2 2.38 Listen to a presentation by a university student. Choose the correct ending (a or b) to complete the sentences, according to his presentation. In two sentences, both endings are correct.

1 Davi is from ....
  a Brazil
  b the USA
2 He talks about Earth Day in the ....
  a past
  b present
3 People in China planted 600,000 ....
  a flowers
  b trees
4 In Brazil, people picked up rubbish in the ....
  a cities
  b countryside
5 Davi thinks Earth Day is ....
  a important
  b fun

3 2.38 Listen again. Complete these sentences from the presentation.

MAKING A PRESENTATION

Good morning, and 1 .... for coming.
My name's Davi, and 2 .... Brazil.
Today, 3 .... to talk about an important day.
4 .... all, Earth Day began on April 22nd in 1970.
5 .... , more than 175 countries have an Earth Day.
And 6 .... , in my country lots of people picked up rubbish in the cities and in the countryside.
7 .... , I really think Earth Day is important.
Thank you very much 8 ....

Friends at 'Earth Day' in Washington, D.C.

April 22nd is Earth Day. For one day every year, people in different countries help the Earth. For example, they clean parks, pick up rubbish or plant trees. The first Earth Day was on April 22, 1970 in the USA. Over 20 million people went to an Earth Day in their city. There were politicians, teachers, artists and musicians. As one person said, 'We had fun, but we also wanted to help the Earth and the environment.'

4 Pronunciation pausing on commas

a 2.39 Listen to and repeat these sentences from a presentation. Notice how the speaker pauses on commas. Then listen again and repeat.

1 Today, I'd like to talk about my company.
2 First of all, we started the company in 1999.
3 In conclusion, I think it's very important.

b Read sentences 1–7 in Exercise 3 and practise pausing on a comma.

5 Prepare a short presentation. Choose one of these topics and follow the instructions (1–4).

- your local club or organisation
- an important day in the year
- your company or place of study
- something you think is important

1 introduce yourself and your subject
2 talk about its history
3 talk about now
4 say why you like it or why you think it's important

6 Work in groups and give your presentations.

12e Planning an event

Writing a poster

1 Look at the poster for Earth Day. Where do people normally put posters? What are the best places so people can see a poster?

2 Look at the poster. Which of the following questions does it answer?

1 Who is organising it?
2 What is it?
3 What date is it on?
4 What activities are there?
5 Is there car parking or transport?
6 Where is it?
7 What time does it start and end?
8 How much does it cost?
9 Why is it happening?
10 What can you buy?
11 Is there food and drink?
12 Where can you read more information?

3 Writing skill important words and information

a We don't normally write full sentences on posters, notices and adverts. Look at the highlighted words in these sentences. They are the words and information on the poster. Which words does the writer use on the poster? Which kind of words doesn't the writer use?

1 Everyone is welcome to our Earth Day celebration at Newmarket Park on April 22.
2 We are going to plant 100 trees around Newmarket town centre.

b Underline the key words and information in these sentences. Then compare your ideas with the poster.

1 There will be presentations about how to help the environment.
2 You can watch theatre, listen to music and look at art by local performers and artists.
3 Shops are going to be selling environmentally-friendly products.
4 You can also buy hot and cold food.
5 Entrance to the event is free.
6 Visit our website at NECG.org/earthday for more information.

4 Work in groups. You are going to design a poster for an Earth Day in your town or city. Look at this list of activities that many people do on Earth Day. Discuss each activity and choose one.

- plant lots of trees in the city centre
- pick up plastic bags and rubbish in the parks
- have a party in the park with local musicians
- sell energy efficient light bulbs to local people
- visit local schools and talk to school children about Earth Day
- your own idea

5 Prepare and design a poster for your Earth Day. Include some or all the information in Exercise 2. Use short sentences.

6 Put your posters on the wall in your classroom. Look at the posters by other groups. Do they include all the important information? Do they use short sentences?

12f Volcanoes

Lava from a volcano

Before you watch

1 Work in pairs. Look at the photo of a volcano and read the caption. Follow the instructions.

1 Write three words to describe it.
2 Compare your words with other students in your class.

2 Discuss the questions as a class.

1 Are there any volcanoes in your country? Are they active?
2 Have you ever seen a volcano?

While you watch

3 Watch the video. Number these things in the order you see them (1–7).

a the Earth from space
b a map of the Ring of Fire
c a group of tourists
d a volcano in the middle of the sea
e a picture of Mount Vesuvius and Pompeii
f a diagram of the inside of a volcano
g an animal

4 Watch the video again. Match these names and words (1–8) with the descriptions (a–h).

1 mountains of fire	5 lava
2 'the Ring of Fire'	6 Kilauea
3 tectonic plates	7 Vesuvius
4 magma	8 Pompeii

a the surface of the Earth are made of these large pieces of rock
b a name for volcanoes in the past
c volcanoes around the Pacific ocean
d a volcano in Hawaii
e a famous and dangerous volcano in history
f this hot rock melts under the ground where the tectonic plates meet
g a volcano buried this city two thousand years ago
h magma at the surface of the Earth

5 Watch the video again. Are these sentences true (T) or false (F)?

1 Volcanoes are openings in the surface of the Earth.
2 There are 1,500 active volcanoes around the Pacific Ocean.
3 Tectonic plates are moving all the time.
4 Tourists cannot go near Kilauea because it's dangerous.
5 Two thousand people died in Pompeii.
6 Volcanoes always destroy life.

6 At the end of the video, the narrator says volcanoes are important for life. What are the reasons?

After you watch

7 Complete the text about Mount Vesuvius with these words.

active eruption lava magma
tectonic plates volcano

Mount Vesuvius is a famous [1] .... in southern Italy, near the city of Naples. Vesuvius began because the two [2] .... of Africa and Europe meet in this region. Nowadays, it's still an [3] .... volcano, but there hasn't been an [4] .... for many years. Visitors can see where the [5] .... ran down the sides of the mountain in the past, but now trees and vineyards grow here. No one knows if Vesuvius will erupt in the future, but there is still hot [6] .... under the mountain so it's always possible.

8 Group presentation a presentation about volcanoes

Work in groups. Prepare a group presentation about volcanoes. You can use information from the video and from other places (e.g. the Internet). Your presentation should include the following:

1 Volcanoes on the Earth today (where most of them are)
2 The science of a volcano (why and how it's made)
3 Some examples of active volcanoes you can visit
4 Why volcanoes are dangerous
5 Why we need volcanoes

9 Work with another group. Take turns to give your presentations.

- How similar or different were the presentations?
- Did you learn something new about volcanoes from the other group?

active (volcano) (adj) /'æktɪv/ a volcano that can produce lava at any time
eruption (n) /ɪ'rʌpʃn/ when lava comes out of the top of a volcano

Grammar

1 Complete the conversations with *'ll*, *will* or *won't*.

A: I think we [1] .... live on the Moon in the future.
B: No, we [2] .... It's impossible.

A: [3] .... the Earth get warmer?
B: Yes, I think it [4] ....

A: In some parts of the world it [5] .... rain this year.
B: [6] .... deserts get larger?
A: Yes, they [7] ....

2 Write *the* or Ø (no article) for these places.

1 .... Polynesian Islands
2 .... Michigan
3 .... Atlantic Ocean
4 .... Atlas Mountains
5 .... Africa
6 .... Yangtze River
7 .... Mount Kilimanjaro
8 .... United Arab Emirates
9 .... Gobi Desert
10 .... Polynesian Islands
11 .... Iceland
12 .... Arctic Circle

3 In the future, where would you like to visit on the Earth? Write your top three destinations. Then compare your list with a partner.

I CAN
- make predictions with *will* ☐
- use the definite article or no article with places ☐

Vocabulary

4 Complete the text with these abbreviations.

°C   m   kg   %   km²

Easter Island is in the south-eastern Pacific Ocean and its area is 163 [1] .... The climate is warm with an average temperature of about 20 [2] .... The island is famous for 887 statues called Maoi. The largest Maoi weighs 74,389 [3] .... and it's 9.8 [4] .... tall. 3,790 people live on the island. 60 [5] .... of the population are Rapanui. The ancestors of this people built the Maoi.

5 Complete the questions about Easter Island with these words. Then find the answers in the text.

tall   big   many   warm

1 How .... is Easter Island?
2 How .... is the climate?
3 How .... is the largest Maoi?
4 How .... people live on the island?

6 Choose the correct option to complete these sentences.

1 I'm from Poland and my family always spends the summer by the Baltic *Ocean / Sea*.
2 The *Lake / River* Plate is between Argentina and Uruguay.
3 Greenland is the largest *forest / island* in the world.
4 We all think they are cold places, but the Arctic and the Antarctic are also *deserts / mountains*.

7 Work in pairs. Which of the eight areas of land and water in Exercise 6 do you have in your country? Tell your partner.

I CAN
- use abbreviations ☐
- talk about large areas of land and water ☐

Real life

8 Delete the extra word in each sentence from a presentation.

1 Good morning ~~you~~, and thank you for coming.
2 My name's Eva, and I'm from the Germany.
3 Today, I'm am going to talk about my company.
4 First of all, the company has began in 1965.
5 In conclusion, I think the company will to grow in the future.
6 Thank you very much for your listening.

I CAN
- make a presentation ☐

Speaking

9 You have reached the end of the book! Work in groups and prepare a quiz about facts in *Life*. Look at each unit and write one question about the information in it.

10 Work with another group and ask your twelve questions. Which group answered the most questions correctly?

Unit 7c Exercise 9, page 14

1 Mercury
2 Venus
3 Neptune
4 Earth
5 Venus

Unit 7a Exercise 11, page 11

Student A

Read about the journey. Make questions in the past simple with the question words. Then take turns to ask your partner your questions and complete the text.

> Peter McBride, Mark Rebholz and John LaNoue are modern pilots. They flew from England to Cape Town in [1] ________ (when?). Their aeroplane was from the 1920s and very similar to the Silver Queen. They took off from England. They arrived in [3] ________ (where?) three weeks later. They couldn't fly over parts of Africa so they flew over [5] ________ (which sea?) and they arrived in Saudi Arabia. Their plane had mechanical problems at Mount Kilimanjaro because of [7] ________ (why?). But they fixed the plane and they landed in Cape Town. They flew 5,600 kilometres, but they didn't receive any money! They just wanted to relive the past.

Unit 7d Exercise 8, page 16

Unit 10b Exercise 2, page 48

Student B

Memorising numbers

Do you often forget new numbers? For example a telephone number, a house number or a PIN number. Some people 'see' the number in their brain. Maybe the numbers are in colour or they see the numbers like a picture. You can also repeat the number a few times or learn the numbers in groups. So you remember the first two numbers because it's your age. And the next three numbers is the house number of a friend. We remember better when we make it personal.

Unit 11a Exercise 2, page 58

What do your answers mean?

Tourist A: You don't have much spare time so your holidays last a week or two weeks. Your favourite holidays are going on cruises or bus tours. You like taking lots of clothes and staying in comfortable hotels. You usually travel with groups of people.

Tourist B: You go on long holidays (a month or more) and you don't like planning them. Your favourite holidays are backpacking or hiking. You enjoy meeting local people, eating local food and staying at small hotels or camping. You usually travel on your own or with one other friend.

Unit 7a Exercise 11, page 11

Student B

Read about the journey. Make questions in the past simple with the question words. Then take turns to ask your partner your questions and complete the text.

Peter McBride, Mark Rebholz and John LaNoue are modern pilots. They flew from England to Cape Town in 1999. Their aeroplane was from the 1920s and very similar to the Silver Queen. They took off from [2] .... (where?). They arrived in Egypt [4] .... (when?). They couldn't fly over parts of Africa so they flew over the Red Sea and arrived in Saudi Arabia. Their plane had mechanical problems at [6] .... (where?) because of the strong wind. But they fixed the plane and they landed in Cape Town. They flew [8] .... (how many kilometres?) but they didn't receive any money! They just wanted to relive the past.

Unit 10b Exercise 2, page 48

Student A

Memorising names and faces

Do you often forget names and faces? When you meet someone for the first time, listen to them. Repeat their name and use it in the conversation. For example, 'It's nice to meet you, Elaine.' Look at their face and the clothes they wear. Introduce them to another person and make conversation. With new work colleagues, write down their name, their job and where you met them.

Unit 10b Exercise 2, page 48

Student C

Memorising directions and addresses

Taxi drivers learn hundreds of roads and addresses. How do they do it? Some people see the directions in their head. They see a picture of the roads or the buildings. Other people repeat the names of the roads, or the directions. For example, 'Turn left at the end, turn right at the cinema.' You can also draw the directions on paper. When you draw, use different colours – the brain remembers more when it sees colour.

Unit 8d Exercise 6, page 28

Discuss these things.

- The subject of the photo
- Location of people and things
- The people (their appearance and what they are doing or wearing)
- Your opinion of the photo

UNIT 7

Past simple: negatives, questions and short answers

Form and use

Negatives
I/you/he/she/it/we/they **didn't travel** by train.

Questions
Did I/you/he/she/it/we/they travel **by** train?

Short answers
Yes, I/you/he/she/it/we/they **did**. No, I/you/he/she/it/we/they **didn't**.

Wh- questions
Why/When **did** I/you/he/she/it/we/they **travel** by train?

We use the auxiliary verb *did/didn't* for negatives and questions.
Kate didn't take the train.
Did you use a map?

We also use *did/didn't* for short answers.
Did they drive? Yes, they did.

Remember, we use the infinitive form of the verb.
We didn't go. (not ~~*We didn't went*~~.)

Practice

1 Complete the conversations with *did or didn't*.

1 A: *Did* you bring a map?
B: Yes, I .... It's here.
2 A: How much .... the bus ticket cost?
B: I don't know. I .... pay.
3 A: .... you have a good trip?
B: Yes, we .... It was great.
4 A: Who .... you travel with?
B: Just my wife. My children .... come.
5 A: What time .... the plane take off?
B: I'm not sure. I .... look at my watch.
6 A: .... the Mayflower sail to the New World?
B: Yes, it .... Its first journey there was in 1620.
7 A: .... you visit the transport museum in London?
B: No, we .... We .... have time.
8 A: .... you take a bus to the airport?
B: Yes, we .... It was very easy.

Comparative adjectives

Form

Adjective	Spelling rule	Example
one-syllable adjectives	+ *-er* + *-r* if the adjective ends in *-e*	*warm* → ***warmer*** *safe* → ***safer***
adjectives ending in one vowel + one consonant	double the consonant and + *-er*	*big* → ***bigger***
two or more syllable adjectives	*more* + adjective	*boring* → ***more boring*** *interesting* → ***more interesting*** *easy* → ***easier***
two-syllable adjectives ending *-y*	change *-y* to *-ier*	
irregular adjectives	e.g. *good, bad, far*	*good* → ***better*** *bad* → ***worse*** *far* → ***further***

We use *than* after a comparative sentence.
An aeroplane is faster ***than*** *a ship.*

Use

We use comparative adjectives to compare two things or people.

Practice

2 Write sentences with comparative adjectives.

1 Travel by air / by road (safe)
Travel by air is safer than by road.
2 My car / your car (old)
....
3 Trains / buses (expensive)
....
4 A bike / a car (slow)
....
5 Geese / small birds (fast)
....
6 Learning a language / learning a musical instrument (difficult)
....
7 Male elephants / females (big)
....
8 My journey to work / your journey to work (long)
....

Superlative adjectives

Form

Adjective	Spelling rule	Example
one-syllable adjectives	+ -*est* + -*st* if the adjective ends in -*e*	*near* → *nearest* *large* → *largest*
adjectives ending in one vowel + one consonant	double the consonant and + -*est*	*big* → *biggest*
two or more syllable adjectives	*the most* + adjective	***the most** amazing*
two-syllable adjectives ending –y	change -*y* to -*iest*	*easy* → *easiest*
irregular adjectives	e.g. *good, bad, far*	*good* → ***the best*** *bad* → ***the worst*** *far* → ***the furthest***

We use *the* before a superlative.
Neptune is **the** *furthest planet from the sun.*

Use

We use the superlative form to compare something to other things (*the biggest, best,* etc.) in a group.

Practice

3 Complete the sentences with the superlative form of the adjectives.

1 The HSR (high-speed rail) is *the fastest* (fast) train in the world.
2 The London Underground is .... (old) metro system in the world.
3 My car is .... (small) car in the street.
4 Who's .... (good) driver in your family?
5 Neil Armstrong is one of .... (famous) astronauts in history.
6 Fridays and Sundays are .... (expensive) days to travel by plane.
7 My road trip across the USA was .... (amazing) journey of my life.
8 Atlanta has .... (busy) airport in the world.

UNIT 8

have got / has got

Form

Affirmative	Negative
I/you/we/they**'ve got** (**have got**) brown eyes.	I/you/we/they **haven't got** (**have not got**) any hair.
He/she/it**'s got** (**has got**) brown eyes.	He/she/it **hasn't got** (**has not got**) any hair.

Questions	Short answers
Have I/you/we/they **got** a camera?	Yes, I/you/we/they **have**. / No, I/you/we/they **haven't**.
Has he/she/it **got** a camera?	Yes, he/she/it **has**. / No, he/she/it **hasn't**.

We do not use the auxiliary *do/does* with *have got*.
I haven't got a key. (not ~~*I don't have got a key*~~.)
Have you got any money? (not ~~*Do you have got any money*~~?)

Use

We use *have got* to talk about appearance, possessions and relationships.
Has your sister got dark hair?
I've got three children.
He hasn't got a bicycle.

We can also use *have* to talk about possession, family and appearance.
They have a house in Italy.

We use *have got* in spoken and informal written English. We don't use *have got* in American English. We use *have*.

We don't usually use *have got* in the past simple.
I had long hair when I was young. (Not ~~*I had got long hair when I was young*~~.)

Practice

1 Write sentences with the correct form of *have got*.

1 Jake / two brothers
Jake's got two brothers.
2 I / not / any climbing boots
....
3 Lily / curly hair?
....
4 Her parents / a furniture business
....
5 your car / air-conditioning?
....
6 you / a new phone?
....
7 Rob and Helen / not / children
....
8 Our house / two bathrooms
....

Present continuous

Form

Affirmative	Negative	Interrogative
I'm (am) working.	I'm not (am not) working.	Am I working?
You/we/they're (are) working.	You/we/they aren't (are not) working.	Are you/we/they working?
He/she/it's (is) working.	He/she/it isn't (is not) working.	Is he/she/it working?

We form the present continuous with the present simple of the verb *to be* + verb + *-ing* form of the verb.

Use

We use the present continuous to talk about:

- things happening now. *I can't come now. I'm eating my dinner.*
- things happening around now, but not necessarily at the moment. *She's walking to work a lot these days.*
- We don't usually use stative verbs (*be, have, like, love*, etc.) in the present continuous.

Present continuous and present simple

We use present simple (not present continuous) to describe a habit or routine.
He usually wears trainers, but today he's wearing formal shoes.

We use different time expressions with the present continuous and present simple:

Present continuous
now, these days, at the moment, today, this week/month/year

Present simple
usually, often, every day, once a week, never

Notes

Notice the spelling rules for the *-ing* form.

- for most verbs, add *-ing*: *walk → walking, play → playing, read → reading*
- for verbs ending in a consonant + vowel + consonant, double the last letter of the verb and add *-ing*: *sit → sitting, run → running, put → putting*
- for verbs ending in *-e*, delete the final *e* and add *-ing*: *make → making, come → coming, write → writing*

Practice

2 Complete the sentences with the present simple or present continuous form of the verbs.

1 Why *are you wearing* (you wear) gloves? Are you cold?
2 I .... (read) a very good book at the moment.
3 She .... (not work) today.
4 .... (you usually have) a shower in the morning or the evening?
5 Who .... (you wait) for?
6 He .... (not like) wearing hats.
7 It's not a good time to speak. I .... (make) dinner.
8 Our cousins .... (stay) with us today and tomorrow.

UNIT 9

going to (for plans)

Form

Affirmative	Negative
I'm (am) going to see a film.	I'm not (am not) going to see a film.
You/we/they're (are) going to see a film.	You/we/they aren't (are not) going to see a film.
He/she/it's (is) going to see a film.	He/she/it isn't (is not) going to see a film.

Questions	Short answers
Am I going to see a film?	Yes, I am. / No I'm not.
Are you/we/they going to see a film?	Yes, you/we/they are. / No, you/we/they aren't.
Is he/she/it going to see a film?	Yes, he/she/it is. / No, he/she/it isn't.

Use

We use *going to* to talk about our plans for the future.
We're going to watch a DVD this evening.

With the verb *go* we can say *going to go* or *going*.
I'm going to go to out tonight. = *I'm going out tonight.*

We often use future time expressions with *going to* (e.g. *next week, tonight, tomorrow, this evening*).
We're moving house next month.

Practice

1 Complete the sentences with *going to* and these verbs.

come ~~meet~~ not have not pay see
study visit write

1 We *'re going to meet* Abigail outside the cinema.
2 What .... they .... at the theatre?
3 .... Flavia .... to our party?
4 He .... a novel next year.
5 .... you .... your cousin in Australia?
6 I .... a holiday this summer.
7 He .... French at university next year.
8 I .... extra money to see the film in 4D.

Present continuous for future reference

We can use the present continuous to talk about the future and to make future arrangements with another person.

I'm meeting my friends at ten.
He isn't working tomorrow.
Where are you eating out tonight?

Infinitive of purpose

Form and use

We can use an infinitive to talk about why we do something. This is called an infinitive of purpose.
I'm going to Madrid to visit the Prado Museum.
(not ~~*I'm going to Madrid for visit the Prado Museum.*~~)

We often use the infinitive of purpose to answer the question *Why?*
Why are you going to the shop? To get a newspaper.

Practice

2 Complete the answers to these questions with infinitives of purpose. Use these verbs.

change drive get invite learn make see ~~take~~

1 Why are you going to get up early tomorrow?
To take Ben to the airport.
2 Why is she going to Mexico?
.... Spanish.
3 Why are you going to call the doctor's surgery?
.... the time of my appointment.
4 Why are they going to the cinema early?
.... good seats.
5 Why are you going to call Jim?
.... him to dinner.
6 Why are you going to buy apples?
.... a fruit salad.
7 Why are you going to the art gallery?
.... a photography exhibition.
8 Why are you going to rent a car?
.... to the coast.

UNIT 10

Present perfect

Form

Affirmative	Negative
I/you/we/they**'ve (have) sent** a letter.	I/you/we/they **haven't (have not) used** a public telephone.
He/she/it**'s (has) gone** to Spain.	He/she/it **hasn't (has not) come** back.

Questions	Short answers
Have I/you/we/they **seen** that film?	**Yes,** I/you/we/they **have.** **No,** I/you/we/they **haven't.**
Has he/she/it **arrived?**	**Yes,** he/she/it **has.** **No,** he/she/it **hasn't.**

We form the present perfect with *have/has* + the past participle (*lived*, *sent*, etc.).

With regular verbs, past participles end in *-ed*. They are the same as the past simple: *book → booked, telephone → telephoned, play → played*

Many verbs have irregular past participles. They are often, but not always, different from the past simple: *see → saw → seen, write → wrote → written, buy → bought → bought*

Go has two past participles:
She's been to China. (= She went to China and came back.)
She's gone to China. (= She went to China and is in China now.)

Use

We use the present perfect to talk about experiences in the past. We don't say exactly when they happened.
I've made a YouTube video.
I haven't booked a holiday at a travel agent.

With the present perfect we often use *ever* (= in your life) in questions and *never* (not in your life).
Have you ever been to Brazil?
He's never downloaded a film.

We use the affirmative form with *never.*
I've never been to Greece. (not ~~*I haven't never been to Greece.*~~)

Practice

1 Complete the sentences with the present perfect form of the verbs.

1 I *'ve downloaded* (download) a lot of music.
2 My mother .... (travel) to several countries in South America.
3 My 90-year-old neighbour .... (never/ use) a computer.
4 We .... (go) to the new science museum. It was amazing.
5 I .... (not write) many letters by hand.
6 .... you ever .... (cook) Indian food?
7 She .... (not read) any plays by Shakespeare.
8 He .... (never / buy) a CD.

Present perfect and past simple

Use

Present perfect

We use the present perfect to talk about something in the past and we don't say exactly when it happened.
I've been to Costa Rica.
We often use words like *ever* and *never* because they do not talk about an exact time.
Have you ever learned a new language?

Past simple

We use the past simple to talk about something in the past and we say when it happened. We often use it with past time expressions e.g. *last week, yesterday, in 2012.*
We went to Beijing in 2008. (not ~~*We have been to Beijing in 2008.*~~)

We use the past simple with the question *When …?*
When did he win the competition? (not ~~*When has he won the competition?*~~)

Practice

2 Choose the correct option to complete the conversations.

1 A: *Have you ever been / Did you ever go* to Rome?
B: Yes, I *have / did*. I *have worked / worked* there between 2005 and 2008.
2 A: Can you remember his name? I*'ve forgotten / forgot* it.
B: It's Roger. He *was / has been* at university with me last year.
3 A: *Have you seen / Did you see* Mark yesterday?
B: Yes, I *did / have*. I *saw / have seen* him in the library.
4 A: What *have you done / did you do* last night?
B: Some friends *have come / came* round for dinner.
5 A: What *have you learned / did you learn* in your guitar lesson last week?
B: The teacher *taught / has taught* us some new chords.
6 A: *Have you ever studied / Did you ever study* a foreign language?
B: Yes, I *have / did*. I *'ve learned / learned* Arabic last year.
7 A: My husband's a journalist. He *'s visited / visited* a lot of countries.
B: *Have you ever travelled / Did you ever travel* with him?
8 A: *Have you won / Did you win* a prize in the dance competition last month?
B: No, I *haven't / didn't*, but I *had / have had* a lot of fun.

UNIT 11

should

Form

Affirmative	Negative
I/you/he/she/it/we/they **should** take an umbrella.	I/you/he/she/it/we/they **shouldn't** take a lot of cash.
Questions	**Short answers**
Should I/you/he/she/it/we/they buy a ticket in advance?	**Yes,** I/you/he/she/it/we/they **should.** **No,** I/you/he/she/it/we/they **shouldn't.**

Should is a modal verb. Remember that this means:

- There is no third person -*s*.
  He should go. (not ~~*He shoulds go.*~~)
- There is no *to* before the verb.
  You should do it. (not ~~*You should to do it.*~~)
- The negative is with *not* (*n't*).
  You shouldn't do it. (not ~~*You don't should do it.*~~)
- There is no auxiliary *do* in questions.
  Should I come? (not ~~*Do I should come?*~~)

Use

We use *should* to give advice.
You should put sun cream on. = I think it's a good idea.
You shouldn't go on your own. = I think it's a bad idea.

Practice

1 Complete the sentences with *should or shouldn't* and these verbs.

~~do~~ eat get go learn stay watch wear

1 He *should do* some exercise. He's not very fit.
2 You .... gloves. It's very cold.
3 You .... a tango show when you're in Buenos Aires.
4 I .... some Italian phrases before I go to Sicily.
5 You .... at that restaurant. The food's terrible.
6 I .... a new job. This one's very stressful.
7 They .... at that hotel. It's noisy at night.
8 I .... to bed late tonight. I've got an exam tomorrow.

have to / don't have to, can/can't

Form

Affirmative	Negative
I/you/we/they **have to** show a passport.	I/you/we/they **don't have to** show a passport.
He/she/it **has to** show a passport.	He/she/it **doesn't have to** show a passport.
Questions	**Short answers**
Do I/you/we/they **have to** buy a ticket?	**Yes,** I/you/we/they **do.** **No,** I/you/we/they **don't.**
Does he/she/it **have to** buy a ticket?	**Yes,** he/she/it **doesn't.** **No,** I/you/we/they **don't.**

Affirmative	Negative
I/you/he/she/it/we/they **can** take one bag onto the plane.	I/you/he/she/it/we/they **can't** smoke on the plane.

Use

We use *have to, don't have to, can* and *can't* to talk about rules and possibilities.

- We use *have to* + infinitive to say that something is necessary.
  You have to turn off your mobile phone on the plane.
- We use *don't have to* to say or that something is not necessary.
  You don't have to show your passport on domestic flights.

- We use *can* to say that something is possible.
  You can check in online.
- We use *can't* to say that something is not possible.
  Air passengers can't take knives in their hand luggage.

Practice

2 Choose the correct option (a–c) to complete the sentences.

1 Air passengers ______ check in online.
 a have to b can't (c) can
2 Pilots ______ wear a uniform.
 a have to b can't c can
3 We ______ check in at the desk. I checked in online yesterday.
 a have to b don't have to c can
4 You ______ smoke on an aeroplane.
 a can b can't c don't have to
5 You ______ pay for food on aeroplanes.
 a can often b can't often c often have to
6 You usually ______ book plane tickets before you fly.
 a have to b don't have to c can't
7 You ______ stand up when a plane is taking off.
 a have to b can c can't
8 Air passengers ______ take more than 100 ml of liquid in their hand luggage.
 a don't have to b can c can't

everywhere, somewhere, nowhere, anywhere

Form

	-where	-thing	-body
every-	everywhere	everything	everybody
some-	somewhere	something	somebody
no-	nowhere	nothing	nobody
any-	anywhere	anything	anybody

Use

- Use these words with the verb in the singular form.
  Everybody likes travelling. (not ~~*like*~~)
- Use *any-* in negative sentences and questions.
  I didn't buy anything at the shops.
  Is there anywhere to stay in this town?

Practice

3 Write in the missing part of the word.

1 There are cafés every *where* in Paris.
2 He needs to buy some______ in this shop.
3 I telephoned the airline, but no______ answered the phone.
4 Hello? Is any______ there?
5 I think ______body needs a holiday. It's really important.
6 I put my sunglasses ______where and I can't find them.
7 I don't like holidays on the beach. There's ______thing to do!
8 I haven't been ______where on holiday this year.

UNIT 12

will/won't

Form

Affirmative	Negative
I/you/he/she/it/we**'ll** (**will**) change.	I/you/he/she/it/we **won't** (**will not**) change.
Interrogative	**Short answers**
Will I/you/he/she/it/we/they **live** for a long time?	**Yes,** I/you/he/she/it/we/they **will.** **No,** I/you/he/she/it/we/they **won't.**

Will is a modal verb. This means:

- There is no third person *-s*.
  He will go. (not ~~*He wills go*~~.)
- There is no *to* before the verb.
  It will get hotter. (not ~~*It will to get hotter.*~~)
- The negative is with *not* (*n't*).
  It won't be there for ever. (not ~~*It don't will be there for ever*~~.)
- There is no auxiliary *do* in questions.
  Will they come? (not ~~*Do they will come*~~?)

Use

We use *will* and *won't* to talk about what we think or know about the future, i.e. to make predictions.
The Earth will get warmer.
He won't buy an apartment.

We often use *think* or *don't think* before *will* when we make predictions.
I think it'll snow tomorrow.
I don't think we'll go to Scotland this year.

We usually say *I don't think* + *will* not *I think* + *won't*.

Practice

1 Complete the sentences with *will* (*'ll*) or *won't*.

1 We *won't* buy an electric car. They're too expensive.
2 Do you think it ______ snow this weekend?
3 I don't think humans ______ go to the Moon again.
4 It's a national holiday tomorrow so the shops ______ be open.
5 I'm doing my homework now because I ______ have time this evening.
6 I'm going to the doctor's at 9 a.m. so I ______ miss the meeting. Sorry.
7 Sheena ______ move to the countryside. She loves city life.
8 Don't worry about your interview. You ______ be fine.

Definite *the* or no article before names

Form and use

the	no article
• deserts: the Sahara desert • seas: the Mediterranean (Sea) • oceans: the Atlantic (Ocean) • rivers: the Nile • plural names or groups of places: the United States/The USA, the Alps, the Philippines, the Netherlands	• continents: Africa • countries: Mexico • states: California • towns and cities: Milan • places in towns and cities (streets, buildings, etc.): George Street, Oxford University, Waterloo Station • lakes: Lake Tahoe • a single mountain: Mount Everest

Practice

2 Add *the* to the correct place (or places) in the sentences. If the sentence is correct, put a tick (✓).

1 We went to Andes when we were in Argentina.
2 Africa is bigger than Europe.
3 Mississippi is the longest river in United States.
4 Mont Blanc is the highest mountain in Alps.
5 Would you like to go to Lanzarote in Canary Islands?
6 Have you ever swum in Atlantic Ocean?
7 I'd love to visit Atacama desert.

Unit 7

2.1

In 1620, one hundred and twenty people travelled across the Atlantic Ocean. The ship was called the Mayflower. It left England on September 6th. At first, the weather was good, but later, there were bad storms at sea. Eventually, after 2,750 miles, the Mayflower arrived in the 'New World' (now America) on November 11th. The people on the ship were the first Europeans to live in the 'New World'. After this journey, the Mayflower sailed across the Atlantic ocean four more times. On its final journey, it left England, but it never arrived in America.

2.2

I = Interviewer, H = Historian

I: This week's programme is about a famous journey nearly one hundred years ago. In 1920, an aeroplane called the Silver Queen travelled from England to Cape Town. It was the first aeroplane to travel on this journey. Here in the studio to tell us about this journey is travel historian Nigel Ross.
H: Hello.
I: So Nigel, in 1920, this was a small aeroplane and there weren't many airports in Africa at that time. How dangerous was this journey?
H: Oh, it was very dangerous for the two pilots.
I: Yes, the two pilots were Pierre Van Ryneveld and Quintin Brand. Did they have maps for this journey?
H: Yes, they did. Well, for some parts of the journey. For example, they had maps for Europe, Egypt and South Africa. But they didn't have maps for other parts of Africa.
I: And why did they go on this journey? Was it for the money?
H: All travellers and explorers go for different reasons. But Van Ryneveld and Brand didn't go for the money. I think they flew there because it was new. They wanted to be the first.

2.3

1 The saiga lives in Central Asia. In the spring, it walks to higher places. A male saiga can walk thirty-five kilometres a day and it's faster than a female. The journey is more difficult for a female saiga because she has her calf in the spring.
2 Many turtles swim longer distances than other sea animals, but the loggerhead turtle has a longer journey than other turtles. It leaves the beach as a baby and it swims around fourteen thousand kilometres. Fifteen years later, the female turtle returns to the same beach and lays eggs.
3 Tree frogs go on shorter journeys than other animals, but for a small tree frog the journey isn't easier. Every spring it climbs down a tree. That's about thirty metres. It lays eggs in water and then returns up the tree. For a tree frog that's a very long journey.

2.5

Conversation one

C = Dr Cunningham, E = Dr Egan

C: Doctor Egan? Doctor Egan?
E: Yes, are you Doctor Cunningham?
C: That's right. Nice to meet you. But please, call me Sonia.
E: Nice to meet you too, Sonia. I'm Charles.
C: How was your flight?
E: Not bad. A bit tiring because we were delayed for ten hours.
C: That's right. I got your message.
E: Oh that's good. But I had a good night's sleep at the airport hotel.
C: Oh was it comfortable?
E: Yes, very. I feel fine now.
C: Great! OK. My car is outside.
E: Right. Let's go.

Conversation two

F = Friend, E = Dr Egan

F: Hello Charles. How was your trip?
E: Very interesting. And I had some very useful meetings with Doctor Cunningham.
F: Good. Did you try the local food?
E: Yes, I did. It was delicious. I ate fresh seafood every night.
F: And what was the weather like?
E: Terrible! On the second day we couldn't travel anywhere.
F: Why? What happened?
E: There was a terrible storm. It rained for twenty-four hours and all the roads were closed.

Unit 8

2.7

I was in the city of Iloilo in the Philippines last month. I wanted to see the Dinagyang Festival. The festival is always on the fourth Sunday in January. It's the most famous festival in the Philippines and thousands of local people and tourists come to the city. Groups of local people wear colourful clothes and make-up. Then they dance through the streets. The music was really loud. I also ate lots of local food – it was delicious!

2.8

A: I've got some photographs here from my holiday in Spain.
B: Oh, let me see.
A: This one is from a town called Banyoles. It's in Catalonia.
B: What's this one?
A: This is of three children in masks. It was a special festival. They always have it in the summer. People come from all over for the food and music.
B: Why have they got these masks?
A: It's part of the festival. The masks are called *capgrossos* in the local language. I think they're a bit ugly.
B: Oh no! I don't think so. He's got a fantastic white face. And look at those red cheeks.
A: Yeah, but he hasn't got any eyebrows.
B: Oh, that's right. Well, he's got one. So are they brothers and sister?
A: Yes, that's right. I think this one's the oldest brother. Or maybe he's tall because he's got that big hat. And she's his little sister. She's got great big blue eyes.
B: She's similar to my daughter with that blonde hair and the red ribbon.
A: I hope she isn't!

2.9

This Polga tribesman is a dancer at a festival in Papua New Guinea. All the men are tall and handsome and they've got colourful clothes with red hats over their short, dark hair. They've got white faces and black lines around their brown eyes, on their eyebrows, and on their cheeks. The man in the photo has got red on his lips and nose, and he's got black on his chin and a string of seashells around his neck.

2.11

S = Sam, G = Gilliam

S: Hello?
G: Hi Sam. I'm calling from Tokyo.
S: Sorry, who's speaking?
G: Sam. It's me. Gillian.
S: Oh sorry, Gillian. It's a really bad line. Give me the number of your hotel and I can call you back.
G: No, I'm not staying in Tokyo. I'm waiting for my flight at the airport.
S: Where are you going now?
G: To Vietnam. Ho Chi Minh City.
S: Oh I see. Are you travelling on your own?
G: No, Jess is with me. We're working on a project together. It's about fashion in Asia.
S: Great. Can you email me some of your photographs?
G: Sure, but my email isn't working at the moment.
S: OK, send them tomorrow… Bye.

2.12

Reinier Gerritsen is one of my favourite photographers. He's from the Netherlands, but you can often see his photos around the world, in magazines and sometimes in galleries. I've got some books by him as well. His photos are very interesting. They often show people in their everyday life. This one is on the New York subway. It's early morning so I think most of the people are travelling to work. They're all standing close together, but they aren't talking to each other. Well, on the right, the man and woman are talking, but the others aren't. The woman in the middle is reading her book. And in front of her the woman with blonde hair is listening to music. Then the other blonde woman on the left is watching her. I'm not sure what she's thinking, but she looks a bit sad. Oh and look at the other woman at the back. She's looking straight at the photographer. I take the train to work every day, but I never think about the other people. I like it because I don't normally look at people very closely. But Gerritsen does.

Unit 9

2.14

For a visitor to the city of Sydney, it's a strange sight. You are driving past the harbour with its fantastic view of the opera house, when you suddenly see the huge face of a sleeping woman. But for local people, this outdoor cinema is popular during the long hot summer evenings. The screen is the same size as a large building and it's above the water. The audience can sit on the beach or in their cars as they watch their favourite actors in the latest film.

2.15

C = Charles, B = Beata

C: Hey! Beata. Stop!
B: Hi Charles. Sorry, but I'm going to buy a ticket for the next film. It starts in five minutes. It's called *My Wedding and Other Secrets*. Are you going to see it too?
C: No, I'm not, but what are you doing afterwards? Didier, Monica and I are going to have dinner at a Japanese restaurant. Do you want to come?
B: Sorry, but I'm not going to stay out late tonight. I'm tired.
C: Sure.
B: Oh, I must go. Bye.
C: Bye. See you later.

2.17

I = Interviewer, A = Adrian Seymour

I: Doctor Adrian Seymour is a film director and a wildlife biologist. He travels to different parts of the world to film animals in the wild. You can see his films on television and on the Internet. Today I'm talking to Adrian about his films. So, Adrian, how do you plan a film?
A: At the beginning, there is a lot of planning for the journey. You have heavy camera equipment so it's expensive to travel. And you often need special visas to film in some countries.
I: How many people work on the film?
A: It depends on the film. But there's always a director and a camera person. On bigger films you need more people.

I: And how long does it take to make a film?
A: Well, I'm planning a film at the moment and we're going to film it in the summer. Then I'm going to edit it in the autumn. So in total, it takes about a year.
I: So tell us about your next film project. Where are you going?
A: To Malaysia.
I: Why are you going there?
A: I'm going to Malaysia to make a film for television. It's about a man called Alfred Russell Wallace. He was a famous explorer in the nineteenth century. After that, I'm going to Indonesia for three weeks.
I: Why are you going there?
A: To have a holiday!

2.18

R = Rachel, A = Adriana

Conversation one

R: Hi Adriana. It's Rachel.
A: Hi. Sorry, but I'm at work. I can't talk now.
R: I know, but I'm going to the theatre tonight. I've got two tickets for *Phantom of the Opera*. My friend works at the theatre and sometimes he gets free tickets.
A: Great.
R: So would you like to come?
A: Thanks, I'd love to. When is it?
R: Tonight!
A: Tonight?
R: Yes, are you free?
A: I'm sorry, but I'm working late tonight.
R: Oh. Can't you ask your manager?
A: I can try.
R: OK. Bye.

Conversation two

R: Hello?
A: Hi Rachel. It's me again. Do you still have the extra ticket?
R: Yes, why? Do you want to go?
A: Yes, my manager said I can finish early. What time does it start?
R: At seven thirty so let's meet at seven outside the theatre.
A: That's great. See you at seven.

Unit 10

2.20

People often compare the brain with a computer. And it's true, there are similarities. For example, both of them need energy. But both use different types of energy. A computer needs electrical energy, but the brain uses chemicals and chemical energy. Another similarity is they both store information. One big difference is that computers are easy to fix. OK, so sometimes you have problems with your laptop. Maybe it gets a virus and you can't fix it, but the man at the computer shop knows how. With the brain, it's generally more difficult to fix a brain because doctors don't know everything about it. In fact, there's more we DON'T know about the brain than what we do know. The other difference is that a computer can shut down, but a brain never stops. Even when you are sleeping, your brain is working.

2.21

A: Hello, I'd like to ask you a few questions about how technology has changed your life.
B: OK. Go ahead.
A: So, have you ever booked a holiday at a travel agent?
B: Yes, I have but it was a long time ago. Nowadays I always book online.
A: Right. Thanks. Here's the next question. Have you ever bought a CD?
B: Actually, yes, I have bought a CD. Normally I download music but last week I bought a CD for my father. It was his birthday and he doesn't know how to download music.
A: I see. And before a car journey, have you ever used a map?
B: Yes, I have. Well, I did in the past but now I use a sat nav, you know, a GPS, because I drive a lot for my job.
A: OK. And what about money? Have you ever paid for something by cheque?
B: No, because I've never had a cheque book. I pay for everything with a credit card. Oh, and I also bank online.
A: Right. And TV. Have you ever watched a programme at the time it's on TV?
B: Yes, of course. I do that every night.
A: So you never watch TV programmes online?
B: Oh, I see what you mean. Err, well, I have watched videos on YouTube.
A: OK. And finally, have you ever sent a letter in an envelope?
B: Err. I'm not sure. Let me think. Err. No, I haven't because I send emails or texts.

2.22

1 Have you ever sent a letter?
2 Yes, he has.
3 I haven't telephoned from a public telephone.
4 No, she hasn't!
5 We've never written letters by hand.
6 She's bought a CD.
7 No, I haven't.
8 The computer hasn't printed your photo.

2.23

Do you always forget names and faces? All the time? And how many numbers such as telephone numbers can you remember? Not many? Well, meet Nelson Dellis. Nelson can listen to 99 names and look at their faces. Then he can memorise every one of them. He can also hear 300 different numbers and then repeat them.

Because of his special memory, Nelson has won the USA Memory Championship twice. He won the competition in 2011 and again in 2012. The USA Memory Championships are like the Olympic Games, but the athletes train their brains and they take different memory tests.

So how does Nelson do it? He says he doesn't have a special memory. Like normal people, he's forgotten names, dates and numbers but in 2010 he studied memory techniques and he practised for hours and hours and hours every day. Since then, he's won competitions and he's taught his techniques to people all over the USA.

2.24

R = Richard, O = Omar

R: Hello, Omarox Engineering.
O: Hello, Richard. This is Omar.
R: Hello, Omar. Where are you now?
O: I'm in Kuala Lumpur.
R: Great. What time is it there?
O: Err, it's three o'clock.
R: Is that three in the morning?
O: No, in the afternoon. I've just arrived but my mobile isn't working. I'm calling from a telephone at the hotel.
R: I see.
O: So I want to give you the name of my hotel for the next two days. It's the Ancasa Hotel.
R: One moment. I need a pen. OK. Sorry was that the Encasa Hotel?
O: No, the Ancasa Hotel. A for apple.
R: Oh sorry. Ancasa.
O: And the number is six oh three, two one six nine, double two double six.
R: So that's six zero three, two one six nine, two two, six six.
O: That's right.
R: Is there anything else?
O: Yes, one thing. Have you called our colleagues about tomorrow?
R: Yes, I have. They can meet you at three.
O: Good. And have you emailed me all the designs?
R: No, I haven't because your email wasn't working. The email came back three times this morning.
O: That's because my mobile isn't receiving emails. Ermm, can you put them on the company website and I can download them?
R: Yes, I've done that.
O: Oh, great. Thanks. Bye for now.

2.27

V = Voicemail, R = Richard

V: Hello. This is the Ancasa Hotel. Please leave a message after the tone.
R: Hello. This is Richard Sanger calling. That's S-A-N-G-E-R. This is a message for Doctor Omar Al Harbia. Please tell him I can't email the designs so they are on a website. He can download them from this address. It's omarox – that's O-M-A-R-O-X – dot com slash e dash one, once again that's omarox dot com slash e dash one. And can he call me back on my mobile number? That's 0770 234 3785. Or email me at r_sanger@omarox.com. Please give him this message before he leaves this morning. It's urgent.

2.28

1 Can you call Jim back this evening?
2 I'd like you to email the date of the meeting.
3 Can you meet Mrs Rivers at the airport?
4 Would you book a room for two nights at the hotel?
5 Can you buy two new mobile phones?

Unit 11

2.29

When I was nineteen, I took a gap year between school and university. I saved some money and then I went backpacking around the world. My favourite memory is when I was travelling in the desert in Jordan and I met some local people. They were called Bedouin and they lived in tents in the desert. They were very friendly and invited me for tea. It was a hot afternoon, but they put the table outside and made hot tea. We all sat in the middle of the desert, drank tea and watched the sun go down. It was wonderful!

2.30

I = Interviewer, J = Jan

I: Hello and welcome to your weekly podcast from indietravelinfo.com. With me today is travel writer Jan Lanting with some more suggestions on holidays for the independent traveller. So Jan, today I want to start with your advice for travellers this month. We're sitting in London and it's the end of March. Can you give me some suggestions for good places to visit?
J: Well actually, you don't have to leave England. There are some nice places to visit. Last week I was in a place called Thurlestone. It's in the south-west of England and it's a beautiful part of the country.
I: What's the best way to travel there?
J: Good question. You can buy a return ticket on the train but actually I think you should rent a car. Then you can drive along the coast.
I: And what's the weather like at this time of year?
J: Sometimes it rains so you should take a coat.

I: OK. So after England, let's travel somewhere warmer.
J: OK. Well, Malaysia is good for this time of year. It's very hot.
I: Great, maybe I should take a holiday there. What about the language? Do people speak English?
J: Yes, a lot of people speak some English. But of course, when you travel you should take a phrase book and learn a few phrases in the local language as well.
I: And what about hotels?
J: In the big cities, hotels are often busy so you should book in advance. But in the countryside it's no problem. You can always find a room. I also recommend a tour in to the jungle.
I: The jungle?!
J: That's right. You can go walking through the jungle and see lots of amazing animals and plants.
I: Should I go on my own or with a tour guide?
J: You shouldn't go into the jungle on your own. Always go with a local guide because it can be dangerous.
I: Sure. Now for our final destination. The Arctic?
J: That's right. The Arctic.
I: But it's very cold.
J: Yes, you shouldn't go in the winter because it's very cold and very dark. At the end of March, it's sunny and the days are longer so you should go then.
I: Yes, but how do you get there?! Should I go on my own or with a tour?
J: It's very difficult on your own, but you can take a ship with a lot of travel companies now. They offer special tours. So it is possible. If you want more details, there are links on my blog at www …

2.32

A: That looks interesting.
B: Yes, it's a holiday brochure.
A: Oh really?
B: Yes, I've got a month in South America so I'm looking at places to go.
A: I went there last year. It's an amazing part of the world. I went on a cruise all the way from Brazil to Argentina. You should go on that.
B: Yes, but I'm interested in the wildlife.
A: How about visiting the Andes? That was part of my bus tour in Chile.
B: But the disadvantage is that there are lots of other people with a bus tour. I like travelling on my own.
A: But the advantage is that you see more with a tour guide. And you visit places other tourists don't normally go to.
B: Hmm. Maybe you're right.
A: Can I make a suggestion? If you have a month, why don't you go on a tour for two weeks AND then you could travel on your own afterwards.
B: Actually, that's a really good idea.

Unit 12

2.35

Ira Block took this photo of an Inuit man near his home in the Arctic circle. He lives on Baffin Island in Canada. That's about two and half thousand kilometres from the North Pole. The Inuit man is also holding another photo by Ira Block. Ira took this photo in the US state of South Carolina which is about two and half thousand kilometres from the equator. Ira took the two photos because about fifty-six million years ago, the Arctic Circle probably looked like South Carolina today. The temperature at the Arctic Circle was around twenty-five degrees Celsius. Nowadays, the average temperature in the Arctic is around minus ten degrees.

2.36

1 It'll rain here tonight.
2 I will visit space in my life time.
3 I think I'll learn Spanish.
4 Will you visit me one day?
5 The percentage of people in the countryside will decrease.
6 I don't think there'll be more snow this winter.

2.37

A: It's the deepest place on the Earth and before now, nobody has ever been to the bottom. But the film director and *National Geographic* explorer James Cameron has travelled down to the bottom of the Mariana Trench. With me in the studio is our science expert Jenny Walters to tell us how he did it.
B: Good evening.
A: So Jenny. First of all, how deep is the Mariana Trench?
B: It's eleven kilometres to the bottom. That's a long way down.
A: Indeed, and how long did the journey take?
B: James Cameron took over two hours to get to the bottom and then he spent about four hours down there.
A: And how did he travel there? In some kind of submarine?
B: That's right. It was a special one-man submarine.
A: I see. How big is it exactly?
B: It's seven metres long but it has a big engine so there isn't much space for a human.
A: So you're in a small space and it's dark down there. I couldn't do it. How well could he see?
B: It's very dark but the submarine has lights, of course. So Cameron could see small sea creatures. He described it as a 'desert'. He also had film cameras on the submarine and he plans to make a 3D-film about the adventure.
A: And of course he isn't the first explorer, is he? How many other explorers have been there?
B: There was one other. Don Walsh went down in 1960, but he didn't go to the bottom. In fact he was on the ship when Cameron went down.
A: Wow! How old is he now?
B: I think he's in his eighties.
A: That's amazing! And I have one last question that everyone wants to know the answer to. How much did James Cameron spend on this? Thousands? Millions?
B: I'm afraid I don't know, but films like *Titanic* and *Avatar* made a lot of money at the cinema so I think he could afford it.

2.38

Good morning, and thank you for coming. My name's Davi and I'm from Brazil. Today, I'd like to talk about an important day in my year called Earth Day.

First of all, Earth Day began on April 22nd in 1970. Over 20 million people went to Earth Day in different cities across the USA. There were politicians, teachers, artists and musicians. Since that day in 1970, Earth Day has become famous all over the world.

Nowadays, more than 175 countries have an Earth Day. Lots of people do different things. Last year, people in China planted 600,000 new trees. In New Orleans in the USA, they put 300,000 energy efficient bulbs into houses. And finally, in my country lots of people picked up rubbish in the cities and in the countryside.

In conclusion, I really think Earth Day is important. Next year, I hope you will do something on Earth Day. Thank you very much for listening.

NATIONAL GEOGRAPHIC LEARNING
CENGAGE Learning

Life

ELEMENTARY
WORKBOOK

John Hughes

Unit 7 Journeys

7a Famous journeys

Vocabulary travel verbs

1 Complete the sentences with these verbs.

cycle drive fly sail take travel

1 One day I'd like to be a pilot and .... around the world.
2 I can't .... a car because I'm only fifteen.
3 I have a new bicycle so I can .... to work every day.
4 I always .... public transport because the roads in the city centre are very busy.
5 Is it difficult to .... a ship?
6 Do you .... by train or by bus?

2 Vocabulary extra land, sea and air

a Write these words in the correct groups. Use a dictionary to help you.

aeroplane bicycle boat car drive fly hot air balloon sail ship train walk wheels wings

b Can you add more words to the three groups?

Grammar past simple: negatives

3 Complete the three texts with the past simple negative form of the verbs.

A The Spirit of St Louis

The Orteig Prize was $25,000. Raymond Orteig was a rich businessman and he offered the prize in 1919 to the first pilot to fly non-stop from New York to Paris. It was a dangerous journey and before 1927 six pilots tried the journey but they [1] .... (survive). But in 1927, Charles Lindbergh flew from New York to Paris. It took 33 hours. He [2] .... (stop) and so he won the Orteig Prize. Lindbergh and his plane, *The Spirit of St Louis*, became famous. You can see the plane today at the National Air and Space Museum in Washington.

B The Victoria

On 10th August 1519, five ships left Seville in Spain: the *Trinidad*, the *San Antonio*, the *Concepción*, the *Santiago* and the *Victoria*. Ferdinand Magellan was the leader of the five ships. They travelled across the ocean and arrived in a port in Brazil. After Brazil, Magellan's journey is famous because he sailed round the southern tip of South America. But Magellan [3] .... (return) to Spain. He died in the Philippines and only the *Victoria* finished the journey. There is a replica of the ship in Punta Arenas in Chile, at the beginning of the Straits of Magellan.

C Sputnik

Sputnik was the first satellite from Earth into space. Humans [4] .... (travel) inside *Sputnik* but they sent the satellite into space on 4th January 1957. As the satellite started to orbit Earth, people looked for it in the sky. It travelled round Earth 1,440 times and [5] .... (enter) Earth's atmosphere again until 4th January 1958. Nowadays, there are replicas of *Sputnik 1* in different museums. More importantly, there are thousands of satellites orbiting Earth because of *Sputnik 1*'s journey.

Reading three famous journeys

4 Read about the three journeys in Exercise 3 again. Answer the questions for each journey.

1 Where was each journey: on land, sea, air or somewhere else?
A ....
B ....
C ....

2 What transport did they use?
A ....
B ....
C ....

5 Match the sentences (1–8) with the texts (A–C).

1 Other people tried the same journey, but they didn't succeed. ....
2 He didn't stop on the journey. ....
3 He didn't return to his country. ....
4 He won some money because of the journey. ....
5 There were a group of them on the journey. ....
6 The journey took 33 hours. ....
7 You can see it in a museum and it isn't a replica. ....

Grammar past simple questions

6 Write questions for these answers about the three journeys.

1 What .... in 1919?
A prize of $25,000 to the first pilot to fly non-stop from New York to Paris.

2 When ....?
In 1927.

3 How long ....?
33 hours.

4 When .... Spain?
On 10th August 1519.

5 Where ....?
In the Philippines.

6 At night, what .... in the sky?
Sputnik.

7 How many times ....?
1,440 times.

8 When .... Earth's atmosphere?
On 4th January 1958.

7b Land, sea and air

Vocabulary journey adjectives

1 Match the pairs of adjectives (1–4) with the four pictures (a–d).

1 short and easy ....
2 long and slow ....
3 fast and dangerous ....
4 difficult but safe ....

a

b

c

d

Listening animals on land, in the sea and in the air

2 2.1 Listen to a nature documentary about these three animals. Answer the questions with a number.

Albatross

1 How far does an albatross fly in its lifetime? .... kilometres
2 How long are the wings of an adult albatross? .... metres
3 How far can it fly to feed a chick? .... kilometres

Zebra

4 How many zebras are in the middle of Africa? ....
5 How far is their migration? .... kilometres

Elephant seal

6 How far can an elephant seal travel on a journey? .... kilometres
7 How far can it dive? .... metres

Glossary

chick (n) /tʃɪk/ a baby bird

3 2.1 Listen again. Complete these sentences.

1 The wings of an albatross ....

on Earth.

2 These beautiful animals are famous for their black and white coats, but their lives ....

because of their long journey.

3 The ocean around Antarctica ....

but for the elephant seals it is their home.

4 They can stay under the water ....

and only come up for air for a few minutes.

Grammar comparative adjectives

4 Look at the sentences in Exercise 3. Underline examples of comparative adjectives.

SPELL CHECK comparative adjectives

- Add *-er* to short adjectives to form the comparative: *old* → *older*
- Add *-r* to adjectives ending in *-e*: *large* → *larger*
- Change adjectives ending in *-y* (after a consonant) to *-i*, and add *-er*: *happy* → *happier*
- Double the final consonant on some adjectives ending with a vowel and a consonant: *hot* → *hotter*

5 Look at the spell check box. Write the comparative form of these adjectives.

1 short ....
2 easy ....
3 big ....
4 busy ....
5 cheap ....
6 sad ....
7 wet ....
8 nice ....

6 Complete these sentences with the comparative form of the adjective in brackets.

1 This laptop is .... (cheap) than that one.

2 I love the summer because it's .... (hot)

3 Everything is .... (expensive) at the airport shops.

4 Your new car is .... (fast) than your old one.

5 The city is .... (safe) during the day. At night it can be dangerous.

6 Are you .... (old) than me?

7 I can speak Japanese but my brother is .... (good)

8 Why are your results from school .... (bad) than last year?

Word focus *than*

7 Use the prompts to make comparative sentences.

1 my brother / short / me
My brother is shorter than me.

2 walking / slow / cycling ....

3 I think / rock climbing / difficult / surfing ....

4 giraffes / tall / elephants ....

5 camping / cheap / staying in a hotel ....

6 Canada / big / Iceland ....

7 a taxi / expensive / a public bus ....

8 cities / crowded / towns ....

8 2.2 Listen and check your answers.

9 **Pronunciation stressed syllables**

2.2 Listen again and underline the stressed syllables in your sentences from Exercise 7.

My brother is shorter than me.

7c Journey to the seamounts

Listening mountains under the sea

1 2.3 Listen to a documentary about seamounts. Number these topics in the order you hear them (1–3).

a the location of Las Gemelas
b a description of seamounts
c the journey to Las Gemelas

2 2.3 Listen again. Are the sentences true (T) or false (F)?

1 You can see seamounts above the sea.
2 About 100,000 seamounts are over a kilometre high.
3 The journey to a lot of seamounts is short and easy.
4 Las Gemelas is an area of seamounts about 500 kilometres from the coast of Canada.
5 There is sea life on the sides of Las Gemelas.
6 Three people went to Las Gemelas in DeepSee.
7 They can't see the bottom of the seamounts.
8 A lot of seamounts are from volcanoes.

Avi Klapfer, Gregory Stone and Brian Skerry in the submersible DeepSee

Grammar superlative adjectives

▶ SPELL CHECK superlative adjectives

- Add *-est* to short adjectives to form the comparative: *old* → *oldest*
- Add *-st* to adjectives ending in *-e*: *large* → *largest*
- Change adjectives ending in *-y* (after a consonant) to *-i*, and add *-est*: *happy* → *happiest*
- Double the final consonant on some adjectives ending with a vowel and a consonant: *hot* → *hottest*

3 Look at the spell check box. Write the superlative form of these adjectives.

1 short ....
2 easy ....
3 big ....
4 slow ....
5 cheap ....
6 fast ....
7 sad ....
8 nice ....

4 Complete the sentences with the superlative form of these adjectives.

busy easy far good high large populated short

1 The .... part of the seamount Las Gemelas is 2,286 metres.
2 The .... view of seamounts is from a submersible.
3 There are five oceans and the Pacific Ocean is the ....
4 In the northern hemisphere of the Earth, the .... day of the year is on 21st December.
5 Shanghai is the .... city on Earth. There are eighteen million people.
6 Neptune is the .... planet from the Sun.
7 Some people think English is the .... language to learn, but I think it's difficult!
8 Atlanta airport is the .... airport in the world. Over 38 million passengers travel through the airport every year.

7d How was your trip?

Vocabulary *journey, travel* or *trip*?

1 Complete these sentences with *journey*, *travel* or *trip*.

1 It's a long .... from Cape Town to Cairo.
2 I don't like to ....
3 My manager is away on a business ....
4 Lots of students .... during their holidays.
5 We went on a .... to Amsterdam last weekend.
6 My .... along the Andes mountains took 30 days.

Real life asking about a trip

2 2.4 Listen to five short conversations. Match the conversations (1–5) with the topics (a–e).

Conversation 1	a the journey
Conversation 2	b the weather
Conversation 3	c the food
Conversation 4	d the hotel
Conversation 5	e business meeting

3 2.4 Listen again. Tick the response (a–c) you hear.

1 How was your flight?
 a Very good, thank you.
 b Very uncomfortable.
 c Tiring.
2 Was your hotel comfortable?
 a No, it wasn't and the Internet didn't work.
 b Yes, it was fine, but the Internet didn't work.
 c No, it wasn't, but the Internet worked.
3 How was your meeting?
 a Really useful.
 b Really interesting.
 c Very interesting.
4 What's the weather like?
 a Not bad.
 b Great!
 c Terrible.
5 Did you try the local food?
 a Yes, it's very hot and spicy.
 b Yes, it's delicious.
 c Yes, but I didn't enjoy it.

4 **Pronunciation intonation in questions**

2.5 Listen to the questions and repeat with the correct intonation.

1 How was your journey?
2 How was your hotel?
3 Did you have dinner at the hotel?
4 What was the food like?
5 How was the meeting?
6 How was the weather?

5 **Listen and respond questions about a trip**

2.6 Listen to the questions again and respond with an answer.

7e Writing about journeys

Vocabulary online writing

1 Complete the pairs of sentences with these words.

1 blog / website

a I have my own .... I write about my life and put pictures of my family on it.

b I buy all my clothes from this ....

2 blogger / writer

a Charles Dickens was a famous English .... in the nineteenth century.

b Andrew Evans is a .... on the *National Geographic* website.

3 homepage / online

a I need to go .... Is there Wi-Fi in the café?

b Can you give me the address for the .... ?

4 upload / download

a I want to .... photos of my holiday so all my family can see them online.

b I can't .... the photos of our holiday. Are you sure they are there?

5 post / comment

a I read your latest blog and wrote a .... afterwards. Did you see it?

b My new .... is about my latest journey through Madagascar.

2 Writing skill *so, because*

Join the sentences with *so* or *because*.

1 The bus was cancelled. We waited for the next one.

The bus was cancelled so we waited for the next one.

2 The flight was cancelled. The weather was terrible.

....

3 The food was hot and spicy. We drank a litre of water with our meal.

....

4 The meeting was long and boring. The managing director spoke for two hours!

....

5 The restaurant didn't take credit cards. I paid with cash.

....

6 The hotel restaurant was closed. We went into the centre of town for a meal.

....

Writing a description of a journey

3 You write a travel blog. Write a short blog post (80–100 words) about the journey in these pictures.

Travel Blog

Wordbuilding *really/very* + adjective

▶ WORDBUILDING *really/very* + adjective

You can make some adjectives stronger or weaker with *really*, *very* or *not very*.

My dinner was really good. (+ +)

My meal was good. (+)

My meal wasn't very good. (– –)

The TV programme was very interesting. (+ +)

The TV programme was interesting. (+)

The TV programme wasn't very interesting. (– –)

You can use *very* and *really* with these adjectives: *good, bad, interesting, comfortable, nice.*

You can only use *really* (not *very*) with these adjectives: *great, amazing, delicious.*

1 Read the sentences and look at the symbols in brackets. Rewrite the sentences using *very* or *really*.

1 The journey was good. (+ +)
The journey was very/really good.

2 The food wasn't good. (+ +)

3 The meetings were interesting. (– –)

4 The party was great! (+ +)

5 The weather was bad. (+ +)

6 It was sunny. (– –)

7 The meal wasn't very nice. (+ +)

8 The hotel was amazing! (+ +)

Learning skills draw pictures

2 Pictures are a good way to learn new language. Look at these pictures in a learner's notebook. Match the language points (1–3) with the pictures (a–c).

1 opposite adjectives
2 comparative adjectives
3 superlative adjectives

3 Choose eight new words you learned in Unit 7 of the Student's Book. Write them in your notebook and draw pictures to help you remember them.

Check!

4 What is the connection between the names on the left and the numbers on the right? Can you remember? Check your answers in Unit 7 of the Student's Book.

Mayflower and 17th century. They sailed to America in the Mayflower in the 17th century.

1 Mayflower	30 metres
2 Mayflower II	35 kilometres
3 Silver Queen	1977
4 Saiga	17th century
5 Tree frog	349,000 kilometres
6 Loggerhead turtle	1957
7 Voyager	14,000 kilometres
8 Jupiter	44 days

Unit 8 Appearance

8a Describing appearance

1 Vocabulary extra adjectives about festivals

Replace the words in bold with these adjectives.

~~boring~~ colourful crowded fun noisy

1 The festival was**n't interesting**.
boring

2 The musicians and their instruments were very **loud**.
....

3 The streets were **full of people**.
....

4 The people's clothes were **lots of different colours**.
....

5 We had **a good time** at the festival.
....

Reading the face of Cleopatra

2 Read the article. Are the sentences true (T) or false (F)?

1 When Cleopatra was born, she was the queen.
2 Nowadays, people don't learn about Cleopatra.
3 We don't know what Cleopatra looked like.
4 Archaeologists find objects from Alexandria under the water.
5 There are pictures of Cleopatra under the water.
6 Two thousand years ago, writers often described her appearance.
7 Her face was on coins.
8 It's easy to see her appearance on the coins.

The face of Cleopatra

Cleopatra was born in Egypt over two thousand years ago. She was eighteen when her father died and she became a famous queen. In the modern world, she is still famous. Schoolchildren read about her in books. We watch her in films at the cinema and on TV. In modern pictures and old paintings she is always beautiful.

But what did Cleopatra look like? No one knows exactly. She lived in the ancient city of Alexandria. But over time, a lot of Alexandria disappeared and nowadays most of this region is underwater. Some archaeologists study the objects under the water, but there isn't a face of the queen.

Some historians from the period wrote about the queen. But they describe her power and do not tell us about her appearance. The only real picture of Cleopatra is on some metal coins from Alexandria. One coin shows a woman's face with a large nose. Another coin shows a long neck. But none of the coins are clear, so the face of Cleopatra is still a mystery.

Vocabulary face and appearance

3 Match these words with the parts of the face.

lips	....	ear	....
eyebrow	....	eye	....
cheek	....	chin	....
nose	....		

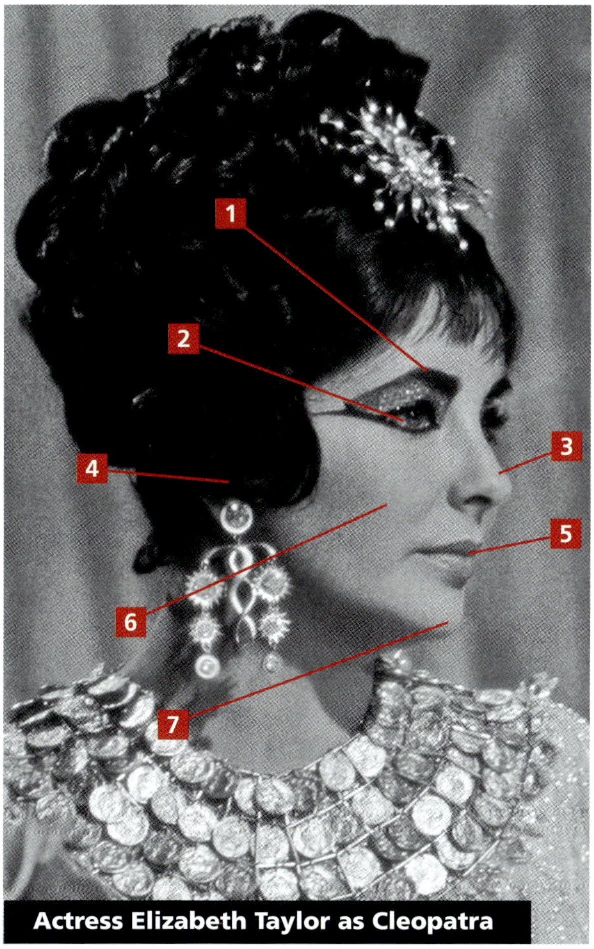

Actress Elizabeth Taylor as Cleopatra

4 Choose the correct option to complete the description of the actress in the photo.

This is a [1] *beautiful / handsome* woman. She's got [2] *short / long*, [3] *straight / curly* hair. It's [4] *blonde / dark*.

Grammar *have got / has got*

5 Complete the description of the photo with these verbs.

has got (x2) 's 're have got

I was in Venice last year so I took a lot of photos. At the Venice Carnival, people [1] .... amazing costumes. They [2] .... always very beautiful. This man [3] .... a great mask, and his costume [4] .... big blue and gold wings. I think he [5] .... a handsome butterfly!

6 **Pronunciation** groups of consonants

2.7 Listen to these words. Write the missing letters.

1 li_ _
2 eye_ _ow
3 u_ _ _
4 ma_ _
5 _ _ee_ _
6 _ _ _ai_ _ _
7 _ _o_ _e
8 ha_ _ _ome

8b Global fashion

Listening clothes around the world

1 2.8 Listen to descriptions of these photos. Match the descriptions (1–5) with the photos (a–e).

Description 1 ....

Description 2 ....

Description 3 ....

Description 4 ....

Description 5 ....

a

b

c

d

e

2 2.8 Listen again and answer the questions for each description.

Description 1

1 Are the women at work?

....

2 Which country are they in?

....

Description 2

3 Which country is the police officer in?

....

4 Does he work in a city or on a reservation?

....

Description 3

5 What colours are their clothes?

....

6 Why is the purple robe good in the mountains of Nepal?

....

Description 4

7 What colours are Masai clothes?

....

8 How does the speaker describe the Masai man's hair?

....

Description 5

9 What is the woman doing on the side of the road?

....

10 Which clothes does the speaker describe?

....

Word focus *like*

3 Put the words in order to make sentences with *like*.

1 we clothes buying like new

....

2 dress like your is mine new

....

3 my old ones these shoes like are

....

4 my uniform like I don't

....

5 like a cowboy hat this hat is

....

6 jeans Jason wearing likes

....

4 Look at the sentences from Exercise 3. Answer the questions.

1 Which sentences use *like* as a verb? ...., ... and ....

2 Which sentences use *like* with the meaning 'similar to'? ...., ... and ....

Grammar present continuous

5 Look at these pictures. Then complete the sentences with the affirmative or negative present continuous form of the verbs in brackets.

1

2

3

4

1 He *isn't wearing* (wear) normal clothes. He *'s wearing* (wear) a uniform because he's in the army.

2 Trisha .... (buy) clothes. She .... (sell) clothes.

3 Georgio .... (make) a dress. He .... (design) one.

4 He .... (play) a computer game. He .... (read) a book.

6 Use the prompts to write questions for these answers about the pictures in Exercise 5.

1 what / he?

....?

A uniform.

2 Trisha / or / clothes?

....?

She's buying them.

3 what / Georgio?

....?

A dress.

4 play / a computer game?

....?

No, he isn't.

7 Complete the sentences with the present simple or present continuous form of these verbs.

come know learn like stand stay take walk

1 My family .... from Vietnam.

2 We .... with friends in Japan for two weeks.

3 I sometimes .... photos of ordinary people in interesting clothes.

4 Why .... you .... here? Let's go!

5 .... you .... Peter? Yes, I do. He works in my office.

6 I .... to work today because the weather is nice.

7 How is your English course? .... you .... a lot?

8 .... you .... my new shirt? Yes, I do. It's very nice!

Vocabulary clothes

8 Read the clues and complete the crossword with clothes words. What's the mystery word?

1 Wear this on your head.

2 Women wear this.

3 We put on a pair of these and walk outside.

4 Wear this over a shirt so you are warm.

5 At home I wear a T-.......... and at work I wear a .... and tie.

6 This holds your trousers up!

7 It's like a dress, but it's only the bottom half.

8 Wear these on your feet when it's cold.

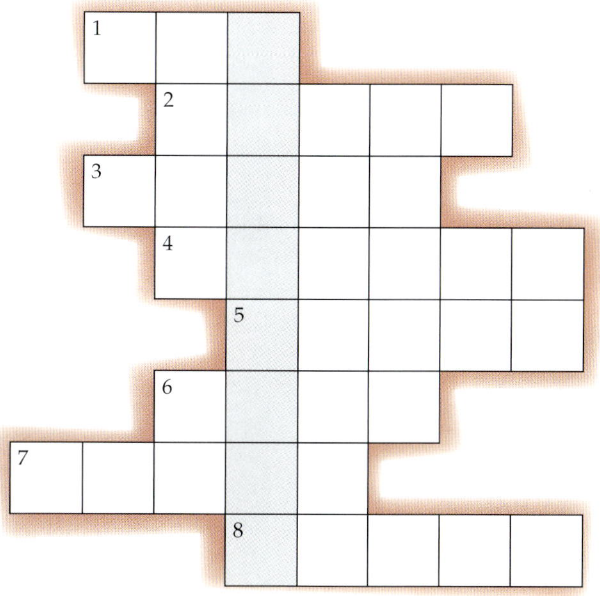

Mystery word: ....

8c Changing your appearance

Listening animal camouflage

1 2.9 Listen to part of a nature programme about how animals use their appearance. Tick the animals they talk about.

2 2.9 Listen again. Answer the questions with *Yes*, *No* or *Don't know* (because the speaker doesn't say).

1 Are a lot of animals the same colour as the landscape?
2 Is a deer easy to see in the forest?
3 Are zebras the same colour as the landscape?
4 Are zebras colour blind?
5 Do lions look for one zebra?
6 Are the large, round colours on some butterfly wings like eyes?
7 Does a chameleon change colour for camouflage?
8 Is an Arctic fox white in the autumn?

Vocabulary parts of the body

3 Complete the sentences with these words.

arm back foot hand knee leg neck shoulder

1 Kick the ball with your ________.
2 When you meet someone, shake their ________ and say, 'Pleased to meet you.'
3 She's got beautiful jewellery around her ________. Is it gold?
4 You look tired. Lie down on your ________ and go to sleep.
5 Why are you standing on one ________?
6 Carry this bag over your ________.
7 Bend your leg at the ________.
8 Your hand is at the end of your ________.

1 deer ☐

2 squirrel ☐

3 zebra ☐

4 elephant ☐

5 lion ☐

6 butterfly ☐

7 chameleon ☐

8 polar bear ☐

9 Artic fox ☐

10 giraffe ☐

Glossary

camouflage (n) /ˈkæməˌflɑːʒ/ when animals or humans use or change their appearance so their enemies cannot see them

colour blind (n) /ˈkʌləˌblaɪnd/ when you can't see the difference between some colours

danger (n) /ˈdeɪndʒə/ the possibility that something will hurt you

enemy (n) /ˈenəmi/ a person or an animal that wants to hurt another person or animal

landscape (n) /ˈlændˌskeɪp/ the appearance of the land in a natural area

8d Photos

Real life talking about pictures and photos

1 2.10 Listen to a student. She is describing this photo for an English exam. Answer the questions.

1 What does she think the photo shows?

....

....

2 What are the children waiting for?

....

....

3 Who is looking through a telescope?

....

....

4 How does the family look?

....

....

5 How does she know they are from Lapland in northern Norway?

....

....

2 Complete the description with these phrases.

I think   in front of her   in the middle
on the right   the family looks
the photo is interesting   they are wearing
this photo

[1] .... shows a family, I think. [2] .... is the grandmother and on the left is the mother, maybe. The two children [3] .... are waiting for dinner. The girl is looking at something and, [4] ...., the boy is looking through a telescope. But I think it's the wrong way round!
[5] .... serious, but perhaps they are hungry.
[6] .... special clothes.
[7] .... they are from Lapland in northern Norway because the women's hats and clothes are from this region.
[8] .... because it shows people in their everyday life.

3 2.10 Listen again and check your answers.

4 **Pronunciation silent letters**

2.11 These letters are silent in some words. Listen to the words (1–8). Which letter is silent?

b   d   e   h   k   n   t   w

1 listen ....*t*....
2 who ....
3 Wednesday ....
4 climb ....
5 what ....
6 knee ....
7 blonde ....
8 autumn ....

8e How RU? ☺ tks

1 Writing skill textspeak

Match the textspeak with these words or phrases.

2day	CU	@	GR8	atm	4get	b4
l8	pls	:-)	RU	w/e	UR	4u	sry
thx	Weds	<3				

1 your ....
2 for you ....
3 see you ....
4 today ....
5 before ....
6 Wednesday ....
7 at ....
8 are you ....
9 great ....
10 please ....
11 late ....
12 sorry ....
13 thanks ....
14 love ....
15 forget ....
16 at the moment ....
17 happy ....
18 weekend ....

2 Write these sentences using textspeak.

1 Please come on Wednesday.
pls come on weds
2 Are you happy today?
....
3 Sorry I'm late.
....
4 Are we meeting at the weekend?
....
5 I love the film.
....
6 I have great news!
....
7 Call me before you leave.
....
8 See you later.
....

Writing texts and online messages

3 Read the situation and write a text message conversation between two friends.

Two friends (A and B) are meeting, but A is on a train and he's late for the meeting. He wants to change the time of the meeting. B is waiting outside a cinema but she wants to meet in a café.

A:

B:

A:

B:

A:

B:

A:

B:

Wordbuilding phrasal verbs

▶ WORBUILDING phrasal verbs

A phrasal verb is a verb with a particle. For example:

*put + on = **put on***

*take + off = **take off***

Some phrasal verbs are transitive and some phrasal verbs are intransitive.

- Transitive = verb + particle + something: *Put on your coat.*
- Intransitive = verb + particle: *Get up!*

1 Complete the sentences with these phrasal verbs.

eat out	get up	go back	look at
look up	put on	take off	turn off

1 It's cold outside! .... your hat and coat!
2 I always .... at six o'clock and have fruit for breakfast.
3 I'm hungry. Can we .... at a restaurant tonight?
4 .... this photo of some people on a train. It's interesting.
5 I can't hear! Please .... that music!
6 You forgot your homework! .... and get it.
7 It's hot in here. .... your coat and hat!
8 You can .... words in your dictionary.

Learning skills dictionary skills (2)

2 You can look up phrasal verbs in your dictionary. Look at these examples. [T] means the verb is transitive and [I] means the verb is intransitive.

put on /ˌpʊtˈɒn/ [T] to start wearing something
She put on her hat and coat and she went outside.

eat out /ˌiːtˈaʊt/ [I] to have a meal in a restaurant
We always eat out at the weekend.

3 Look at the sentences in Exercise 1. Five of the phrasal verbs are transitive. Three are intransitive. Write T or I. Check your answers in a dictionary.

1 *T (put on)*
2 *I (get up)*
3 ....
4 ....
5 ....
6 ....
7 ....
8 ....

Check!

4 Do the quiz. You can find the answers in Unit 8 of the Student's Book.

1 Where is the Dinagyang Festival?
....
2 What are the children wearing at the festival in Catalonia?
....
3 Where can you see a Polga tribesman?
....
4 Where did archaeologists find a five-thousand-year-old man?
....
5 What decorations are important in Polynesia?
....
6 Who wrote the book *Ancient Marks*?
....
7 Which photographer takes photos of people in their everyday life?
....
8 What do you call the faces in texts and online messages?
....

Unit 9 Film and the arts

9a At the cinema

1 Vocabulary extra at the cinema

Label the picture with these words.

actor aisle actress audience
back row front row screen seat

Vocabulary films

2 Complete the sentences with these types of film.

animation comedy documentary horror
romantic comedy science fiction

1 *When Harry met Sally* is a famous .... about two friends. In the end, they fall in love.

2 It's a .... film about a man. He's driving his car in the middle of the night. Suddenly the engine stops, so he goes into an old house and never returns!

3 I learned a lot about lions and how they live in the wild from the ....

4 My children love .... films, especially the ones by Disney.

5 .... films are usually in space.

6 I like the two actors but I didn't like the film. Normally they are very funny but they weren't in this .... It was boring and I didn't laugh.

Listening films

3 2.12 Listen to extracts from four different films. Match the films (1–4) with the types of film (a–d).

Film 1	a romantic comedy
Film 2	b documentary
Film 3	c action film
Film 4	d science fiction

4 2.12 Listen again. Choose the correct option (a–c) to complete these sentences.

Film 1

1 The mountains are ....

a red   b white   c black

2 A .... is moving fast towards the man.

a spaceship   b light   c planet

Film 2

3 The animals normally .... at night.

a come out   b eat   c sleep

4 The mother is looking for ....

a a place to live   b her children   c food

Film 3

5 .... says, 'Don't move!'

a A police officer   b The bank manager   c The man

6 The man says he didn't take the ....

a money   b gold   c credit card

Film 4

7 The woman says she is ....

a not bad   b not very well   c fine

8 The man thinks the woman is ....

a older   b beautiful   c older and beautiful

Grammar *going to* (for plans)

5 Match sentences 1–6 with sentences a–f to make pairs.

1 The children are hungry.
2 My brother wants to be a film director.
3 Mike and I like to be near the screen.
4 The book is very good.
5 I need some money.
6 Anousheh has got some money.

a She's going to buy our tickets.
b He's going to Hollywood!
c Steven Spielberg is going to make a film of it.
d They're going to eat lunch.
e We're going to sit in the front row.
f I'm going to get a job.

6 Look at the pictures. Write their plans with *going to* and these verbs.

buy   have   make   meet   play   watch

1 I .... a film.
2 You .... tennis.
3 He .... shoes.
4 She .... a friend.
5 We .... dinner.
6 They .... a film.

7 Pronunciation /tə/

a 2.13 Listen to these two sounds: /tə/ and /tuː/.

b 2.14 Listen to eight sentences. Tick the sound you hear: /tə/ or /tuː/.

1 /tə/   /tuː/
2 /tə/   /tuː/
3 /tə/   /tuː/
4 /tə/   /tuː/
5 /tə/   /tuː/
6 /tə/   /tuː/
7 /tə/   /tuː/
8 /tə/   /tuː/

9b Film-makers and artists

Vocabulary art and entertainment

1 Complete the diagram with these words. You can use some words more than once.

actor artist audience film music musical musicians
novel painting screen writer

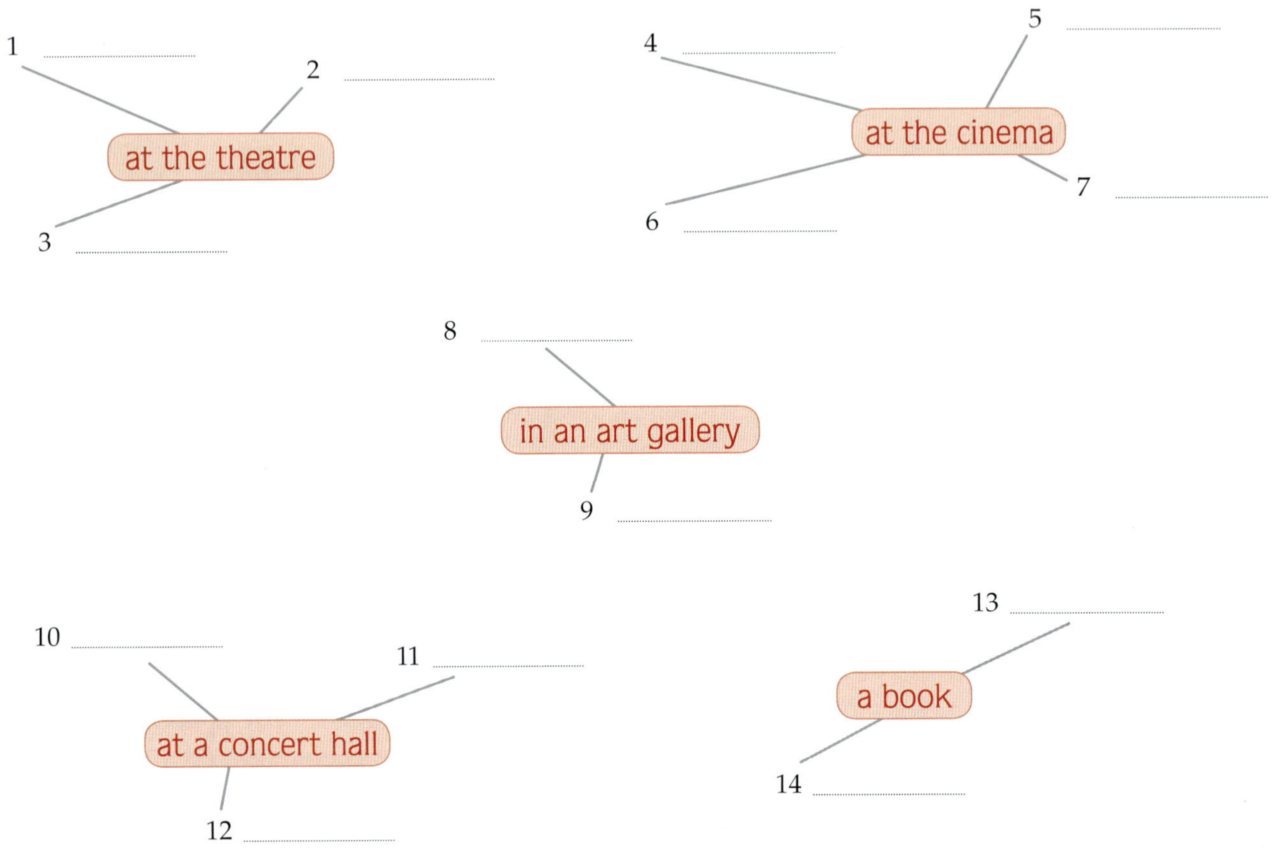

2 Pronunciation word stress

2.15 Listen to the stress pattern in these words. Then complete the table with the words.

actresses artist cinema director
gallery musical musician novel
painting theatre writer

●•	●••	•●•
....	....	....
....	....	....
....	....	
....	....	
....		

Reading an interview with a documentary film-maker

3 Complete the article about the film-maker Bryan Smith with these questions (a–h).

a What types of film does he make?
b What are his other interests?
c How did he become a film-maker?
d Why does he like adventure film-making?
e Where does he live?
f What does he do in his free time?
g What was his favourite film project?
h What is his normal day?

Filmmaker: Bryan Smith

1 ....

In a city called Squamish in Canada.

2 ....

He didn't go to film school. He became an adventurer and athlete and then he learned camera skills. He worked with other film-makers and they taught him.

3 ....

Because he loves exploring places and he films the lives of some very interesting people.

4 ....

He doesn't have a normal day.

5 ....

Documentaries. His first film was *49 Megawatts*. He also films adventure sports for *National Geographic*. Next he's going to make a TV series for the Internet about sportspeople.

6 ....

The Kamchatka Project expedition in 2010. It was a wild and remote place.

7 ....

He loves kayaking and skiing.

8 ....

In the film business people don't have much time, so he spends his free time with his family.

Grammar infinitive of purpose

4 Combine phrases from each list to make *I'm going to* + infinitive of purpose sentences.

1 borrow this book	study acting
2 download this song	read about film-making
3 book tickets	listen to it
4 buy this film	watch it later
5 evening classes	learn French
6 drama school	see a play

1 I'm going to *borrow this book* to *read about film-making*.
2 I'm going to .... to ....
3 I'm going to .... to ....
4 I'm going to .... to ....
5 I'm going to .... to ....
6 I'm going to .... to ....

5 Dictation arts news

2.16 Listen to and read this article. Complete the article with infinitives of purpose.

Film, music and arts news

We look at the latest news from the world of film, music and art.

Josh Roberts is going to work in Hollywood [1] ....

The young Irish film director is going to buy a house in Los Angeles [2] .... He said, 'I'm not going there forever.'

The band Stronger are going to be on TV next week [3] .... Switch on at seven on Wednesday evening [4] .... about the group.

There is going to be an exhibition of Javier Bowman's art at the National Gallery [5] .... The exhibition opens on 10th January. Phone this number (0845 4785) [6] ....

9c Nature in art

Vocabulary nature

1 Choose the correct option to complete the sentences.

1 I like watching the *birds / butterflies* around the flowers and looking at their coloured wings.
2 The forest has hundreds of tall, old *trees / leaves*.
3 Bananas are a type of *grass / fruit*.
4 Australia is famous for its *kangaroos / polar bears*.
5 We prefer walking in the *rocks / mountains* to walking in the forest.
6 In the autumn the *grass / leaves* fall from the trees.
7 In parts of Australia, some *Rock / Tree* Art is 30,000 years old.
8 Penguins spend a lot of their time in the *sea / sky*.

Listening *War Horse*

2 2.17 Listen to a description of *War Horse*. Number these topics in the order you hear them (1–3).

The play ______ The book ______ The film ______

3 2.17 Listen again. Are the sentences true (T) or false (F)?

1 Michael Morpurgo wrote the book in 1982.
2 The book is for adults.
3 The book is about Joey and the First World War.
4 *War Horse* became a stage play in 2007.
5 In the play, they used real horses.
6 You can see the play in different countries.
7 Spielberg used one horse to play Joey in the film version.
8 The film had large audiences.

The film

The play

9d Making arrangements

Real life inviting and making arrangements

1 2.18 Listen to a telephone conversation between two friends. Answer the questions.

1 Where is Max going?

2 How much are the tickets for the concert?

3 When is the concert?

4 What is Max's problem?

5 What time are they going to meet?

6 Where are they going to meet?

2 2.18 Complete the conversation with these phrases. Then listen again and check.

are you   do you want   I'd love   I'm sorry
let's meet   see you   that's
would you like to

R = Richard, M = Max

R: Hi Max. It's Richard.

M: Hi Richard. Sorry, but I'm going to a meeting now so I don't have long.

R: OK, it's just that a friend gave me some free tickets for a concert. [1] ______ to go?

M: What is it?

R: Some music by Mozart.

M: Hmm, I don't know much about classical music.

R: I don't either but it's free, so [2] ______ come?

M: OK thanks, [3] ______ to. When is it?

R: Tomorrow night. [4] ______ free?

M: [5] ______ but I'm working late tomorrow night.

R: What time do you finish?

M: At seven.

R: That's OK. It starts at eight. [6] ______ at seven outside your work.

M: [7] ______ great. [8] ______ at seven.

3 Pronunciation showing enthusiasm

a 2.19 Listen to these four phrases for responding to invitations. Which two speakers show enthusiasm in their pronunciation? Which two don't?

1 I'd really like to. ☺ ☹
2 I'd love to. ☺ ☹
3 That sounds fantastic. ☺ ☹
4 That's great. ☺ ☹

b 2.20 Listen to the four phrases again. Each speaker shows enthusiasm. Listen and repeat.

4 Listen and respond responding to invitations

2.21 Listen to four invitations. Respond with phrases from Exercise 3.

Grammar present continuous for future reference

5 Complete the sentences with the present continuous form of the verbs.

1 We *'re meeting* (meet) at two this afternoon.
2 Today I ______ (wear) my mother's old dress.
3 They ______ (go) on holiday in June.
4 Where ______ (you / go)? Work doesn't finish until five o'clock.
5 At the moment, she ______ (talk) to someone. Can I help you?
6 I ______ (not take) a holiday this year.
7 He ______ (work) late tonight.
8 We ______ (not play) tennis any more. Jules won the match twenty minutes ago.

6 Do the sentences in Exercise 5 refer to the present (P) or the future (F)?

1 *F*   5 ______
2 *P*   6 ______
3 ______   7 ______
4 ______   8 ______

9e It looks amazing!

1 Grammar extra sense verbs + adjectives

Complete the sentences about the photos with these adjectives.

beautiful delicious loud very old well worried

1 He sounds ....
2 He looks ....
3 I don't feel ....
4 It looks ....
5 That smells ....
6 This dessert tastes .... !

1

2

3

4

5

6

2 Writing skill giving your opinion with sense verbs

Complete these sentences from different online reviews and comments with sense verbs.

1 In my opinion, the music on their second album .... no different to their first.
2 I think the food at this new restaurant .... fantastic!
3 This new horror film is frightening. The audience .... scared from the beginning to the end.
4 Damien Hirst's new paintings .... amazing!
5 I think this perfume .... terrible! Don't put it on!

Writing reviews and comments

3 Write three reviews. Use the notes and write three sentences for each.

1
The Alhambra
new Middle Eastern café
delicious sandwiches
nice mix of old and new furniture
friendly staff

....
....
....
....
....
....
....

2
War Horse
a play at the theatre
horse looks amazing
interesting story
loud music

....
....
....
....
....
....
....

3
Digital Hero II
new computer game
graphics look modern
felt bored
no different to Digital Hero I

....
....
....
....
....
....
....

Wordbuilding suffixes (2)

1 Choose the correct ending to make nouns for jobs or occupations.

1	study	(ent) / or / ian	*student*
2	music	er / or / ian	
3	write	r / ian / tive	
4	paint	ent / er / or	
5	explore	or / nt / r	
6	art	or / ive / ist	
7	direct	or / ive / ist	
8	manage	nt / r / ian	

Learning skills learn from your mistakes

2 Do you often use the wrong word? It's a good idea to write your mistakes in a notebook and write the correct word next to it. Read the page from a student's notebook and write the correct words.

My mistakes

1 I like ~~seeing~~ *watching* TV.

2 Can we ~~hear~~ to the radio?

3 The film is ~~at~~ Friday.

4 We're going to meet ~~on~~ the cinema.

5 How ~~many~~ money is a ticket for the concert?

6 Hamlet is a ~~theatre~~ by William Shakespeare.

7 This novel is very ~~interested~~.

8 The actor Daniel Craig is a ~~beautiful~~ man.

Check!

3 Match these sentences (a–h) with the places on the map (1–10). Check your answers in Unit 9 of the Student's Book.

a There's an outdoor cinema in this harbour. ......

b Where the Chukchi people live. ......

c Andō Hiroshige's paintings show this country. ......

d It's the location of the film *Grandma*. ......

e Damien Hirst is the richest artist here. ......

f The artist Stanislaw Witkiewicz was born here. ......

g It's the location of the film *My Wedding and Other Secrets*. ......

h Adrian Seymour is going to make his next film here. ......

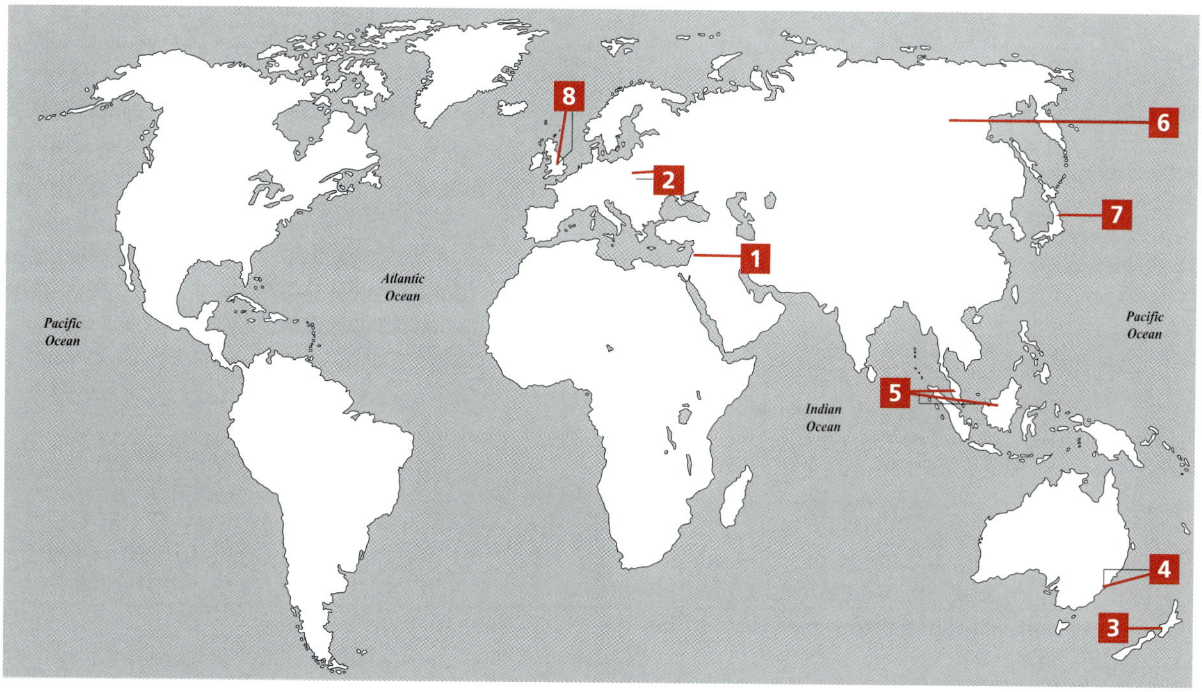

10a Science and technology

Vocabulary science subjects

1 Label the pictures with the types of science.

astronomy biology chemistry physics neuroscience technology zoology

1 ______

2 ______

3 ______

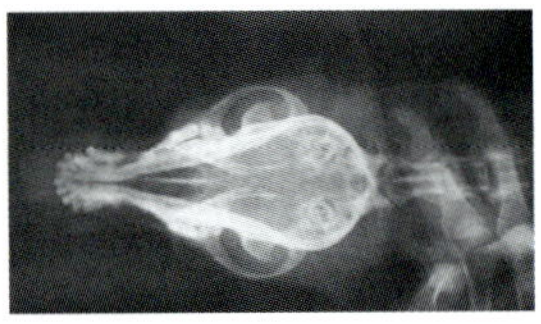

4 ______

5 ______

6 ______

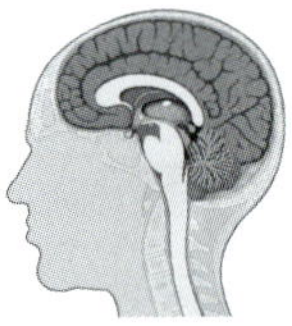

7 ______

Reading science articles

2 Read these extracts from five science articles. Match the extracts (1–5) with the types of science from Exercise 1.

1 ______
With the problem of energy on Earth, some scientists have studied lightning because they want to use the energy in lightning. A single lightning bolt has around five billion joules of energy. Unfortunately, a lightning bolt lasts for seconds, so how do you catch the energy?

2 ______
On the 18th of this month, Mars will be below the Moon and to the right. If it's a clear night, you'll see the red planet without a telescope. It could be the best view this year.

3 ______
We've had PCs, laptops and tablets, so what's next? One team of scientists wants to develop a keyboard on your body. A small device projects the keyboard onto your arm and you type onto your skin.

4 ______
The Durrell Wildlife Conservation Trust is on the island of Jersey. There are a lot of rare animals in the park, but the Trust also gives money to projects with animals in places such as the Galapagos Islands, India, Madagascar and the Caribbean Islands.

5 ______
Mirror neurons help animals to learn. For example, when a young animal watches its mother, it learns how to do something. Scientists believe this is because the mirror neurons in its brain are working.

Vocabulary everyday technology

3 Complete the pairs of sentences with these words.

1 download / CD
  a Listen to this ______ from the Internet.
  b I bought a new ______ in town last week.
2 search engine / library
  a My father still takes books out of the ______.
  b It's quicker to find articles on this topic with a ______.
3 map / sat nav
  a Can you open the ______ and have a look for the town?
  b Switch on the ______ and type in the location.
4 radio / podcast
  a I've downloaded this ______ for you to listen to.
  b Turn up the ______. The news is on.
5 text / send
  a I've got my phone with me so you can ______ me.
  b Why didn't you ______ me a postcard while you were on holiday?

Listening explaining technology

4 2.22 It's Karen's first day in a new job. Her manager helps her with some technology. Match the conversations (1–3) with the technologies (a–c).

Conversation 1 ______

Conversation 2 ______

Conversation 3 ______

a tablet computer

b answering machine

c photocopier

Grammar present perfect

5 2.22 Complete the conversations with the present perfect form of the verbs or *have/haven't*. Then listen again and check your answers.

M = Manager, K = Karen

Conversation 1

M: OK, Karen. [1] ______ (you ever use) this machine before?

K: Yes, of course I [2] ______ (use) one before.

M: No, I mean, [3] ______ (you ever make) copies with this type of machine? It's different from others.

K: Oh, I see. No, I [4] ______, but it looks similar to the one in my previous job.

Conversation 2

M: And this is yours.

K: Oh, I [5] ______ (never see) one like this before.

M: It's very easy. Press this button.

K: OK. I [6] ______ (do) that.

M: Great. Has the screen come on?

K: Yes, it [7] ______.

M: Now you put your finger on the screen.

Conversation 3

K: Someone [8] ______ (leave) a message on my phone.

M: OK. Press play.

K: I [9] ______ (press) play but it doesn't work.

M: [10] ______ (you switch) it on?

K: Ah. Sorry! No, I [11] ______.

6 **Listen and respond** ***Yes, I have / No, I haven't***

2.23 Listen to six *Have you ever …?* questions. Respond with *Yes, I have* or *No, I haven't*.

Have you ever listened to a podcast?

7 **Pronunciation** ***'ve / 's***

2.24 Listen and circle the number of words in each sentence. A contracted form with *'ve* or *'s* is one word (e.g. *I've* or *she's* = one word).

a	3	4	5	e	3	4	5
b	3	4	5	f	3	4	5
c	3	4	5	g	3	4	5
d	3	4	5	h	3	4	5

8 **Dictation**

2.24 Listen again and write the sentences.

a *I've printed the photos.*

b ______

c ______

d ______

e ______

f ______

g ______

h ______

10b Memory and language

Reading London taxi drivers' memories

1 These sentences are missing from the end of the paragraphs in the article. Match the sentences (a–d) with the paragraphs (1–4).

a They can only use the map inside their head.

b That's because taxi drivers in London have memorised the whole city.

c Scientists believe their training for 'The Knowledge' is the reason for changing their brains.

d For 150 years, they have had to pass this test to become a taxi driver.

2 Read the article again and answer the questions.

1 According to the article, what are the two reasons why London is famous?

Reason 1: ....

Reason 2: ....

2 Why is it easier to travel round London in a taxi?

....

....

3 When did London taxi drivers first take the test?

....

4 How long does it take to learn 'The Knowledge'?

....

5 Can they use technology to answer the questions on the test? Yes / No

6 Can they use a map? Yes / No

7 Which part of the taxi driver's brain have scientists studied? What does it do?

....

....

8 How is the hippocampus different in London taxi drivers' brains?

....

....

Taxi!

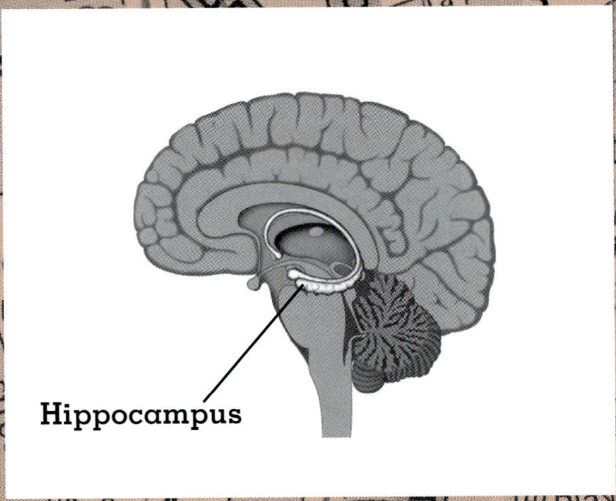

London is famous as a historic city with lots of interesting places to visit. It's also famous for difficult roads. Tourists and visitors to London quickly become lost in the old streets – even with a map or sat nav. It's much easier to catch a taxi. [1] ....

Since 1865, trainee London taxi drivers have studied for a test called 'The Knowledge'. They have learned the names of every street, the location of every police station and the fastest route to every theatre. [2] ....

Learning 'The Knowledge' can take over two years. When they think they are ready, taxi drivers take the test. They answer questions such as 'What's the fastest route from Buckingham Palace to London University?' They can't use a map or a sat nav. [3] ....

Scientists at London University have studied the brains of London taxi drivers. In particular, they have looked at the part of the brain called the hippocampus. It's the part that stores memories. In London taxi drivers, the hippocampus is bigger than in the brains of other people. [4] ....

Vocabulary memory and learning

3 Choose the correct word (a–c) to complete the list of tips for studying for exams.

FIVE TIPS FOR EXAM SUCCESS

- Plan a timetable for studying. Write down the date of the exam and then write the times and days you are going to [1] .... before it.
- [2] .... short lists of information over short periods of time. Take regular breaks.
- Which things do you often [3] ....? Write down that information and study that the most.
- Work with a friend. [4] .... each other with questions.
- Don't study the night before. [5] .... in the evening and go to bed early.

1	a study	b know	c teach
2	a Forget	b Practise	c Memorise
3	a forget	b know	c train
4	a Memorise	b Learn	c Test
5	a Understand	b Relax	c Remember

Grammar present perfect and past simple

▶ SPELL CHECK past simple and past participles

With regular verbs, you add *-ed* (or *-d*/*-ied*) to the end of a verb to make the past simple form or the past participle (see also Unit 6):

Infinitive	Past simple	Past participle
train	*trained*	*trained*
study	*studied*	*studied*

However, irregular verbs have irregular forms. Sometimes the past simple and the past participle have the same irregular form:

Infinitive	Past simple	Past participle
have	*had*	*had*
teach	*taught*	*taught*

Sometimes the past simple and the past participle do not have the same irregular form:

Infinitive	Past simple	Past participle
know	*knew*	*known*
take	*took*	*taken*

4 Complete the table of irregular verbs. You can find the answers in Unit 10 of the Student's Book.

Infinitive	Past simple	Past participle
1	bought	2 ....
pay	3	paid
4	put	5 ....
send	6	sent
7	forgot	forgotten
make	8	made
read	read	9 ....
10	won	won

5 Complete these sentences with the correct form of the verbs from Exercise 4.

1 Have you ever .... any books in other languages?
2 Nelson Dellis .... the Memory Championships in 2010 and 2011.
3 When did you .... these tickets?
4 Did you .... me a text or an email?
5 I've .... the advert for the car in the local newspaper.
6 Have you ever .... for something with online banking?
7 We've .... the rule for the present perfect. Can you remind us?

6 Complete these short conversations. Use the same verb twice.

1 take
A: *Have* you ever *taken* an English exam?
B: Yes, I *took* one last year.

2 study
A: .... you ever .... Spanish?
B: Yes, I .... it when I was a student at university.

3 teach
A: .... you ever .... a subject?
B: Not exactly, but I .... a friend how to use his new computer.

4 learn
A: .... you ever .... a musical instrument?
B: Yes, I .... the violin at school.

5 write
A: .... you ever .... a book?
B: No, but I .... a travel blog when I went round the world.

10c Inventions

Vocabulary science and inventions

1 Write the names of these inventions.

1 i..........

2 v.......... c..........

3 w..........

4 k..........

5 e..........

6 s.......... t..........

7 f..........

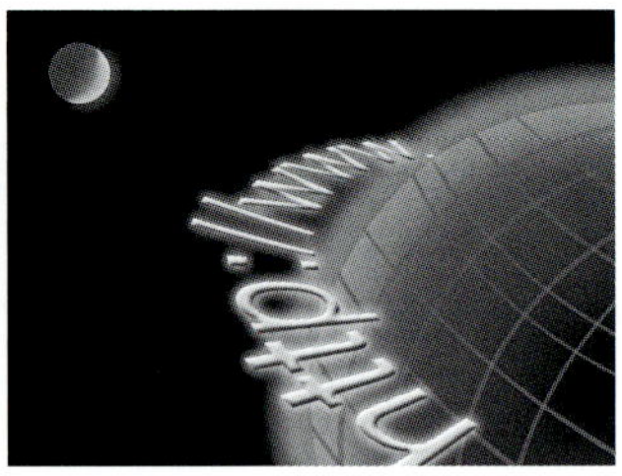

8 the I..........

2 Match the descriptions (a–h) with the inventions (1–8) from Exercise 1.

a It turns. ....
b It plays music. ....
c It sticks paper. ....
d It burns. ....
e It cleans the house. ....
f It gives energy. ....
g It cuts. ....
h It searches for links. ....

Listening a TV quiz

3 2.25 Listen to a radio quiz programme. The host asks three questions. Match the questions with the answers (a–c).

First question ....
Second question ....
Third question ....

a

Morse Code

b

Compass

c

Marconi

4 2.25 Listen again and answer the questions.

1 How many points do the two teams have at the beginning of round five?
....
2 When did Marconi send a radio message across the Atlantic Ocean?
....
3 What is the difference between the sounds in Morse Code?
....
4 When did the Chinese invent the compass?
....
5 Where did it point?
....
6 Does the Green team or the Blue team answer the third question correctly?
....
7 How many points does the Blue team have?
....
8 How many points does the Green team have?
....

10d On the phone

Real life checking and clarifying

1 2.26 Listen to a telephone conversation. Choose the correct option (a–c) to complete the sentences.

1 The name of the company is .... Technologies.
a AGA b EGA c AGI
2 Sophie is at the Science Fair in ....
a Casablanca b Cairo c Cologne
3 The name of the hotel is ....
a Insel b Ensal c Insal
4 The number is ....
a 021 8843 50 b 021 8834 50 c 021 4508 83
5 Sophie wants the new ....
a designs b prices c machines

2 2.26 Complete the conversation (1–8) with the questions (a–h). Then listen again and check.

a Was that zero two one, eight eight three four, five zero?
b What time is it there?
c Have you emailed me a copy of the new prices?
d Is that six in the morning?
e Was that the Ensal Hotel?
f Can you fax it to the hotel?
g Where are you now?
h Is there anything else?

L = Lance, S = Sophie
L: Hello, AGA Technologies. Can I help you?
S: Hello, Lance. This is Sophie.
L: Hello, Sophie. [1] ....
S: I'm at the Science Fair in Cologne.
L: Great. [2] ....
S: Err, it's six o'clock.
L: [3] ....
S: No, in the evening. I want to give you the name of my hotel for the next two days. It's the Insel Hotel …
L: One moment. I need a pen. OK. [4] ....
S: No, the Insel Hotel. I for Italy, N – S – E for England, L.
L: Oh sorry. Insel.
S: And the number is zero two one, eight eight three four, five zero.
L: [5] ....
S: That's right.
L: [6] ....
S: [7] ....
L: No, I haven't because your email wasn't working.
S: That's strange. [8] .... I don't know the number.
L: Don't worry. I've just looked at your hotel website and there's a fax number on that.
S: Great, thank you. I'll call you later. Bye for now.

3 Pronunciation contrastive stress

a Read these five conversations. Which word do you think B stresses? Underline it.

1 A: Is that two in the morning?
B: No, it's three in the morning.
2 A: Was that the Ensel Hotel?
B: No, it was the Insel Hotel.
3 A: Is that I for Italy?
B: No, it's A for Amsterdam.
4 A: Is that two in the morning?
B: No, it's two in the afternoon.
5 A: Was that three double six?
B: No, it was three double seven.

b 2.27 Listen and check your answers.

10e Telephone messages

Vocabulary email addresses and websites

1 Match the parts of the email addresses and websites with the words.

1	@	dot com
2	.com	at
3	/	dash
4	-	dot co dot uk
5	www.	dot org
6	//	underscore
7	:	double slash
8	.org	slash
9	_	www dot
10	.co.uk	colon

2 Read the words of three people saying email addresses and websites. Write the address or website.

1 *So that's h underscore schmitt at hotmail dot co dot de.*

....

2 *The hotel website is www dot concordia dot com.*

....

3 *Download the podcast from www dot instolisten dot org slash dailypod dash 2*

....

3 Writing skill imperatives

Read the speakers' words. Rewrite the sentences so they start with an imperative.

1 Can you call Stacey back?
Call Stacey back.

2 I'd like you to send everyone a letter.

....

3 Can you take Mr D'Souza to the station?

....

4 Would you book a table for two?

....

5 Can you buy more paper?

....

6 Would you print these photographs, please?

....

7 Can you email the designs to g_rich@gmail.com?

....

8 I'd like you to telephone the hotel.

....

Writing a telephone message

4 2.28 Listen to three voicemails. Complete the messages.

1
MESSAGE
Name of caller: ....
Message for: ....
Message: ....
....
....
....
Urgent ....

2
MESSAGE
Name of caller: ....
Message for: ....
Message: ....
....
....
....
Urgent ....

3
MESSAGE
Name of caller: ....
Message for: ....
Message: ....
....
....
....
Urgent ....

Wordbuilding synonyms and antonyms

1 Replace the words in bold with a synonym.

call find memorise search send
show stop working study

1 Please **email** me the photographs. ....
2 **Read** the grammar rules. ....
3 Look at this list of words. How many can you **learn and remember**? ....
4 **Look** for the answer to this question on the Internet. ....
5 Can you **teach** me how to use the photocopier? ....
6 Scientists need to **discover** the answer. ....
7 Did you **telephone** the cinema for film times? ....
8 Robots often **break down**. ....

2 Complete these pairs of sentences with the correct antonym.

1 remember / forget
  a I always .... the Chinese word for 'house'.
  b Can you .... the Chinese word for 'house'?
2 leave/ take
  a Eduardo is out of the office. Do you want me to .... a message?
  b Eduardo is out of the office. Do you want to .... a message for him?
3 teach / learn
  a You're good at playing the guitar! Can you .... me?
  b I'd like to .... how to play the guitar.
4 send / receive
  a Did we .... any emails from any customers today?
  b Did you .... the contracts to our customers?

Learning skills your learning style

3 Students can have different learning styles. Some students are more:

- Visual (They learn by looking.)
- Auditory (They learn by listening.)
- Kinaesthetic (They learn by doing.)

Do this quiz to find out your learning style. Choose the best ending (a–c) for you to complete these sentences.

What's your learning style?

1 When I learn English in class,
  a I like watching the teacher.
  b I like listening to the teacher.
  c I like doing something with other people.

2 When I learn a new word,
  a I draw a picture of it.
  b I repeat the word many times.
  c I imagine it in my head.

3 When I study for an English test,
  a I write notes and use different colours.
  b I talk to myself or other people about my notes.
  c I study and do physical activity at the same time.

What do your answers mean?

Mostly A answers = You are a visual learner.
Mostly B answers = You are an auditory learner.
Mostly C answers = You are a kinaesthetic learner.

Check!

4 Answer the questions. You can check your answers in Unit 10 of the Student's Book.

a What are three words ending with *-ology*?
  1 ....ology
  2 ....ology
  3 ....ology
b What are three ways to send information?
  1 ....
  2 ....
  3 ....
c What three types of new technology do you use every day?
  1 ....
  2 ....
  3 ....
d What three old inventions do you never use?
  1 ....
  2 ....
  3 ....

Unit 11 Tourism

11a Holiday advice

1 Vocabulary extra types of holiday

Put the letters in order to make types of holiday.

1 NGCMAPI ....
2 SISENEGHTIG ....
3 BKANACKPCIG ....
4 KIINGH ....

Vocabulary tourism

2 Replace the words in bold with these words.

book	carry on	check in	rent
~~return ticket~~	sightseeing	souvenirs	
tour guide			

1 I'd like a **ticket to take me there and back**. *return ticket*
2 Let's go **and look at some of the famous places in the city**. ....
3 I have one bag to **put on the plane** and one **bag to take on the plane**. ...., ...
4 When we land at the airport we could **pay money to have** a car for the week. ....
5 The **person who showed us round the city** knew a lot of history and could answer all our questions. ....
6 I bought some **nice objects connected with the city** to give to family and friends at home. ....
7 Did you **telephone the hotel in advance for** a room? ....

Reading Doug Lansky

3 Read the article about travel writer Doug Lansky. Answer the questions with *Yes*, *No* or *Don't know* (because the information isn't in the article).

1 Does Doug still travel nowadays?
2 Does he write for travel magazines?
3 Does he take a backpack?
4 Does he like travelling with other people?
5 Does he often go sightseeing?
6 Does he like meeting local people?
7 Are the photos on his site from all over the world?
8 Can you put any type of travel photo on his website?

Alternative travel

Doug Lansky started travelling when he was young and, as an adult, he never stopped. He's travelled all over the world and he writes about his experiences for magazines. He also writes travel guide books.

Doug doesn't go to places with lots of tourists and he hates travelling with other 'travellers'. He likes to visit new places and spend a lot of time there and meet the local people. He also takes hundreds of photos. In particular, he photographs signs around the world because he thinks they are more interesting than normal travel photos. This was his first photo of a sign:

Now he has a website called www.signspotting.com with hundreds of signs from different countries. Tourists and travellers put up their favourite signs from around the world. The photographs don't have to be great, but they have to be interesting and funny.

Doug Lansky

Word focus *take*

4 Match the sentence beginnings (1–5) with the endings (a–e).

1 I want a photo of us in front of the Eiffel Tower. Can you take
2 We're late for our flight. Let's take
3 I'm so tired of working. It's time to take
4 You're wet! Why didn't you take
5 We don't speak Spanish so we should take
6 The only way to the Antarctic is to take

a a cruise.
b your camera with you on holiday?
c your umbrella?
d a phrase book.
e a taxi to the airport. It's faster.
f a very long holiday!

Grammar *should/shouldn't*

5 Choose the correct options to complete these sentences.

1 You *should* / *shouldn't* buy them!
2 You *should* / *shouldn't* stay there.
3 You *should* / *shouldn't* go home.
4 You *should* / *shouldn't* come here on holiday.
5 You *should* / *shouldn't* watch TV all day!
6 You *should* / *shouldn't* take a photo.

6 Correct the mistake in each sentence.

1 You should to book a hotel room.
You should book a hotel room.
2 He doesn't should work late.
....
3 Do we should buy a ticket here?
....
4 She shoulds check in her bag.
....
5 You don't should rent a car.
....
6 What should we to eat?
....

Writing email advice to a friend

7 You have received this email from a friend. Underline the advice he asks for.

Hi!
I've booked my tickets and I'm arriving on the 21st! Before I arrive at your house, I'm going to travel round the country. Should I rent a car or go by public transport, do you think? Also I'm going to spend some time in the capital. What should I see there? And should I book my hotel in advance? Can you give me any advice? Oh! And what's the weather like? Is it cold? Should I bring lots of clothes?
See you soon!
Mike ☺

8 Write a reply to Mike. Complete this email.

Dear Mike
I'm really happy that you are coming to my country.
Here is my advice:
When you travel round the country, you should
....
....
....
In my capital city, you should ....
....
....
For hotels, I think you should ....
....
....
At the moment the weather is very cold, so you should
....
....
See you soon!

11b Planning a holiday

Listening advice about holidays

1 2.29 Listen to six tourists talking about travel in different countries. Match the tourists (1–5) with the topics (a–f).

Tourist 1 ....
Tourist 2 ....
Tourist 3 ....
Tourist 4 ....
Tourist 5 ....
Tourist 6 ....

a road travel
b weather
c money and currency
d language
e safety and emergencies
f visas and immigration

2 2.29 Listen again. Answer the questions for each tourist.

Tourist 1

1 What type of transport did he take?

....

2 Did he pay for medical costs?

....

Tourist 2

3 Which part of the world does she talk about?

....

4 What clothes does she suggest?

....

Tourist 3

5 Which country did he go to?

....

6 Why was road travel difficult?

....

Tourist 4

7 Who needs a visa to stay longer than three months in the USA?

....

8 Who should you contact for a work visa?

....

Tourist 5

9 What did he take to Mexico?

....

10 Where did he need it?

....

Tourist 6

11 Does she change money before or after she arrives in a country?

....

12 When does she use her credit card?

....

Vocabulary in another country

3 Read the clues and complete the crossword.

Across

1 The .... is hot in the south, but colder in the north.
3 Get a .... from the embassy before you go.
5 Russia has nine different time ....
6 You need a driving .... to drive a car.
7 London is a multi-........ city with people from all over the world.

Down

1 The .... in Canada is the dollar.
2 Drive on the left-........ side in the UK, Australia, Japan, Ireland and Kenya.
4 It's .... to travel without a passport.

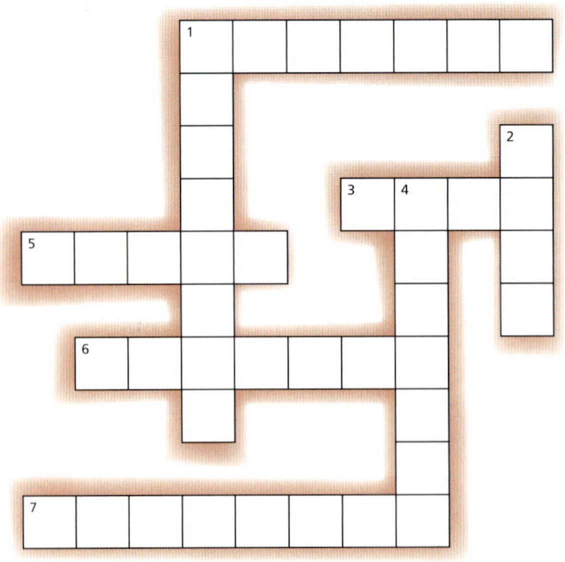

Grammar *have to / don't have to, can/can't*

4 Choose the correct option (a–c) to complete the information from an airline website.

	a	b	c
1	a have to	b have	c don't have to
2	a can't	b don't have to	c can
3	a can	b can't	c have to
4	a have to	b can't	c don't have to
5	a have to	b don't have to	c can't
6	a can	b can to	c have
7	a don't have to	b can't	c have to
8	a can	b can't	c have to

5 Dictation travel announcements

2.30 Listen to four announcements at an airport and complete the sentences.

1 All passengers on ....

....

.... Gate 13 immediately.

2 .... liquids over one hundred millilitres ....

3 Passengers ....

.... this line.

4 Adults .... first.

6 Pronunciation /hæftə/

2.31 Listen to six sentences with the words *have to*. Tick the pronunciation you hear.

1 /hæftə/ ✓ /hæf tuː/
2 /hæftə/ /hæf tuː/
3 /hæftə/ /hæf tuː/
4 /hæftə/ /hæf tuː/
5 /hæftə/ /hæf tuː/
6 /hæftə/ /hæf tuː/

Information for passengers

- You [1] .... check in before going through security. You [2] .... do this online or at the airport.
- You [3] .... take carry-on bags over 10 kg on to the plane. Check these in before you fly.
- Passengers flying to airports in the same country [4] .... show a passport but you must show some form of ID.
- Passengers travelling to foreign countries [5] .... travel without a valid passport.
- On some flights, you [6] .... pay extra to change your seat to one in business class.
- You [7] .... use mobile phones and electronic devices when the plane is taking off and landing.
- When the seatbelt sign is off, passengers [8] .... get up from their seat.

11c Being polite in other countries

Listening customs in other countries

1 2.32 Listen to a radio programme about how to be polite in other countries. Which two countries do they talk about?

2 2.32 Listen again. Read and tick *Do* or *Don't* for the two countries.

	DO	DON'T
First country		
1 Shake hands when you meet people.	....	....
2 Take flowers to someone's house.	....	....
3 Wear your shoes in someone's house.	....	....
4 Join in the dancing.	....	....
Second country		
5 Eat before the oldest person at the table.	....	....
6 Cross your chopsticks.	....	....
7 Shake hands or bow when you meet someone.	....	....
8 Take flowers to someone's house.	....	....

Grammar *everywhere, somewhere, nowhere, anywhere*

3 Complete the sentences with *where, thing* or *body*. Use each word twice.

1 Are you doing any.................... interesting this weekend?

2 I put my passport some...................., but I can't find it now.

3 There's some.................... at the door. I don't who it is.

4 Let's go shopping. There's no.................... to eat in the fridge.

5 Every.................... is here so let's have dinner.

6 Are you going any.................... nice for your holiday this year?

7 I'm so bored! Suggest some.................... to do.

8 I invited some friends for dinner but no.................... could come.

4 Choose the correct option to complete these sentences.

1 I don't know *anybody* / *somebody* in the room. Who are they?

2 I'd like *everything* / *something* to drink.

3 There's *everywhere* / *nowhere* like home.

4 *Everything* / *Something* on the menu looks delicious! I want to eat it all!

5 Let's go to a nightclub because *anybody* / *everybody* likes dancing.

6 Let's go *nowhere* / *somewhere* for lunch. How about that new restaurant on the corner?

7 *Somebody* / *Nobody* telephoned earlier but they didn't leave their name.

8 Did *anything* / *everything* happen while I was away?

11d A holiday in Morocco

Listening holiday plans

1 2.33 Listen to a conversation between Marie and Enzo. Are the sentences true (T) or false (F)?

1 Marie has booked her holiday this year.
2 Marie wants to go somewhere hot.
3 Enzo suggests Morocco.
4 Marie doesn't think it's a good idea.
5 Marie wants to meet other people.
6 Enzo suggests a tour.
7 Enzo thinks a tour is expensive.
8 Enzo suggests a camping holiday.

Real life making suggestions

2 Put the words in order to make suggestions.

1 can suggestion make I a ?
....
2 go to should you Morocco
....
3 you own could on your travel
....
4 why tour go with don't you a ?
....
5 going about how on a package holiday ?
....

3 2.33 Listen to the conversation again and match the suggestions (2–5) from Exercise 2 with these responses (a–c).

a Maybe you're right. ....
b But the disadvantage is that it's more expensive. ....
c That's a really good idea. ....
d Yes, but I'd like to meet people as well. ....

4 Listen and respond responding to suggestions

2.34 Listen to four suggestions. Respond with a phrase from Exercise 3. Then compare your responses with the model answer that follows.

Why don't you travel on your own?

Yes, but I'd like to meet people as well.

5 Pronunciation /ʌ/, /ʊ/ **or** /uː/

2.35 Listen to these words. Tick the vowel sound you hear: /ʌ/, /ʊ/ or /uː/.

1	bus	/ʌ/	/ʊ/	/uː/
2	book	/ʌ/	/ʊ/	/uː/
3	you	/ʌ/	/ʊ/	/uː/
4	but	/ʌ/	/ʊ/	/uː/
5	should	/ʌ/	/ʊ/	/uː/
6	food	/ʌ/	/ʊ/	/uː/
7	cruise	/ʌ/	/ʊ/	/uː/
8	could	/ʌ/	/ʊ/	/uː/

11e Your feedback

1 Writing skill closed and open questions

a Complete the questions with these words.

~~Did~~ What How many Was
Were How Why Would

1 ......*Did*...... you use room service?
2 .... the food of a high standard?
3 .... nights did you stay at the hotel?
4 .... easy was it to park near the airport?
5 .... you recommend this sports centre to friends?
6 .... our staff friendly and polite?
7 .... other suggestions can you make?
8 .... did you choose our restaurant?

b Match the questions (1–8) from Exercise 1 with these responses (a–h).

a Two. ....
b No, I didn't. ....
c It was very easy. ....
d Yes, fairly high. ....
e Yes, I would. ....
f Because of the location and I like Chinese food. ....
g Yes, they were. ....
h You should have a car park at the hotel. ....

Writing a feedback form

2 The local tourist office in your town has this feedback form for tourists. You are a tourist. Fill in the form with your feedback. Answer the questions and write comments.

Tourist Information

1 How helpful were the staff at our tourist information office?
Very helpful and polite ☐ Helpful and polite ☐
Not helpful or polite ☐
Comment:
....
....

2 Did you visit the local historic places? Yes / No
If yes, please comment:
....
If no, please say why not:
....

3 Which hotel did you stay at? Please comment on its level of service.
....
....

4 Which restaurant(s) did you eat at? Please comment on the quality of the food.
....
....

5 Overall, how was your experience of our town?
Excellent ☐ Very good ☐ OK ☐
Not very good ☐
Comment:
....
....

6 Would you recommend our town as a tourist destination? Yes / No
If yes, please comment:
....
If no, please say why not:
....

Wordbuilding word forms (1)

1 Complete this table of word forms. Use a dictionary to help you.

Verb	Noun	Person
manage	management	1 ....
photograph	2	3 ....
4	study	student
backpack	backpack	5 ....
visit	6	7 ....
8	cooker	cook
9	design	10 ....

2 Complete these sentences with words from the table in Exercise 1.

1 I work for a travel company and I .... six people.
2 I took this great .... when I was on holiday.
3 When I was a .... I studied tourism.
4 I can put everything in my .... when I go on holiday.
5 When you are a .... in another country, you should learn their language.
6 Don't forget to switch off the .... in the kitchen.
7 My sister is a fashion .... for Gucci.

Learning skill pronunciation

3 When you learn a new word, remember to answer these questions about the pronunciation.

- How many syllables are there?
- Where is the main stress?
- Does the pronunciation change with other word forms?

Example:
<u>man</u>age (two syllables) <u>man</u>agement (three syllables) <u>man</u>ager (three syllables)

Look at the other words in Exercise 1. Write the number of syllables and mark the stressed syllable.

Check!

4 Match these comments from tourists (1–6) with the suggestions (a–f). You can find all the places in Unit 11 of the Student's Book.

1 'I want to see buildings from the Renaissance.'
2 'I'd like to walk through the jungle.'
3 'We're going hiking in the Andes.'
4 'I've never seen the desert.'
5 'I'd like to see Ayers Rock.'
6 'I want to go somewhere with nobody living there.'

You should go to …

a Malaysia
b Florence in Italy
c Jordan
d Australia
e Antarctica
f South America

12a Earth trends

1 Vocabulary extra the Earth

Label the diagram with these words.

Antarctic Circle Arctic Circle Equator
North Pole Northern hemisphere
South Pole Southern hemisphere

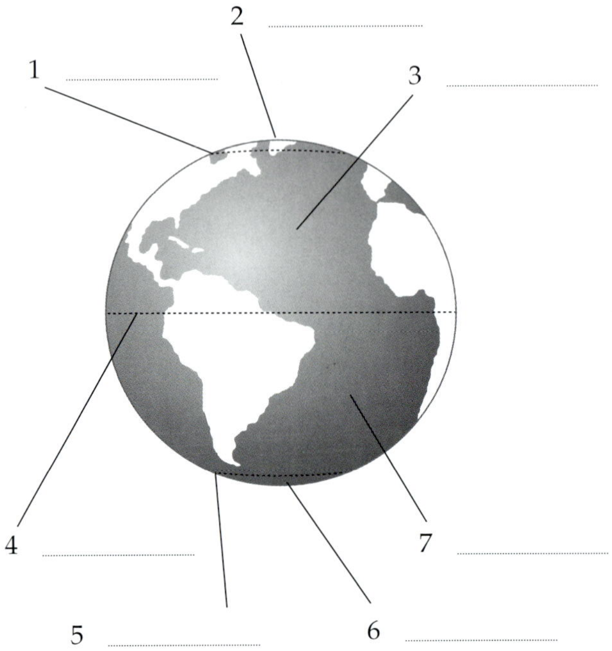

Vocabulary measurements

2 Match the sentence beginnings (1–5) with the endings (a–e).

1 The area of Antarctica is
2 Water becomes ice at a temperature below zero
3 The average adult should drink
4 Thirty per cent
5 The height of the tallest tree on Earth is
6 The weight of the International Space Station (ISS) is

a of the Earth's surface is dry land.
b degrees Celsius.
c fourteen million square kilometres.
d four hundred and nineteen thousand, four hundred and fifty-five kilograms.
e two point five litres of water per day.
f one hundred and thirty metres.

International Space Station

3 Write the measurements in Exercise 2 as numbers and abbreviations.

1 The area of Antarctica: *14,000,000 km²*
2 When water becomes ice: below ....
3 Amount of water for an average adult: ....
4 Earth covered by dry land: ....
5 Height of the tallest tree: ....
6 Weight of the ISS: ....

Listening Earth trends

4 2.36 Listen to four predictions of future trends on Earth. Match the predictions (1–4) with the topics (a–e). There is one extra topic.

Prediction 1 ....
Prediction 2 ....
Prediction 3 ....
Prediction 4 ....

a population
b food and water
c energy
d technology
e travel and tourism

5 2.36 Listen again. Choose the correct option (a–c) to complete these sentences.

1 Experts think immigration will ....
   a increase   b decrease
   c stay the same
2 Tourist destinations and popular cities will have problems because there will be so many ....
   a immigrants   b tourists
   c experts
3 More people live in cities than live in ....
   a houses   b towns
   c the countryside
4 By 2030 there will be .... people on the planet.
   a seven billion   b eight billion
   c nine billion
5 Computers and communication across the Earth have increased in the past ....
   a 50 years   b 40 years
   c 30 years
6 The speed of the technology will ....
   a become faster   b become slower
   c stay the same
7 Farmers need more .... to grow food.
   a money   b workers
   c land
8 Many experts are .... about the future for modern farming.
   a positive   b unhappy
   c worried

Grammar *will/won't*

6 Look at the trends for a small town in England. Write sentences with *will/won't*.

Number of cars

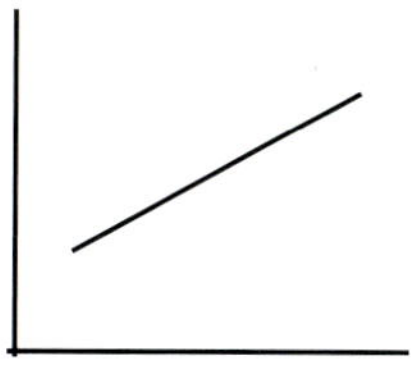

1 The number of ....*cars will*........ increase.

Number of houses

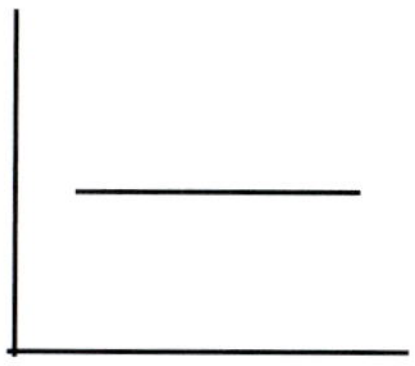

2 The number of .... stay the same.

Number of children

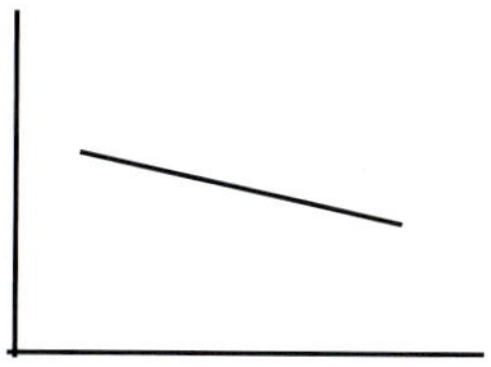

3 The number of .... increase.

Temperature in the summer

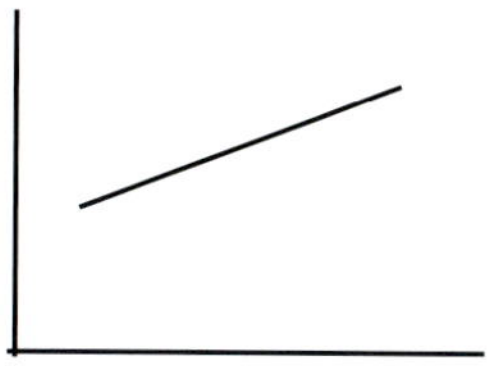

4 The temperature in .... decrease.

Rainfall in the winter

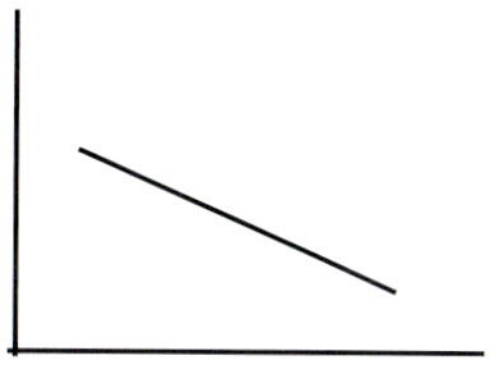

5 The rainfall in .... decrease.

Number of people

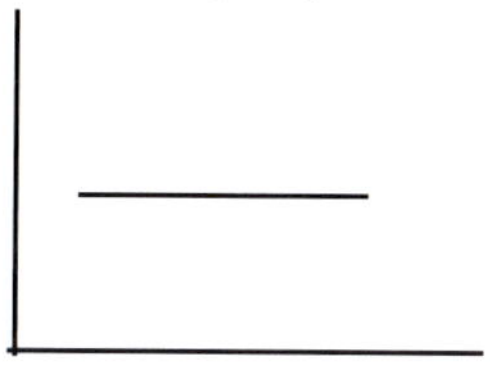

6 The number of .... increase.

7 **Pronunciation *'ll* or *will***

2.37 Listen to eight sentences. Do you hear *'ll* or *will*?

1 'll   will
2 'll   will
3 'll   will
4 'll   will
5 'll   will
6 'll   will
7 'll   will
8 'll   will

12b Exploring places

Vocabulary land and water

1 Complete the sentences about the places with these words.

desert forest island lake mountain ocean river sea

1 Malta is a beautiful __________ in the Mediterranean Sea.
2 The Pacific __________ separates Asia, Australasia and the Americas.
3 30% of all the trees in the world are in the boreal __________ in Canada, Scandinavia and Russia.
4 Kilimanjaro in Tanzania was a volcano and now it's a __________.
5 __________ Urmia is the largest one of its kind in the Middle East.
6 Nine countries are next to the Baltic __________.
7 The __________ Ganges is 2,525 km long and goes from India to Bangladesh.
8 The Gobi __________ covers large parts of southern Mongolia and northern China.

Grammar definite *the* or no article + names

2 Write *the* or Ø (no article) before these names of places.

1 __________ Maldive Islands
2 __________ Atlantic Ocean
3 __________ Europe
4 __________ Mount Kilimanjaro
5 __________ Malta
6 __________ River Nile
7 __________ Lake Balaton
8 __________ Peru
9 __________ Sahara Desert
10 __________ Asia
11 __________ River Mississippi
12 __________ Iceland
13 __________ Mediterranean Sea
14 __________ Black Forest
15 __________ Himalayan Mountains

3 There are three mistakes in this quiz. Cross out the extra word in three of the questions.

How much do you know about the world?
Test your knowledge.

1 What's the longest river?
2 Which ocean is the Madagascar in?
3 What is the nationality of someone from the Netherlands?
4 Where is the Lake Vostok?
5 Which continent are the Alps in?
6 Where is the Mount Ararat?

4 Can you answer the questions in the quiz in Exercise 3? Check your answers on page 138.

Reading the highest place

5 Complete the article about Felix Baumgartner with these sentences (a–e).

a That's faster than the speed of sound.
b Felix Baumgartner is a skydiver.
c He jumped 31 kilometres in 1960.
d The balloon was 100 metres tall.
e 'Felix did a great job.'

Space jump

[1] .... He is 43 years old and he has jumped from the tops of mountains and some of the tallest buildings in the world. On 24th October 2012 he jumped from the highest place above the Earth.

A balloon carried him to a height of 39 kilometres above the surface of the Earth. [2] .... From his special capsule, Baumgartner could see the Earth really well before he jumped back to Earth. The jump took him ten minutes. On the way down, he travelled at a speed of 1,342 kilometres an hour. [3] .... He fell for four minutes twenty seconds before he opened his parachute.

Baumgartner now has the world record for jumping from the highest place above the Earth. Before Baumgartner, Joe Kittinger had the record. [4] .... Kittinger is in his eighties now and he worked with Baumgartner. After the jump, Kittinger said: [5] ....

Word focus *how*

6 Complete the *how* questions with these words.

far fast high long old tall well

1 How .... is Felix Baumgartner?
2 How .... did the balloon carry him?
3 How .... was the balloon?
4 How .... could he see the Earth from his capsule?
5 How .... did the jump take?
6 How .... did he travel down to Earth?
7 How .... did Joe Kittinger jump in 1960?

7 Read the article again. Then answer the questions from Exercise 6.

1 ....
2 ....
3 ....
4 ....
5 ....
6 ....
7 ....

Felix in his capsule above the Earth

12c Planets

Vocabulary the Earth and other planets

1 Complete the text about Pluto with these words.

astronomers orbit planets rock star surface travel

The [1] .... at the centre of our solar system is called the Sun. There are eight [2] .... in our solar system, including the Earth, and they all [3] .... the Sun. But before 2006, there were nine planets. Pluto was the smallest planet in our solar system. [4] .... discovered Pluto in 1930. Through a telescope, the [5] .... of Pluto looks different colours. It is made of [6] .... and ice. Humans could not live on Pluto so we will probably never [7] .... there. In 2006, scientists decided Pluto was not a planet.

Listening space news

2 2.38 Listen to a news programme. Match the numbers (1–4) with the information (a–d).

1 four ....
2 hundreds ....
3 six ....
4 thousands or millions ....

a the number of exoplanets that scientists have found since the nineties
b the number of exoplanets that scientists think are in the universe
c the number of light years between the region in space called Alpha Centauri and the Earth
d the number of exoplanets around a star two thousand light years away

3 Dictation the news

2.38 Listen again and complete the news report.

Here is the news. [1] .... have found the nearest planet to our solar system. It [2] .... a star in the region of space called Alpha Centauri. That's four light years from the [3] .... The planet is similar in size to Earth, but it is very close to its star. For this reason, [4] .... could not live on it. However, stars often have more than one planet, so the [5] .... is exciting. It's possible that there are other planets in the same solar system.

Planets near other stars are called [6] .... and astronomers have found hundreds of them since the nineties. Using powerful telescopes, they look for a [7] .... in another solar system and then they look for planets orbiting it. Recently, astronomers found a star two thousand light years away with six [8] .... around it, and experts think there are probably thousands or millions more exoplanets in the [9] ....

Answers to 12b Exercise 4

1 the River Nile **2** the Indian Ocean **3** Dutch **4** Antarctica **5** Europe **6** Turkey

12d A special day

Listening national tree planting day

1 2.39 Listen to a presentation about a national tree planting day. Answer the questions.

1 Where is Joel from?

....

2 Which Friday in October is National Tree Planting Day?

....

3 How many trees have people planted across the island since 2002?

....

4 Who plants the trees?

....

5 Where do they plant them?

....

6 Where did Joel and the students plant new trees last year?

....

7 What does he hope other countries will do in the future?

....

Real life making a presentation

2 Match the stages of a presentation (1–7) with these sections of Joel's presentation (a–g).

1 Welcome the audience. ....
2 Introduce yourself. ....
3 Introduce the title of your presentation. ....
4 Talk about the history. ....
5 Talk about the present day. ....
6 Conclude the presentation. ....
7 End the presentation. ....

a First of all, National Tree Planting Day is on the first Friday of October every year. The first National Tree Planting Day was in 2002. Since then, people have planted fifty thousand trees across the island.

b Today, I'd like to talk about an important day in my country. It's called National Tree Planting Day.

c Good morning and thank you for coming.

d In conclusion, I really think National Tree Planting Day is important. In the future, I hope other countries will have the same day.

e Thank you very much for listening.

f Nowadays, everyone from schoolchildren to business people are involved in the day. They can get seeds from their local Forestry Department and they can plant the seeds in local parks and communities. Last year, I went with some students from my university and we planted new trees in the gardens of a home for old people.

g My name's Joel and I'm from Jamaica.

3 Pronunciation pausing on commas

2.40 Listen to these sentences from a presentation. Listen for the pause and write in the missing comma.

1 Today I'd like to talk about an important day.
2 First of all my country's national day is on 4th July.
3 Since then people have always celebrated this day.
4 Nowadays everyone has a day off.
5 Next families have a big meal together.
6 In conclusion I really think it's important.

12e A tree planting poster

1 Writing skill important words and information

a Read these sentences for some posters. Delete the unnecessary words so you have the number of words in brackets.

1 Everyone ~~is~~ invited ~~to our~~ New Year's Party! (five words)
2 The Annual Party is at the Town Hall on 1st May. (eight words)
3 There is a huge sale at the Big Bed Shop all this week. (eight words)
4 You can eat delicious sandwiches at Jill's Café. (six words)
5 Visit the website www.greenfest.org for details. (four words)
6 The entrance to the disco is free. (four words)
7 Listen to live music and look at local art at the Mayberry Arts Festival. (nine words)
8 You are welcome to our Midsummer Party at nine. (six words)

b Read this information about National Tree Planting Day. Underline the most important words and information.

You are invited to plant a tree on 7th October for National Tree Planting Day. We will give you free seeds to plant in the local park. There will be lots of people there and lots of entertainment, so bring the whole family. We'll have hot and cold food, and local shops will sell environmentally friendly products. We'll also have presentations about how to help the environment and information about gardening. The event is in Tenant Park, and it starts at two o'clock and it finishes at five o'clock. The entrance is five euros for adults and free for children under 16. You can telephone us on 088 678 4955 for more information.

Writing a poster

2 Write the important information from the text in Exercise 1b on this poster.

Wordbuilding word forms (2)

1 Label the diagram with these words.

height depth length weight width

1 ....

2 ....

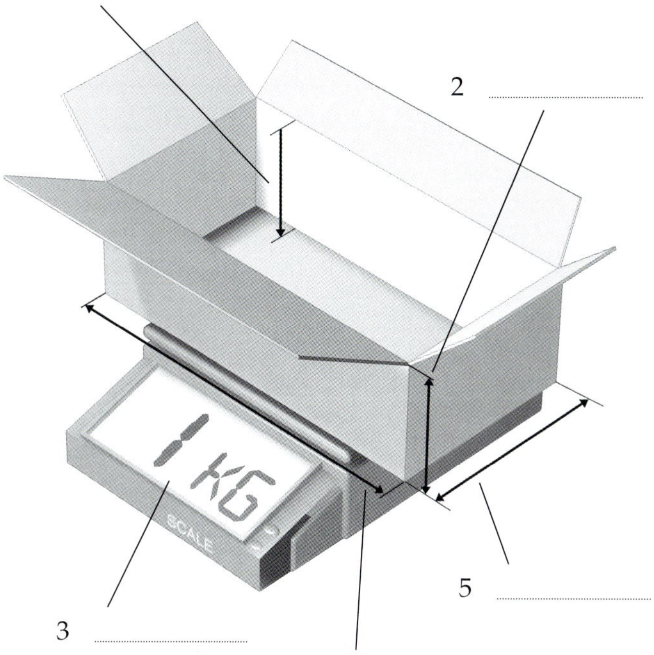

3 ....

4 ....

5 ....

2 Complete the pairs of sentences with the correct form of the measurement words.

1 long / length
 a This film is very ....
 b What is the .... of this film?
2 high / height
 a My son's .... is about one metre.
 b How .... is that mountain?
3 weigh / weight
 a The .... is one kilogram.
 b These potatoes .... one kilogram.
4 deep / depth
 a This swimming pool is very ....
 b Nobody knows the .... of this lake.
5 wide / width
 a In some places, the Amazon River is 40 kilometres ....
 b The .... of the Amazon River is bigger than any other river in the world.

3 Which measurement words in Exercise 2 are adjectives? Which word is a verb?

4 2.41 Listen and repeat the measurement words in Exercise 2.

Learning skills your learning

5 You are at the end of this course. Think about your learning using this questionnaire. Circle the number in Part 1 and answer the questions in Part 2. Then show the questionnaire to your teacher and discuss your answers.

Your learning

4 = Very good 3 = Good
2 = Satisfactory 1 = Not very good

1 How was your progress in …?

Vocabulary	4	3	2	1
Grammar	4	3	2	1
Useful phrases (in 'Real life')	4	3	2	1
Pronunciation	4	3	2	1
Reading	4	3	2	1
Listening	4	3	2	1
Speaking	4	3	2	1
Writing	4	3	2	1

2 What do you want to do in the future? Do you want to do another English course?

Give details:

....

....

Check!

6 What do these numbers refer to in Unit 12 of the Student's Book?

1 914 trillion litres
....
2 47 metres
....
3 2009
....
4 18 trillion
....
5 20 million
....

2.42

LISTENING TEST

Please note that the page reference on the audio refers to the full edition. Stay on this page.

SECTION 1

Questions 1–10

Questions 1 and 2

*Choose the correct letter, **A**, **B** or **C**.*

Example

Ian went to the library to find a book about
A science.
B sport.
C history.

1 At the library, Ian saw
- **A** an exhibition of photos.
- **B** information about a lecture.
- **C** a notice about a club to join.

2 Why is Ian going back to the library?
- **A** to meet someone
- **B** to collect something
- **C** to take part in an activity

Questions 3–10

Complete the notes below.

*Write **NO MORE THAN TWO WORDS AND/OR A NUMBER** for each answer.*

Events at the Library

Day	Name of event	Time	Price per week
Monday	Photography club	7.30 p.m.	£2.50
3	Storytelling workshop	7.00 p.m.	**4** ....
Thursday	**5** .... club	2.00 p.m.	£1.50
6	Film club	7.45 p.m.	**7** ....
Friday	Poetry workshop	**8**	£3.00
Saturday	**9** .... design	10.15 a.m.	£4.75
Saturday	Map reading	2.45 p.m.	**10** ....

Please note that the page reference on the audio refers to the full edition. Stay on this page.

SECTION 2

Questions 11–20

Questions 11–13

*Choose the correct letter, **A**, **B** or **C**.*

11 Which day is Hilary's interview?
- **A** Monday
- **B** Tuesday
- **C** Wednesday

12 Where should Hilary go first?
- **A** the main college reception
- **B** the personnel department
- **C** room number 341

13 Who will Hilary meet at the interview?
- **A** Wendy Bright
- **B** Howard Green
- **C** Diana Cook

Questions 14 and 15

*Choose **TWO** letters, **A–F**.*

What two things should Hilary take to her interview?

A a copy of the application form

B an identity document

C exam certificates

D a written reference

E her invitation letter

F a photo of herself

Questions 16–20

Complete the table below.

*Write **NO MORE THAN TWO WORDS AND/OR A NUMBER** for each answer.*

Job title:	Office assistant
Main duties:	• entering data • **16** .... • dealing with **17** ....
Number of hours per week:	**18** ....
Basic rate of pay per hour:	**19** ....
Paid annual holiday entitlement:	**20** ....

Please note that the page reference on the audio refers to the full edition. Stay on this page.

SECTION 3

Questions 21–30

Questions 21 and 22

Choose the correct letter, ***A***, ***B*** *or* ***C***.

21 Which continent has the largest number of wild rabbits?
- **A** Europe
- **B** Australasia
- **C** North America

22 Wild rabbits usually live for
- **A** five to ten years.
- **B** ten to twelve years.
- **C** fifteen to eighteen years.

Questions 23–30

Complete the table below.

Write ***NO MORE THAN TWO WORDS AND/OR A NUMBER*** *for each answer.*

Keeping rabbits as pets: time and costs involved

Number of rabbits:	2
Total time needed per day:	**23** ....
Daily activities:	• give them food and water • **24** .... their living area • basic **25** .... check • giving them exercise
Cost of buying two rabbits:	£50
Microchipping:	**26** ....
Vaccinations (by vet):	£100
Accommodation:	rabbit house **27** ....
28 .... :	• water bowl £8.00 • food bowl **29** .... • other £20.00
Food:	£16.36 per week
Insurance:	£10.00 per **30** ....
Total cost of two rabbits for life:	£16,000 (10 years)

Please note that the page reference on the audio refers to the full edition. Stay on this page.

SECTION 4

Questions 31–40

Questions 31–34

Choose the correct letter, ***A, B*** *or* ***C.***

31 What should the students do each week?
- **A** Run a fixed distance.
- **B** Run at a constant speed.
- **C** Run for a certain period of time.

32 What does the speaker say about jogging?
- **A** It's best to go with a partner.
- **B** You should always try to feel relaxed.
- **C** Don't try to talk and jog at the same time.

33 Students who already do other sports
- **A** can continue with them during the training.
- **B** need to ask the trainer for advice.
- **C** may not have to train so much.

34 Where should students do the training?
- **A** on a sports track
- **B** on the grass in a park
- **C** on roads and pavements

Questions 35–40

Complete the notes below.

Write ***NO MORE THAN TWO WORDS*** *for each answer.*

TRAINING PROGRAMME

Length of the programme: **35** ....

What to wear:
- the type of shorts that **36** .... usually wear
- **37** .... specially designed for runners

What not to wear: clothes made from **38** ....

If you start to feel hungry, you should **39** .... something.

Stop training if you have caught a **40** ....

READING TEST

SECTION 1

Questions 1–10

Questions 1–10

Look at the six advertisements for part-time jobs, **A–F***.*

For which jobs are the following statements true?

*Write the correct letter (***A–F***) in boxes 1–10 on your answer sheet.*

NB *You may use letters more than once.*

1 You only get one free day per week in this job.

2 This job offers the highest rate of pay.

3 You get free transport to work in this job.

4 You can eat for nothing at work.

5 You have to wear special clothes at work.

6 You have to take money from customers in this job.

7 Language skills are useful in this job.

8 This job only lasts for a limited period.

9 There may be more work available in the future.

10 You have to work closely with other people in this job.

A

Supermarket cashier

Monday to Friday evenings only

No previous experience necessary

£5.30 per hour

10% discount in store (food items only)

Clean and tidy appearance essential

B

Hamburger Chef

Weekend lunchtimes and evenings

Cooking experience an advantage

£5.25 per hour

Free meals when on duty

Uniform provided

C

Coffee bar staff

07.00–09.30 six days a week

To work espresso machine only

Very busy bar – you have to work in a team

£5.50 per hour

Ability to speak French or Spanish an advantage

D

Hotel Receptionist

Weekend lunchtimes only

11.30–15.30

£4.50 per hour

Possibility of extra hours next month

Close to the railway station

E

Suburban Hospital Canteen Porter

- Afternoons: Tuesday to Saturday 16.00–18.00
- £4.75 per hour
- No cooking skills needed
- To take meals to patients
- Weekly bus ticket to the city centre provided

F

Hotel chambermaid

Three mornings a week

08.00–11.00

Temporary contract (six weeks)

£4.50 per hour

City-centre location

SECTION 2

Questions 11–20

Questions 11–20

Read the text on *page 149**.*

Do the following statements agree with the information given in the text?

In boxes 11–20 on your answer sheet, write

TRUE	*if the statement agrees with the information*
FALSE	*if the statement contradicts the information*
NOT GIVEN	*if there is no information on this*

11 The survey was part of the students' course.

12 The people who answered the students' questions all live in the same city.

13 The students sometimes asked different questions.

14 The students were surprised at how difficult the survey was to do.

15 Most people said that walking was their favourite activity.

16 Swimming is more popular than keep-fit exercises.

17 Most people who like walking prefer to do it in the countryside.

18 Walking holidays are more popular than other types of activity holiday.

19 More men than women go on walking holidays.

20 Boating holidays and golfing holidays are equally popular with unmarried people.

Leisure Survey

Recently, students at the city's university carried out a survey about free-time activities and holidays as part of their course. They wanted to find out if city residents like to be active in their free time. They also wanted to find out which sporting activities are the most popular and if different types of people prefer different activities.

The students asked a sample of local inhabitants to take part in the survey and asked them all the same questions. The students were quite surprised by some of the things they found. But if you compare their findings with national statistics, the people taking part in the survey are not unusual.

The first question the students asked people was about their favourite sporting activity. About 12% of the people they asked said that the leisure activity they enjoyed doing most in their free time was walking. This was the most popular activity. In second place in the list was swimming. Nine per cent of the people said that they liked doing that best, and in third place came keep-fit exercises.

The next questions the students asked were about how often people did their favourite activity and how long they spent on it. They discovered, for example, that people who like walking spend 108 minutes each month on average on their hobby. These people walk for an average of about five miles per month. But some walkers do less than that. For instance, a lot of people just go for a walk round their local park after lunch at the weekend. And, of course, some walkers do a lot more. For example, the statistic includes a few very keen walkers who go for long walks in the countryside most weekends.

The students asked the people in their survey about holidays too. Activity holidays, where people go on a holiday to do a sporting activity, are very popular in Britain, and walking holidays are the most popular of all. The students found that this was just as true of local people as it is nationally.

But what type of people take these holidays? The students found out that most people who go on walking holidays are under 35 years of age. The majority of these people have jobs, and more than 50% of them are single. There were an equal number of men and women going on walking holidays, and the same is true of cycling holidays. Golfing holidays, however, were different. Eighty per cent of people who said they went on golfing holidays were male. Boating holidays, on the other hand, are the ones where you find the largest number of single people.

Not everybody likes activity holidays, however. Sixty-two per cent of the people in the survey have not been on this type of holiday in the last five years. However, 12% of these people said they would like to go on one in the future.

SECTION 3

Questions 21–29

Read the text on page 151 and answer questions 21–29.

Questions 21–27

*The text on page 151 has seven sections, **A–G**.*

*Choose the correct heading for sections **A–G** from the list of headings below.*

*Write the correct number (**i–ix**) in boxes **21–27** on your answer sheet.*

List of Headings

i How fit must I be?

ii What about overnight accommodation?

iii Are these holidays expensive?

iv What must I take with me when I'm cycling?

v How far can I cycle on this type of holiday?

vi Are these holidays good for all ages?

vii What can go wrong on cycling holidays?

viii Are cycling holidays good for the environment?

ix Who organises cycling holidays?

21 Section A

22 Section B

23 Section C

24 Section D

25 Section E

26 Section F

27 Section G

Questions 28 and 29

Complete the sentences below.

*Choose **NO MORE THAN TWO WORDS** from the text for each answer.*

The writer gives the example of **28** .... as a place where cycling may be more difficult.

The writer uses the term **29** .... holiday to describe a type of cycling holiday where you sleep in the same place each night.

Eco Escapes: Cycling Holidays

Section A

Are you worried about the amount of pollution you cause when you go away on holiday? Both public transport and cars can cause real damage to places that lots of tourists visit, and some people think that this is wrong. Many British people fly to seaside resorts in places like Spain and Greece on what are called 'package holidays', which can leave quite a big carbon footprint. That's why more and more people are choosing a different type of holiday. Cycling holidays are much greener than holidays by car, train or plane – and you get lots of good exercise as well. So, as well as having a break and seeing different places, you can keep fit too.

Section B

There are different ways of going on a cycling holiday. Of course, there is nothing to stop you going on your own if you want, but often groups of people travel together and plan a route in advance, which may be more fun. Or you may prefer to book a holiday that has been put together by a company which makes all the arrangements in advance, so that you have no worries. On this type of holiday, you also have the chance to make friends with other people who are on the same trip.

Section C

And there are different types of cycling holiday on offer. Serious cyclists sometimes want to travel a long distance every day, because for them the joy of cycling at speed is part of the fun of the holiday. Other people are more interested in seeing the scenery and exploring the places they pass through, and so they are happy to travel more slowly. It's up to you what distance you want to cover every day, and most holiday companies offer a range of possibilities to suit the needs of different types of people.

Section D

Many people who go on cycling holidays use a bicycle regularly and choose this type of holiday because they know that they enjoy cycling. So what about if you have never cycled, or if you haven't been on a bike since you were a young child? It's a good idea to do some training before your holiday, especially if you are new to cycling or out of practice. It isn't necessary to be very strong to ride a bike, but you should be in good health. Cycling in Scotland, for instance, where there are lots of hills, will give you a good physical workout. But if that sounds too much like hard work, choose an area like East Anglia where the landscape is mostly flat.

Section E

There are also a range of options when it comes to how long to stay away and how to make sure you have a bed for the night. Some people prefer what's known as a 'centre-based' holiday, for example, where you return to the same hotel every evening and can have a good meal and a shower. Other people prefer to follow a continuous route – so that they sleep in a different place each night, sometimes carrying a tent with them so that they can go camping.

Section F

Clearly, it is not practical to cycle with lots of luggage. Holiday companies sometimes arrange for your suitcases to be sent on to your next destination, so that they are there waiting for you when you arrive in the evening. This means that you only need to carry a few things with you every day. Some different types of clothing are a good idea in case the weather changes suddenly, and a good map and an emergency repair kit for your bike are essential.

Section G

How much your holiday costs will depend on which type you choose. If you want to explore another country or another continent, like Africa or Australia, then you have to travel there before you can start cycling, and that can be expensive. However, camping can be a way of keeping accommodation costs down. But, generally speaking, you will find there is a cycling holiday to suit every pocket.

SECTION 4

Questions 30–40

Read the text on page 153 and answer questions 30–40.

Questions 30 and 31

Complete the sentences below.

Choose **NO MORE THAN TWO WORDS** *from the text for each answer.*

Cuckoos usually arrive in Europe in the month of **30** ....

Adult cuckoos usually leave Europe in the month of **31** ....

Questions 32–40

For each question 32–40 decide which answer is correct.

Write one letter, **A**, **B** *or* **C**, *next to questions 32–40.*

A	only the bird called Lyster
B	the birds called Chris and Lyster
C	all five birds

Which bird or birds:

32 was (or were) born in England?

33 reached the Congo?

34 flew over Morocco?

35 returned to Norfolk?

36 left England with a satellite tag?

37 successfully crossed the Sahara twice?

38 travelled at least 10,000 miles with a tag?

39 flew over Algeria?

40 only flew over Spain once?

Backpacking cuckoos

The cuckoo is a bird which people all over Europe know from the sound it makes. It doesn't sing, but makes a noise with one high note and one low note – 'coo coo'. People in Europe say that when you hear that sound for the first time each year, you know that spring has arrived. In some years, people hear cuckoos as early as February, and in other years they don't arrive until April. But March is the typical month for the birds to arrive. This is because the cuckoo lives in Africa during the winter months and only comes to Europe when the weather gets better.

People have always known that the cuckoos migrated. They fly thousands of miles across the Sahara desert twice a year – once in the spring and then back again at the end of the summer, normally in July. The young cuckoos are born in England and they leave for Africa a little later. But by mid-August, there are no cuckoos left in Europe. The details of how they make their incredible journey have only recently been understood by scientists.

Last May, scientists caught five male birds in Norfolk in eastern England. They put a tiny satellite tag on each bird's back, and then set them free again. The tag allowed the scientists to see where they went when they left England.

The scientists found that the five tagged birds all travelled about 10,000 miles that summer, and all spent the winter in the Congo region of central Africa. Incredibly, the scientists discovered that the five birds all took different routes to reach their destination in Africa. The first bird, to which the scientists gave the name Lyster, flew across France, Spain and Morocco before crossing the Sahara desert. The second bird, called Chris, went by a completely different route. He flew over Belgium, Germany and Italy before crossing the Sahara desert in Libya. Tunisia and Algeria were countries that the other three birds flew over on their way to Africa.

The scientists were also able to see that all five birds left Africa again, nine months later, to come back to Britain. Incredibly, they each took a different route again. And not only a different route from each other, but a different route from the one they had taken before. For example, Lyster flew back to England via Algeria and France, but this time didn't fly over Spain and Morocco. Chris also crossed the Algerian desert, but then continued his journey via Italy and France. The two birds, however, both returned to the exact place in Norfolk where their satellite tags were fitted the year before. The three other birds did not return to England and the scientists think they died on their return journey.

Next year, the scientists are going to put satellite tags on female birds to see which route they take.

WRITING TEST

TASK 1

You should spend about 20 minutes on this task.

> You recently had lunch in an expensive restaurant, but you didn't like the food. When you told the waiter, he was rude to you.
>
> Write a letter to the manager of the restaurant. In your letter:
>
> - tell the manager why you didn't like the food
> - explain what happened when you told the waiter
> - say what you would like the manager to do.

Write at least 150 words.

You do not need to write any addresses.

Begin your letter like this:

Dear Sir or Madam,

TASK 2

You should spend about 40 minutes on this task.

Write about this topic.

> Some people think it is good to listen to music while they are studying.
>
> Do you agree or disagree?

Give reasons for your answer and include any relevant examples from your own knowledge or experience.

Write at least 250 words.

SPEAKING TEST

PART 1

Let's talk about your family.

- How many people are there in your family?
- What jobs do the people in your family do?
- Do other people in your family speak English?
- What do you do with your family on special occasions?

PART 2

Candidate Task Card

Describe a typical day in your life.

You should say:

- the things you do every day
- what time you do these things
- the things you like and the things you don't like doing
- explain who you meet during the day.

You will have to talk about the topic for one or two minutes.

You will have one minute to think about what you are going to say.

You can make some notes to help you if you wish.

Rounding-off questions

- Which is your favourite part of the day? Why?
- What do you like doing at the weekend?

PART 3

First of all, let's talk about sport in general.

- Which sports do you like? Why?
- Which sports are better to watch and which sports are better to play?
- Do you think everybody should play sport? Why / Why not?

Finally, let's talk about famous sportspeople.

- Do you think that some sportspeople earn too much money? Why / Why not?

Unit 7

2.1

Albatross: This is the albatross. In the life of a 50-year-old albatross, it flies six million kilometres. That's because of its wings. The wings of an albatross are longer than any other bird on Earth. An adult albatross has wings of 3.5 metres and a parent albatross can fly further than 15,000 kilometres to feed a chick.

Zebra: In the middle of Africa, there are 200,000 zebras. These beautiful animals are famous for their black and white coats, but their lives are more dangerous and difficult because of their long journey. Every year they go on a migration of a thousand kilometres across Africa.

Elephant seal: The ocean around Antarctica is colder than other parts of the world, but for elephant seals it is their home. These elephant seals go on journeys of 13,000 kilometres and can dive 1,500 metres. That's deeper than a human submarine. They can stay under the water for longer than two hours and only come up for air for a few minutes.

2.3

Seamounts are mountains that you cannot see above the sea. There are about 100,000 in the Earth's oceans which are over a kilometre high, but we don't know much about them. That's because the journey to a lot of these seamounts is long and difficult.

Las Gemelas is an area of seamounts about 500 kilometres from the coast of Costa Rica. The highest part of Las Gemelas is 2,286 metres and it's interesting for scientists because of the sea life on the sides of the mountains.

Avi Klapfer, Gregory Stone and Brian Skerry took a submersible called the DeepSee to Las Gemelas. It's a small submersible, but it has a lot of scientific equipment. As the DeepSee takes the three men towards Las Gemelas, they can see fish and coral. The higher part of the seamounts is the most perfect home for sea life, but as they travel further down, the ocean is blacker. They switch on the lights of the DeepSee and, finally, there is the bottom of the seamounts. Here they can see how the seamounts began. There's the hole of an old volcano, perhaps millions of years old. Most seamounts come from volcanoes.

After five hours, Klapfer, Stone and Skerry return to their ship and plan their next journey to the seamounts.

2.4

T = Ms Tengku, S = Mr Stewart, C = Colleague of Mr Stewart

Conversation 1

T: Mr Stewart?
S: Yes?
T: My name's Ms Tengku. Nice to meet you.
S: Nice to meet you too.
T: How was your flight?
S: Very good, thank you.

Conversation 2

T: Good morning.
S: Good morning.
T: Was your hotel comfortable?
S: Yes, it was fine, but the Internet didn't work.
T: Oh dear. Do you want to use the connection here?
S: That would be helpful, thanks.

Conversation 3

C: Hi, how's your trip?
S: It's fine so far.
C: How was your meeting?
S: Really interesting. We had a very good discussion today and we have another one tomorrow. I think we can do business with them.
C: Great!

Conversation 4

C: It's really sunny here. What's the weather like?
S: Terrible. It's rained every day. Last night there was a storm. I didn't sleep at all.

Conversation 5

S: Jane took me to an excellent restaurant last night. It was in a beautiful old building.
C: Did you try the local food?
S: Yes, it's very hot and spicy. They eat a lot of fish as well.
C: I don't think I'd like it. I don't eat hot food.
S: Yes, I drank a lot of water with it!

Unit 8

2.8

1 These women are at a festival. They are wearing colourful Indian clothes called saris and they are carrying something on their heads. But this isn't in India. It's in Oxford, England.

2 This one is obvious. It's a police officer in the United States. He has a uniform with a motorcycle helmet and white gloves. He's a Navajo police officer. That means he's from the north American Indian tribe called the Navajo Indians. They live on a place called a reservation and he works as a police officer on the reservation.

3 These two young boys are from Nepal. They are monks so they wear these special clothes. Everyone in Nepal knows they are monks because of their famous red and yellow clothes. And they have a purple robe. It's very practical and it's very warm in the cold mountains of Nepal.

4 The Masai people live in Tanzania in Africa. They are famous for their red and black clothes and this man is wearing them. He's also got long, black hair and wears jewellery around his neck.

5 This woman is from Peru. She's selling things on the side of the road in the mountains. Her clothes are traditional, with a red dress and a white hat on her head.

2.9

P = Presenter, S = Sheena Turner

P: Welcome to The Nature Show. This week's programme is about how some animals use their appearance so their enemies cannot see them. We call this camouflage and some animals are very good at it. With me to talk about this is nature expert Doctor Sheena Turner. Doctor Turner, can you give an example of an animal camouflage?

S: Yes, of course. A lot of animals are the same colour as the landscape. So, for example, a deer in the forest is difficult to see. That's because it's brown and the trees are also brown.

P: Yes. Is that true for all animals?

S: No, not at all. Zebras aren't the same colour as the landscape of central Africa but they use camouflage.

P: Zebras? But you can always see a zebra because of its black and white stripes. It's easy for a lion to see a zebra, isn't it?

S: Well, lions are colour blind, so they can't see the difference between the black and white stripes of a zebra and the brown and green landscape of central Africa. But there's a good reason for the black and white stripes. Zebras are social animals. They live in big groups. When they stand together, you can't see a single zebra.

P: Why is this important?

S: Because when a lion looks for one zebra, it can't see it. All it can see is a large group.

P: I see. Very clever. And how do other animals use their appearance?

S: Some butterflies have large, round colours on their wings. To other animals, these look like the eyes of a large animal, so they don't go near the butterfly.

P: That is good camouflage! But what animals change their appearance? For example, the chameleon can change its colour.

S: That's true, but chameleons don't change colour for camouflage. A chameleon changes colour when a dangerous animal is near because it wants to tell other chameleons about the danger. But another animal called the Arctic fox changes colour. In the winter, it is white because there is snow. In spring and summer, it's brown because there isn't snow and the landscape is brown and green.

P: That's amazing, Doctor Turner, and thank you for coming in today.

2.10

This photo shows a family, I think. On the right is the grandmother and on the left is the mother, maybe. The two children in the middle are waiting for dinner. The girl is looking at something and, in front of her, the boy is looking through a telescope. But I think it's the wrong way round! The family looks serious, but perhaps they are hungry. They are wearing special clothes. I think they are from Lapland in northern Norway because the women's hats and clothes are from this region. The photo is interesting because it shows people in their everyday life.

Unit 9

2.12

1

A = Astronaut, M = Mission control

A: I'm stepping onto the planet now. I'm down.
M: What can you see?
A: Mountains. They're very red. And there's a light about a kilometre away.
M: Is it the sun?
A: No, but it's moving closer. It's moving very fast.
M: What is it?
A: I don't know. But I'm not alone on this planet!

2

These animals live in the mountains and they usually come out at night. So we're very lucky to see the mother with her young today. They are hungry so the mother is looking for food.

3

P = Police officer, C = Criminal

P: Don't move! This is the police.
C: But I didn't take the gold.
P: I said, 'Don't move'. What are you doing at the bank?

4

M = Man, W = Woman

M: So, how are you?
W: Fine. You look great.
M: I'm older.
W: No, you look the same.
M: Well, you look older.
W: Oh.
M: But still beautiful.
W: Thanks.
M: Can I ask you something?
W: Sure.
M: Why did you leave me?

2.14
1 I'm going to the shops.
2 Chris is going to meet friends.
3 I'd like two DVDs, please.
4 They're going to make a film.
5 The film starts in two minutes.
6 She's going to watch a documentary.
7 Can I have two tickets?
8 We're going to buy tickets.

2.16
Film, music and arts news
We look at the latest news from the world of film, music and art.

Josh Roberts is going to work in Hollywood to make his next film. The young Irish film director is going to buy a house in Los Angeles to live there for two years. He said, 'I'm not going there forever.'

The band Stronger are going to be on TV next week to play their new songs. Switch on at seven on Wednesday evening to watch a TV documentary about the group.

There is going to be an exhibition of Javier Bowman's art at the National Gallery to show the artist's most famous paintings. The exhibition opens on 10th January. Phone this number 0845 4785 to book tickets.

2.17
In 1982, the author Michael Morpurgo wrote a book called *War Horse*. It was a book for children about a horse called Joey. Joey lives on a farm, but the army want horses because it is the First World War. Joey goes to France and we learn about the war through the life of Joey.

Michael Morpurgo's book was very popular and in 2007, the National Theatre of Great Britain made the book into a stage play. At the time, people didn't know how they could make a story about a horse into a play. How would they show the horse? In the theatre, the horses are giant puppets. Like the book, the play was very popular and there are theatre productions of *War Horse* in London, New York, Toronto, Australia and Germany.

War Horse became even more famous in 2011 because Steven Spielberg made a film version. Spielberg trained horses for the film. He used fourteen different horse 'actors' to play Joey. The film critics liked the film and thousands of people around the world went to the cinema to see it.

2.18
R = Richard, M = Max
R: Hi Max. It's Richard.
M: Hi Richard. Sorry, but I'm going to a meeting now so I don't have long.
R: OK, it's just that a friend gave me some free tickets for a concert. Do you want to go?
M: What is it?
R: Some music by Mozart.
M: Hmm, I don't know much about classical music.
R: I don't either but it's free, so would you like to come?
M: OK thanks, I'd love to. When is it?
R: Tomorrow night. Are you free?
M: I'm sorry, but I'm working late tomorrow night.
R: What time do you finish?
M: At seven.
R: That's OK. It starts at eight. Let's meet at seven outside your work.
M: That's great. See you at seven.

2.21
1 Would you like to go to the cinema?
2 Are you free tonight? I've got tickets for a musical.
3 Do you want to go to a concert?
4 Would you like to meet for dinner?

Unit 10

2.22
M = Manager, K = Karen
Conversation 1
M: OK, Karen. Have you ever used this machine before?
K: Yes, of course I've used one before.
M: No, I mean, have you ever made copies with this type of machine? It's different from others.
K: Oh, I see. No, I haven't, but it looks similar to the one in my previous job.

Conversation 2
M: And this is yours.
K: Oh, I've never seen one like this before.
M: It's very easy. Press this button.
K: OK. I've done that.
M: Great. Has the screen come on?
K: Yes, it has.
M: Now you put your finger on the screen.

Conversation 3
K: Someone has left a message on my phone.
M: OK. Press play.
K: I have pressed play but it doesn't work.
M: Have you switched it on?
K: Ah. Sorry! No, I haven't.

2.23
1 Have you ever listened to a podcast?
2 Have you ever learned a subject online?
3 Have you ever used a sat nav?
4 Have you ever downloaded an ebook?
5 Have you ever booked a ticket online?
6 Have you ever used online banking?

2.24

a I've printed the photos.
b She hasn't sent a letter.
c They've booked tickets.
d Have you ever learned Spanish?
e No, I haven't.
f Has he sent the email?
g Yes, he has.
h It hasn't worked today.

2.25

H = Host, G = Green team, B = Blue team

H: After round four, let's look at the scores. The Green team has ten points and the Blue team also has ten points.
So, on to round five and the questions are about science and technology. Green team, it's your question first. In 1901, an Italian physicist sent a radio message across the Atlantic from England to Canada. What was his name?
G: Marconi.
H: Marconi is correct. Two points for the Green team. The next question is for the Blue team. You can send messages using a series of short and long sounds. This is a type of code. What is the name of the code and its inventor? I'll have to hurry you for an answer, Blue team.
B: Morse Code?
H: Is correct! Two points. And the next question is for the Green team. In the first century, the Chinese invented an object. It pointed north and south. What was the invention?
Do you have an answer? No? OK, Blue team, for two points. In the first century, the Chinese invented an object. It pointed north and south. What was the invention?
B: Was it the compass?
H: It was! That gives the Blue team fourteen points and the Green team twelve points.

2.26

L = Lance, S = Sophie

L: Hello, AGA Technologies. Can I help you?
S: Hello, Lance. This is Sophie.
L: Hello, Sophie. Where are you now?
S: I'm at the Science Fair in Cologne.
L: Great. What time is it there?
S: Err, it's six o'clock.
L: Is that six in the morning?
S: No, in the evening. I want to give you the name of my hotel for the next two days. It's the Insel Hotel …
L: One moment. I need a pen. OK. Was that the Ensal Hotel?
S: No, the Insel Hotel. I for Italy, N – S – E for England, L.
L: Oh sorry. Insel.
S: And the number is zero two one, eight eight three four, five zero.
L: Was that zero two one, eight eight three four, five zero?
S: That's right.

L: Is there anything else?
S: Have you emailed me a copy of the new prices?
L: No, I haven't because your email wasn't working.
S: That's strange. Can you fax it to the hotel? I don't know the number.
L: Don't worry. I've just looked at your hotel website and there's a fax number on that.
S: Great, thank you. I'll call you later. Bye for now.

2.28

1

V = Voicemail, L = Lisa

V: Hello. This is the Insel Hotel. Please leave a message after the tone.
L: Hello. This is Ms Lisa Farrell. That's F-A-R-R-E-L-L. This is a message for Doctor Nakao. That's N-A-K-A-O. I'm in Cologne tomorrow at two o'clock in the afternoon. Can I meet him in the hotel reception area. Thank you.

2

V = Voicemail, R = Richard

V: Hello. This is AGA Technologies. I'm sorry, but we are now closed. Please leave a message after the tone.
R: Hello. This is Richard Nowitz. That's N-O-W-I-T-Z. This is a message for Dan Moore in Design. Can he email me the designs before twelve o'clock tomorrow? My email is r underscore nowitz at nowitz dot com. It's very urgent.

3

V = Voicemail, M = Max

V: Hello. This is Christine. Sorry I can't answer my phone, but leave a message and I'll get back to you.
M: Hi. This is a message for Christine. My name's Max Lloyd. That's L-L-O-Y-D. You don't know me, but I'm a friend of George's. He gave me your number. I'm interested in renting the room in your apartment. Is the room still available? You can call me on 0990 768 2238 or you can email me at m thirty-six dot lloyd at hotmail dot co dot uk. Thanks. Bye.

Unit 11

2.29

1 Once I rented a motorbike, but I crashed. I was in hospital for two weeks. Fortunately, I had medical insurance so it didn't cost me anything. It's really important in case something bad happens.

2 At this time of year in Asia it's always hot, so you don't need many clothes. But it can be quite cold later in the year, so you should bring a coat for the rain and take an extra jumper.

3 I rented a car in England, but it was scary. Everybody drives on the wrong side of the road! I wanted to drive on the right and it was difficult to understand all the signs. My advice is you should take public transport! It's much easier.

4 When you go to the USA, you sometimes need a visa. Some nationalities can stay for three months without a visa, but everyone needs one to stay longer. And if you work, you definitely need to contact the US embassy in your country.

5 The first time I went to Mexico I took a phrase book. In the big cities a lot of people spoke English, but I wanted to travel to smaller towns, so I needed it there. When I got back home I took lessons in Spanish, so that next time I won't have any problems.

6 I usually change money a few weeks before I go. It's much cheaper than using an exchange office at the airport. I also carry a credit card to pay for big things like a hotel or a meal in a restaurant.

2.30

1 All passengers on flight DL3345 have to go to Gate 13 immediately.
2 You cannot carry liquids over one hundred millilitres in your bag.
3 Passengers in business class do not have to wait in this line.
4 Adults with children can get on the plane first.

2.31

1 I have to leave now.
2 We have to check in at three o'clock.
3 Do you have to go?
4 Yes, I have to.
5 Do we have to show our passports here?
6 No, you don't have to.

2.32

P = Presenter, S = Suzy Trudeau

P: The best travel experiences are when we meet local people. It's a great way to discover what a country is really like. However, if you visit someone's home, it's important to be polite, so you need to know about their customs. With me today is Suzy Trudeau. Suzy is an expert in communication skills. So, Suzy, can you give us an example of what a tourist or traveller needs to know in certain countries?
S: Sure. For example, let's imagine we are going on holiday to Greece. If you meet someone in Greece, you shake hands with both adults and children. And if you go to their house, you can take flowers or a small gift. Oh, but don't wear shoes in someone's house. Take them off at the door.
P: OK, but those things are normal in lots of countries. Is there anything very different you need to do in Greece?
S: There is one thing. Greeks love dancing. You can be in a restaurant and people start dancing. You should join in, so don't eat too much before you start dancing!
P: I see. So that's a European country. What about another part of the world?
S: OK. Let's go to South Korea. Mealtimes are also important there. Wait for the oldest person at the table to eat first. And don't cross your chopsticks.
P: What about meeting people? Do you shake hands?
S: Yes, you can, or you can also bow. This is the traditional greeting.
P: What about presents?
S: Like in Greece, flowers are a nice present. And take your shoes off in South Korea as well when you go inside someone's house.
P: What about dancing?
S: Err, actually I don't know. But South Koreans enjoy socialising. They are happy to talk about most topics, especially about sport.

2.33

E = Enzo, M = Marie

E: Marie, are you going anywhere interesting for your holiday this year?
M: I don't know, Enzo. I want to go somewhere hot and with lots of interesting places to visit.
E: Can I make a suggestion? You should go to Morocco.
M: That's a really good idea.
E: Yes, it's a beautiful place. And the public transport is good, so you could travel on your own.
M: Yes, but I'd like to meet people as well.
E: OK. Why don't you go with a tour?
M: But the disadvantage is that it's more expensive.
E: How about going on a package holiday? Often they're cheap.
M: Maybe you're right.

2.34

F = Friend, MA = Model answer

1 F: Why don't you travel on your own?
MA: Yes, but I'd like to meet people as well.
2 F: How about going with a group?
MA: That's a really good idea.
3 F: You should stay in a really nice hotel.
MA: But the disadvantage is that it's more expensive.
4 F: You could go on holiday in this country. It's cheaper.
MA: Maybe you're right.

Unit 12

2.36

1 People are moving round the Earth more than ever before. Workers from different countries go to work on other continents and experts think immigration will increase. As air travel becomes cheaper, more of us will also go on holiday overseas. However, this trend will also cause problems for tourist destinations and popular cities because there will be so many tourists.

2 For the first time, more people on Earth live in cities than in the countryside. And this trend will continue in the future. By the year 2030, there will be eight billion people on the planet and many will live in cities.

3 In the past 30 years, communication across the Earth has increased. Every year, humans have new and more powerful devices. We can watch news from other countries, text friends on the other side of the Earth and share documents with work colleagues on other continents. In the future, more and more people will use this technology and the speed of the technology will become faster and faster.
4 Will there be enough water and food in the future? That's the big question for many scientists. We need a lot of food to feed all the people and this needs a lot of water. As people need more food and farmers need more land to grow the food, we need new ways of growing food. In fact, many experts are working on this problem and they are positive about the future. They think modern farming can solve the problems of food for seven billion people.

2.37

1 I'll be 50 years old next year.
2 We'll need more water.
3 The Earth will get hotter, I think.
4 It'll rain tonight.
5 I'm sure your English will improve.
6 Will you visit me?
7 Who'll win the football match?
8 They'll move to the city.

2.38

Here is the news. Astronomers have found the nearest planet to our solar system. It orbits a star in the region of space called Alpha Centauri. That's four light years from the Earth. The planet is similar in size to Earth, but it is very close to its star. For this reason, humans could not live on it. However, stars often have more than one planet, so the discovery is exciting. It's possible that there are other planets in the same solar system.

Planets near other stars are called exoplanets and astronomers have found hundreds of them since the nineties. Using powerful telescopes, they look for a star in another solar system and then they look for planets orbiting it. Recently, astronomers found a star two thousand light years away with six planets around it, and experts think there are probably thousands or millions more exoplanets in the universe.

2.39

Good morning and thank you for coming. My name's Joel and I'm from Jamaica. Today, I'd like to talk about an important day in my country. It's called National Tree Planting Day.

First of all, National Tree Planting Day is on the first Friday of October every year. The first National Tree Planting Day was in 2002. Since then, people have planted 50,000 trees across the island.

Nowadays, everyone from schoolchildren to business people are involved in the day. They can get seeds from their local Forestry Department and they can plant the seeds in local parks and communities. Last year, I went with some students from my university and we planted new trees in the gardens of a home for old people.

In conclusion, I really think National Tree Planting Day is important. In the future, I hope other countries will have the same day. Thank you very much for listening.

IELTS practice test

2.42

Presenter: IELTS practice test. In this test, you'll hear a number of different recordings and you'll have to answer questions on what you hear. There will be time for you to read the instructions and questions, and you will have a chance to check your work. The recording will be played once only. The test is in four sections.

Now turn to Section 1 on page 100 of your book. You will hear a student called Ian telling his friend about the public library. First you have time to look at questions 1 and 2. You will see that there is also an example which has been done for you.

Now we shall begin. You should answer the questions as you listen because you will not hear the recording a second time. Listen carefully and answer questions 1 and 2.

Woman: Hi Ian. I was looking for you. Where have you been?

Ian: I went to the public library in the town centre. There's a book I need for my science project. They haven't got it at the college library, so I went to see if they had it in the public library instead. It's much bigger than the college library and I soon found what I was looking for. But they've got a really good sports section and so I decided to have a look round. I found a really good book on the history of cricket.

Woman: Gosh. I never thought of going in there. What else have they got?

Ian: Well, not just books actually. There's online access, of course, but also newspapers and magazines you can read, and a noticeboard with lots of information about local events. Actually, I saw a notice about a photography club that meets there every week – sounds interesting. There's a room there where they have lectures and meetings and stuff.

Woman: Right. I didn't know that. I'll have to go in one day.

Ian: Come with me tomorrow if you like. I'm going back to pick up a book I ordered. If they haven't got the one you want, they can get it from another library in 48 hours. So, I ordered one I need to read for my course.

Woman: Wow. That's brilliant! So, are you going to join the photography club?

Ian: I haven't decided yet. I want to ask how much it costs. So, are you going to come tomorrow?

Woman: Yeah, why not!

Presenter: Before you listen to the rest of the conversation, you have some time to read questions 3 to 10. Now listen carefully and answer questions 3 to 10.

Ian: Oh look, here's a leaflet I picked up about events at the library. You see the photography club is on Mondays, at seven thirty in the evening.

Woman: Oh, right. And look, it tells you how much you have to pay – £2.50 a week.

Ian: That's not much, is it?

Woman: No, in fact all the events are quite cheap. Look. On Tuesday evening there's a storytelling workshop at seven o'clock, and that's only £1.50.

Ian: Oh, I wouldn't be interested in that.

Woman: No, but I am. My friend Jane's really into storytelling. I must tell her. And look, on Thursday at two p.m. there's an Internet club, and that's only £1.50.

Ian: But everyone knows how to use the Internet. Who would go to that?

Woman: Well, it's in the afternoon, so it's probably for old people.

Ian: Yeah, you're right. Look, on Thursday evening there's a film club. It starts at quarter to eight. That sounds more like our sort of thing.

Woman: But look at the price – £8.50 a week. The college film club's only £5.00 and I expect they have the same films.

Ian: Yeah, you're right.

Woman: But look, on Friday, they have a poetry workshop. That's at seven forty-five too, and only £3.00. I think I'd like to go to that.

Ian: OK. And on Saturday mornings there's a course in website design. That sounds more interesting than the Internet one, and it only costs £4.75 a week.

Woman: But look, it starts at ten fifteen in the morning. You never get up before lunchtime on Saturdays! Look, there's map reading in the afternoon. That would be better for you. It's cheaper too – only £2.75 – and you'll be awake by then because it doesn't start till a quarter to three.

Ian: Very funny. I can get up early if I need to.

Woman: Really?

Presenter: Now turn to Section 2 on page 101 of your book. You will hear a woman called Hilary talking on the phone about a job interview she is going to have. First you have some time to look at questions 11 to 15. Now listen carefully and answer questions 11 to 15.

Man: Hello. Southdown College, personnel department. Jon speaking.

Hilary: Oh, hello. My name's Hilary Brown. I've applied for a job in the accommodation office at the college.

Man: Ah yes, and we've invited you for interview, haven't we? On Tuesday, I think.

Hilary: That's right. Only in your voicemail message you said it would be on Monday.

Man: Ah, yes. Here it is. Yes, some people are coming on Tuesday and Wednesday, but your interview is actually on Monday at ten o'clock in the morning.

Hilary: Oh good. I was actually ringing to ask where I should come to. How do I find the personnel department? Is it in the main building?

Man: Well, the personnel department is in another building actually, but we're not holding the interviews here. When you arrive at the college, go to the main reception and ask for room 341. They will give you directions.

Hilary: I see. Thank you. And will I meet the accommodation officer? Diana Cook is her name, I think.

Man: Not on Monday, actually. One of her assistants, Howard Green, will be interviewing you, and Wendy Bright will be interviewing the people on the other days. She's the other assistant. Did you particularly want to meet Mrs Cook?

Hilary: No, no, I just wanted to know the name of the person.

Man: I see.

Hilary: And another question. What should I bring with me to the interview?

Man: Let me see. Ah yes. I have your application form here.

Hilary: Do I need to bring a copy of the form?

Man: No, that's not necessary. But I see you haven't attached a photograph. So if you could bring one with you, that would be useful. Just a passport-sized one is enough.

Hilary: Oh yes, of course. Do I need to bring an identity document at all?

Man: Yes please. We have checked your qualifications online, so we don't need to see certificates or anything, but we do need to check your identity.

Hilary: And written references?

Man: We have those here on your file already. So I think that's everything. Shall I send you an invitation letter confirming all these details?

Hilary: Oh, yes please. That would be great. Thank you.

Man: No problem.

Presenter: Before you hear the rest of the conversation, you have some time to look at questions 16 to 20. Now listen carefully and answer questions 16 to 20.

Hilary: And could I just ask you one or two questions about the job itself?

Man: Of course you can. What would you like to know?

Hilary: So the job title is office assistant?

Man: That's right.

Hilary: And what will I actually have to do each day?

Man: Well, the office assistant is responsible for entering data onto the computer network. There is some photocopying to do, that's the other main activity, and there will be telephone calls to deal with. But the office assistant does not deal directly with students or with the accommodation providers.

Hilary: I see. And the hours?

Man: Well, it's only a part-time post. Let me see. We said ten hours a week on the advertisement.

Hilary: Oh yes, that's right. I'd forgotten. And how much per hour would I earn?

Man: The basic rate of pay is £8.00 per hour. If you work evenings or weekends, it goes up to £8.50, but that doesn't apply to this job, because it's just weekday mornings.

Hilary: And do I get paid holidays?

Man: Yes. Twenty-two days a year, plus public holidays if they fall on days when you would normally be working.

Hilary: I see. Thank you, you've been very helpful.

Man: That's OK.

Presenter: Now turn to Section 3 on page 102 of your book. You will hear part of a talk about keeping rabbits as pets. First you have some time to look at questions 21 and 22. Now listen carefully and answer questions 21 and 22.

Nancy: Hi there. I'm Nancy Ronson and the subject of my talk this evening is keeping rabbits as pets. Rabbits are very cute animals, and we often think that they make great pets, especially for young children, because they're easy to look after. But actually, they need looking after quite carefully and this takes up quite a bit of time and costs quite a bit of money. So before buying one as a pet for a child, you need to think quite carefully.

First of all, however, a few facts about rabbits. Wild rabbits are very common animals that you can find living in many parts of the world. The rabbit is very common in Europe, and is also found in Asia and Australia, but most of the world's rabbits, around 50% of them, actually live in North America. This is strange because in South America there aren't very many at all!

In the wild, rabbits live for quite a long time. The oldest wild rabbit ever recorded lived to be eighteen years old, but ten to twelve years is more normal. This surprises people. When they buy a pet rabbit, they think it's going to live for maybe five years or so, but actually pet rabbits live just as long as wild ones and so you need to think about this before you buy one.

Presenter: Before you hear the rest of the talk, you have some time to look at questions 23 to 30. Now listen carefully and answer questions 23 to 30.

Nancy: So now I want to tell you exactly how much time you need to look after a pet rabbit properly and how much it costs to keep one.

First of all, don't just buy one rabbit. They feel sad and lonely living alone, that's why it's always better to buy two. So, if a child has two rabbits to look after, how long does that take? Well, I would say it's going to take one hour every day, because there are a number of things to do.

Firstly, you have to give the animals their food and water. Then it is necessary to clean the place where they live. This is something you have to do every day if you want the animals to stay well. Indeed, you need to check their basic health every single day, and make sure that they get some exercise in a safe area where they can run up and down.

So what about costs? Actually buying two rabbits in the first place is going to cost you about £50. Then having microchips fitted, to identify them if they get lost or stolen, will cost another £50. The young rabbits will then need vaccinations to protect them against common diseases – the vet has to do these – and those will cost £100.

Then your rabbit will need somewhere to live. A good rabbit house costs £250 to buy, and you do need a good one if you want your pet to be comfortable and secure. Then you need to buy equipment to go inside the house. A bowl for water costs £8 and one for food costs £12. These are the essential things, but if you want to buy other things, like toys or ramps to walk up, you could spend another £20 very easily.

The food that the rabbit eats, a mixture of green vegetables and special pellets, costs £16.36 each week. Fortunately, the water comes free, and so does the newspaper you can put down each day to help keep the house clean.

The other major expense is insurance. You need this in case your rabbit gets ill and needs to go to the vet. An insurance policy will cost £10 per month. But it is worth it because the vet can be very expensive.

Therefore, if your rabbits live for ten years, and you add up all these costs, then buying two rabbits and looking after them for their whole lives will cost you an incredible £16,000! Think about that, and the time needed to look after them properly, before you go down to the pet shop to buy one!

Presenter: Now turn to Section 4 on page 103 of your book. You will hear a sports coach giving a lecture to some students about training for a five-mile running race. First you have some time to look at questions 31 to 34. Now listen carefully and answer questions 31 to 34.

Man: Hi there. Thanks for coming. I know that you're all planning to run the five-mile race for charity that's taking place later this term. I want to give you a training programme that will help you to develop your fitness and stamina gradually. This means running every week, or actually a combination of walking, jogging and running to begin with, so that you can build up to your target distance.

So, what should you do each week? Well, the important thing is the time you spend training. It doesn't matter what distance you run, or how fast you run at the beginning. But what is important is to spend a fixed period of time each day.

Now this doesn't have to be fast running. At the beginning, jogging is much better. So, what do I mean by jogging? Jogging is something you can do alone or with a partner, and if you do it with a friend you can talk as you jog. If it's difficult to talk, then you're running not jogging – so slow down! Jogging is a relaxed type of activity, it shouldn't make you feel tired or out of breath.

Now at first, you should go jogging every day. People always ask me about other sports training, but my advice is simple. If you do, say, football training one day a week, then you still need to go jogging that day as usual, but you don't have to give up the football training!

And people also ask me about the best place to go jogging. Well, it isn't necessary to run around a sports track. The local park is fine. And jogging on grass is much better for your feet than jogging on hard roads and pavements. It's better to be away from the traffic too!

Presenter: Before you hear the rest of the lecture, you have some time to look at questions 35 to 40. Now listen carefully and answer questions 35 to 40.

Man: So, how does the training programme continue? Basically the programme lasts for eight weeks. Gradually, over that time, you will do more running and less jogging, so that by weeks six and seven you're getting close to running your target distance comfortably.

People often ask me what they should wear for this type of activity, and there are some simple rules to follow. You should wear shorts – the type that you see cyclists wearing are best – rather than the type that footballers usually wear.

You will need good shoes, but the ones you usually wear for sports training are best. You should, however, buy special socks. There are some on the market that are specially designed for runners and they will help you to keep your feet in good condition.

In general, don't wear clothes made out of cotton as they will make you feel too hot. There are suitable clothes for runners made in different types of man-made fibres, and they're not too expensive.

When you're training, you need to look after yourself. For example, if you start to feel hungry this probably means that you need something to drink. Generally speaking, water is the best thing in this situation and it can be a bad idea to eat anything.

If, however, you find that you've caught a cold, then you should stop training until you feel better. If you force yourself to continue, it will be longer before you feel better. You can soon make up for lost time once you're well again.

OK, so before I go on to …

Answer key

Unit 7

7a (pages 94 and 95)

1
1 fly 2 drive 3 cycle 4 take 5 sail 6 travel

2a
Land: bicycle, car, drive, train, walk, wheels
Sea: boat, sail, ship
Air: aeroplane, fly, hot air balloon, wings

3
1 didn't survive 2 didn't stop 3 didn't return
4 didn't travel 5 didn't enter

4
1 A air B sea C somewhere else (space)
2 A aeroplane B ship C satellite

5
1 A 2 A 3 B 4 A 5 B 6 A 7 A

6
1 What did Orteig offer in 1919?
2 When did Charles Lindbergh fly from New York to Paris?
3 How long did the journey take?
4 When did five ships leave Spain?
5 Where did Magellan die?
6 At night, what did people look for in the sky?
7 How many times did it travel round Earth?
8 When did it enter Earth's atmosphere?

7b (pages 96 and 97)

1
1 d 2 b 3 a 4 c

2
1 6 million 2 3.5 3 15,000 4 200,000 5 1,000
6 13,000 7 1,500

3 and 4
1 are longer than any other bird
2 are more dangerous and difficult
3 is colder than other parts of the world
4 for longer than two hours

5
1 shorter 2 easier 3 bigger 4 busier 5 cheaper
6 sadder 7 wetter 8 nicer

6
1 cheaper 2 hotter 3 more expensive 4 faster 5 safer
6 older 7 better 8 worse

7 and 9
1 My brother is shorter than me.
2 Walking is slower than cycling.
3 I think rock climbing is more difficult than surfing.
4 Giraffes are taller than elephants.
5 Camping is cheaper than staying in a hotel.
6 Canada is bigger than Iceland.
7 A taxi is more expensive than a public bus.
8 Cities are more crowded than towns.

7c (page 98)

1
a 2 b 1 c 3

2
1 F 2 T 3 F 4 F 5 T 6 T 7 F 8 T

3
1 shortest 2 easiest 3 biggest 4 slowest 5 cheapest
6 fastest 7 saddest 8 nicest

4
1 highest 2 best 3 largest 4 shortest 5 most populated
6 furthest 7 easiest 8 busiest

7d (page 99)

1
1 journey 2 travel 3 trip 4 travel 5 trip 6 journey

2
1 a 2 d 3 e 4 b 5 c

3
1 a 2 b 3 b 4 c 5 a

7e (page 100)

1
1 a blog b website 2 a writer b blogger
3 a online b homepage 4 a upload b download
5 a comment b post

2
1 The bus was cancelled so we waited for the next one.
2 The flight was cancelled because the weather was terrible.
3 The food was hot and spicy so we drank a litre of water with our meal.
4 The meeting was long and boring because the managing director spoke for two hours!
5 The restaurant didn't take credit cards so I paid with cash.
6 The hotel restaurant was closed so we went into the centre of town for a meal.

3
Example answer:
I took a train across the country. We went past mountains and there was snow. Suddenly we stopped. The train couldn't move because there was snow on the line. It was night. We spent hours on the train and it was very cold. Fortunately, a man on the train had a guitar and he played songs. Everyone sang to the music. In the morning it was sunny and finally the train started moving again.

Wordbuilding / Learning skills (page 101)

1
1 The journey was very/really good.
2 The food was very/really good.
3 The meetings weren't very interesting.
4 The party was really great!
5 The weather was very/really bad.
6 It wasn't very sunny.
7 The meal was very/really nice.
8 The hotel was really amazing!

2
1 c 2 a 3 b

4
1 They sailed to America in the *Mayflower* in the 17th century.
2 The *Mayflower II* sailed to America in 1957.
3 The *Silver Queen* took 44 days to fly from to Cape Town.
4 The saiga travels 35 kilometres per day.
5 The tree frog migrates 30 metres.
6 The loggerhead turtle travels 14,000 kilometres in fifteen years.
7 Voyager took off in 1977.
8 Jupiter is 349,000 kilometres from Earth.

Unit 8

8a (pages 102 and 103)

1
1 boring 2 noisy 3 crowded 4 colourful 5 fun

2
1 F 2 F 3 T 4 T 5 F 6 F 7 T 8 F

3
1 eyebrow 2 eye 3 nose 4 ear 5 lips 6 cheek 7 chin

4
1 beautiful 2 long 3 curly 4 dark

5
1 have got 2 're 3 has got 4 has got 5 's

6
1 lips 2 eyebrow 3 ugly 4 mask 5 cheeks 6 straight
7 blonde 8 handsome

8b (pages 104 and 105)

1
1 b 2 e 3 a 4 c 5 d

2
1 No. 2 England. 3 The United States. 4 A reservation.
5 Red, yellow and purple. 6 It's very warm.
7 Red and black. 8 Long, black hair. 9 Selling things.
10 Her dress and her hat.

3
1 We like buying new clothes. 2 Your new dress is like mine.
3 These shoes are like my old ones. / My shoes are like these old ones. 4 I don't like my uniform.
5 This hat is like a cowboy hat. 6 Jason likes wearing jeans.

4
1 Sentences 1, 4, 6 2 Sentences 2, 3, 5

5
1 isn't wearing, 's wearing 2 's buying, isn't selling
3 isn't making, 's designing 4 isn't playing, 's reading

6
1 What's he wearing?
2 Is Trisha buying or selling clothes?
3 What is Georgio designing?
4 Is he playing a computer game?

7
1 comes 2 're staying 3 take 4 are (you) standing
5 Do (you) know 6 'm walking 7 Are (you) learning
8 Do (you) like

8
1 hat 2 dress 3 shoes/boots 4 jumper 5 shirt
6 belt 7 skirt 8 socks
Mystery word: trousers

8c (page 106)

1
1 deer ✓ 2 squirrel 3 zebra ✓ 4 elephant 5 lion ✓
6 butterfly ✓ 7 chameleon ✓ 8 polar bear 9 Arctic fox ✓
10 giraffe

2
1 Yes 2 No 3 No 4 Don't know 5 Yes 6 Yes 7 No
8 Don't know

3
1 foot 2 hand 3 neck 4 back 5 leg 6 shoulder
7 knee 8 arm

8d (page 107)

1
1 A family. 2 Dinner. 3 The boy.
4 Serious (and perhaps they are hungry).
5 Because of the women's hats and clothes.

2
1 This photo 2 On the right 3 in the middle
4 in front of her 5 The family looks 6 They are wearing
7 I think 8 The photo is interesting

4
1 t 2 w 3 d 4 b 5 h 6 k 7 e 8 n

8e (page 108)

1
1 UR 2 4u 3 CU 4 2day 5 b4 6 Weds 7 @ 8 RU
9 GR8 10 pls 11 l8 12 sry 13 thx 14 <3 15 4get
16 atm 17 :-) 18 w/e

2
1 pls come on weds
2 RU :-) 2day?
3 Sry I'm l8
4 R we meeting @ w/e?
5 I <3 the film
6 I have GR8 news!
7 Call me b4 U leave
8 CU l8er

3
Example answer:
A: Sry I'm l8 :-(
B: Where RU?
A: On the train atm. Where RU?
B: I w8ing 4U @ the cinema
A: Can we meet l8er?
B: What time?
A: @ 2?
B: 2 is ok. I'll w8 in the café
A: OK. CU there.
B: tks

Wordbuilding / Learning skills (page 109)

1
1 Put on 2 get up 3 eat out 4 Look at 5 turn off
6 Go back 7 Take off 8 look up

3
T: put on, look at, turn off, take off, look up
I: get up, eat out, go back

4
1 In the Philippines. 2 'Capgrossos' or large masks.
3 In Papua New Guinea. 4 In ice. 5 Tattoos.
6 Chris Rainier. 7 Reinier Gerritsen. 8 Emoticons.

Unit 9

9a (pages 110 and 111)

1
1 actor 2 actress 3 screen 4 audience 5 front row
6 aisle 7 back row 8 seat

2
1 romantic comedy 2 horror 3 documentary
4 animation 5 Science fiction 6 comedy

3
1 d 2 b 3 c 4 a

4
1 a 2 b 3 a 4 c 5 a 6 b 7 c 8 c

5
1 d 2 b 3 e 4 c 5 f 6 a

6
1 'm going to watch 2 're going to play 3 's going to buy
4 's going to meet 5 're going to have 6 're going to make

7b
1 /tə/ 2 /tə/ 3 /tu:/ 4 /tə/ 5 /tu:/ 6 /tə/ 7 /tu:/ 8 /tə/

9b (pages 112 and 113)

1
1–3 actor, audience, musical
4–7 actor, audience, film, screen,
8–9 artist, painting
10–12 audience, music, musicians
13–14 novel, writer

2
●•: artist, novel, painting, theatre, writer
●••: actresses, cinema, gallery, musical
•●•: director, musician

3
1 e 2 c 3 d 4 h 5 a 6 g 7 b 8 f

4
1 I'm going to borrow this book to read about film-making.
2 I'm going to download this song to listen to it.
3 I'm going to book tickets to see a play.
4 I'm going to buy this film to watch it later.
5 I'm going to evening classes to learn French.
6 I'm going to drama school to study acting.

5
1 to make his next film
2 to live there for two years
3 to play their new songs
4 to watch a TV documentary
5 to show the artist's most famous paintings
6 to book tickets

9c (page 114)

1
1 butterflies 2 trees 3 fruit 4 kangaroos 5 mountains
6 leaves 7 Rock 8 sea

2
The book: 1 The play: 2 The film: 3

3
1 T 2 F 3 T 4 T 5 F 6 T 7 F 8 T

9d (page 115)

1
1 To a meeting. 2 They are free. 3 Tomorrow night.
4 He's working late. 5 At seven. 6 Outside Max's work.

2
1 Do you want 2 would you like to 3 I'd love 4 Are you
5 I'm sorry 6 Let's meet 7 That's 8 See you

3
1 ☺ 2 ☹ 3 ☺ 4 ☹

4
Students' own answers.

5
1 're meeting 2 'm wearing 3 're going 4 are you going
5 's talking 6 'm not taking 7 's working
8 aren't playing

6
1 F 2 P 3 F 4 P 5 P 6 F 7 F 8 P

9e (page 116)

1
1 loud 2 worried 3 well 4 very old 5 beautiful
6 delicious

2
1 sounds 2 tastes 3 feels / felt 4 look 5 smells

3
Example answers:
1 The Alhambra is a new Middle Eastern café in the centre of town. Its sandwiches taste delicious. There's a nice mix of old and new furniture and the staff are very friendly.

2 *War Horse* is a play at the theatre about a horse called Joey in the war. The horse looks amazing on stage and also it's a really interesting story. My only negative comment is the music. It sounds very loud.

3 *Digital Hero II* is a new computer game. The graphics on the screen look modern but I felt a bit bored at times. I think that's because it isn't very different to *Digital Hero I*.

Wordbuilding / Learning skills (page 117)

1
1 student 2 musician 3 writer 4 painter 5 explorer
6 artist 7 director 8 manager

2
1 watching 2 listen 3 on 4 at 5 much 6 play
7 interesting 8 handsome

3
a 4 b 6 c 7 d 1 e 8 f 2 g 3 h 5

Unit 10

10a (pages 118 and 119)

1
1 technology 2 astronomy 3 zoology 4 biology
5 physics 6 chemistry 7 neuroscience

2
1 physics 2 astronomy 3 technology 4 zoology
5 neuroscience

3
1 a download b CD 2 a library b search engine
3 a map b sat nav 4 a podcast b radio 5 a text b send

4
1 c 2 a 3 b

5
1 Have you ever used 2 've used 3 have you ever made
4 haven't 5 've never seen 6 've done 7 has 8 has left
9 have pressed 10 Have you switched 11 haven't

6
Students' own answers.

7
a 4 b 5 c 3 d 5 e 3 f 5 g 3 h 4

8
a I've printed the photos.
b She hasn't sent a letter.
c They've booked tickets.
d Have you ever learned Spanish?
e No, I haven't.
f Has he sent the email?
g Yes, he has.
h It hasn't worked today.

10b (pages 120 and 121)

1
1 b 2 d 3 a 4 c

2
1 Reason 1: as a historic city with lots of interesting places to visit. Reason 2: for difficult roads.
2 Because visitors become lost in the old streets.
3 In 1865. 4 Two years. 5 No. 6 No.
7 The hippocampus. It's the part that stores memories.
8 It's bigger than in the brains of other people.

3
1 a 2 c 3 a 4 c 5 b

4
1 buy 2 bought 3 paid 4 put 5 put 6 sent 7 forget
8 made 9 read 10 win

5
1 read 2 won 3 buy/win 4 send 5 put/read
6 paid 7 forgotten

6
1 Have, taken, took 2 Have, studied, studied
3 Have, taught, taught 4 Have, learned, learned
5 Have, written, wrote

10c (page 122)

1
1 iPod 2 vacuum cleaner 3 wheel 4 knife 5 electricity
6 sticky tape 7 fire 8 Internet

2
a 3 b 1 c 6 d 7 e 2 f 5 g 4 h 8

3
First question: c
Second question: a
Third question: b

4
1 Ten points each. 2 In 1901. 3 They are short and long.
4 In the first century. 5 North and south. 6 Blue team.
7 Fourteen. 8 Twelve.

10d (page 123)

1
1 a 2 c 3 a 4 b 5 b

2
1 g 2 b 3 d 4 e 5 a 6 h 7 c 8 f

3
1 three 2 Insel 3 A 4 afternoon 5 seven

10e (page 124)

1
1 at 2 dot com 3 slash 4 dash 5 www dot
6 double slash 7 colon 8 dot org 9 underscore
10 dot co dot uk

2
1 h_schmitt@hotmail.co.de
2 www.concordia.com
3 www.instolisten.org/dailypod-2

3
1 Call Stacey back.
2 Send everyone a letter.
3 Take Mr D'Souza to the station.
4 Book a table for two.
5 Buy more paper.
6 Print these photographs, please.
7 Email the designs to g_rich@gmail.com.
8 Telephone the hotel.

4
1 Name of caller: Lisa Farrell
Message for: Dr Nakao
Message: Meet her in the hotel reception at 2pm.
2 Name of caller: Richard Nowitz
Message for: Dan Moore
Message: Email the designs before 12 tomorrow.
His email is r_nowitz@nowitz.com
Urgent ✓
3 Name of caller: Max Lloyd
Message for: Christine
Message: Friend of George. He's interested in renting the room. Call him on 0990 768 2238 or email him: m36.lloyd@hotmail.co.uk

Wordbuilding / Learning skills (page 125)

1
1 send 2 Study 3 memorise 4 Search 5 show 6 find
7 call 8 stop working

2
1 a forget b remember 2 a take b leave 3 a teach b learn
4 a receive b send

4
Example answers:
a biology, technology, zoology
b email, text, letter
c email, search engine, satellite navigation
d public telephone, postcard, sticky tape

Unit 11

11a (pages 126 and 127)

1
1 camping 2 sightseeing 3 backpacking 4 hiking

2
1 return ticket 2 sightseeing 3 check in, carry on 4 rent
5 tour guide 6 souvenirs 7 book

3
1 Yes 2 Yes 3 Don't know 4 No 5 Don't know 6 Yes
7 Yes 8 No

4
1 b 2 e 3 f 4 c 5 d 6 a

5
1 should 2 shouldn't 3 should 4 should 5 shouldn't
6 should

6
1 You should book a hotel room.
2 He shouldn't work late.
3 Should we buy a ticket here?
4 She should check in her bag.
5 You shouldn't rent a car.
6 What should we eat?

7
Hi!
I've booked my tickets and I'm arriving on the 21st! Before I arrive at your house, I'm going to travel round the country. Should I rent a car or go by public transport, do you think? Also I'm going to spend some time in the capital. What should I see there? And should I book my hotel in advance? Can you give me any advice? Oh! And what's the weather like? Is it cold? Should I bring lots of clothes?
See you soon!
Mike ☺

8
Example answer:
Dear Mike
I'm really happy that you are coming to my country. Here is my advice:
When you travel round the country, you should go by public transport because it's cheaper than a car and there are lots of buses and trains.
In my capital city, you should see the parliament buildings and the old castle.
For hotels, I think you should book the hotel online. It's very easy.
At the moment the weather is very cold, so you should bring a warm coat!
See you soon!

11b (pages 128 and 129)

1
1 e 2 b 3 a 4 f 5 d 6 c

2
1 A motorbike. 2 No. 3 Asia. 4 A coat and a jumper. 5 England. 6 People drive on the left (or 'the wrong side') and the signs were difficult to understand. 7 Everyone. 8 The US embassy in your country. 9 A phrase book. 10 In smaller towns. 11 Before. 12 For 'big things' like a hotel or a meal in a restaurant.

3
Across: 1 climate 3 visa 5 zones 6 licence 7 cultural
Down: 1 currency 2 hand 4 illegal

4
1 a 2 c 3 b 4 c 5 c 6 a 7 b 8 a

5
1 flight DL3345 have to go to
2 You cannot carry, in your bag.
3 in business class do not have to wait in
4 with children can get on the plane

6
1 /hæftə/ 2 /hæftə/ 3 /hæftə/ 4 /hæf tuː/ 5 /hæftə/
6 /haef tuː/

11c (page 130)

1
They talk about Greece and South Korea.

2
1 Do 2 Do 3 Don't 4 Do 5 Don't 6 Don't 7 Do
8 Do

3
1 thing 2 where 3 body 4 thing 5 body 6 where
7 thing 8 body

4
1 anybody 2 something 3 nowhere 4 Everything
5 everybody 6 somewhere 7 Somebody 8 anything

11d (page 131)

1
1 F 2 T 3 T 4 F 5 T 6 T 7 F (Marie thinks it's expensive.) 8 F

2
1 Can I make a suggestion?
2 You should go to Morocco.
3 You could travel on your own.
4 Why don't you go with a tour?
5 How about going on a package holiday?

3
a 5 b 4 c 2 d 3

5
1 bus /ʌ/ 2 book /ʊ/ 3 you /uː/ 4 but /ʌ/ 5 should /ʊ/
6 food /uː/ 7 cruise /uː/ 8 could /ʊ/

11e (page 132)

1a
1 Did 2 Was 3 How many 4 How 5 Would 6 Were
7 What 8 Why

1b
a 3 b 1 c 4 d 2 e 5 f 8 g 6 h 7

Wordbuilding / Learning skills (page 133)

1
1 manager 2 photograph/photo 3 photographer
4 study 5 backpacker 6 visit 7 visitor 8 cook
9 design 10 designer

2
1 manage 2 photograph/photo 3 student 4 backpack
5 visitor 6 cooker 7 designer

3
photograph (3) / photo (2) photographer (4)
backpack (2) backpacker (3)
visit (2) visitor (3)
study (2) student (2)
cook (1) cooker (2)
design (2) designer (3)

4
1 b 2 a 3 f 4 c 5 d 6 e

Unit 12

12a (pages 134 and 135)

1
1 Arctic Circle 2 North Pole 3 Northern hemisphere 4 Equator 5 Antarctic Circle 6 South Pole 7 Southern hemisphere

2
1 c 2 b 3 e 4 a 5 f 6 d

3
1 14,000,000km^2 2 0°C 3 2.5 l 4 30% 5 130m 6 419,455kg

4
1 e 2 a 3 d 4 b

5
1 a 2 b 3 c 4 b 5 c 6 a 7 c 8 a

6
1 cars will 2 houses will 3 children won't
4 the summer won't 5 the winter will 6 people won't

7
1 'll 2 'll 3 will 4 'll 5 will 6 will 7 'll 8 'll

12b (pages 136 and 137)

1
1 island 2 Ocean 3 forest 4 mountain 5 Lake 6 Sea 7 River 8 Desert

2
1 the 2 the 3 Ø 4 Ø 5 Ø 6 the 7 Ø 8 Ø 9 the 10 Ø 11 the 12 Ø 13 the 14 the 15 the

3
2 Which ocean is ~~the~~ Madagascar in?
4 Where is ~~the~~ Lake Vostok?
6 Where is ~~the~~ Mount Ararat?

5
1 b 2 d 3 a 4 c 5 e

6
1 old 2 high 3 tall 4 well 5 long 6 fast 7 far

7
1 43 2 39km 3 100m 4 really well 5 ten minutes 6 1,342km/h 7 31km

12c (page 138)

1
1 star 2 planets 3 orbit 4 Astronomers 5 surface 6 rock 7 travel

2
1 c 2 a 3 d 4 b

3
1 Astronomers 2 orbits 3 Earth 4 humans 5 discovery 6 exoplanets 7 star 8 planets 9 universe

12d (page 139)

1
1 Jamaica. 2 The first Friday. 3 50,000 4 Everyone from schoolchildren to business people. 5 In local parks and communities. 6 In the gardens of a home for old people. 7 Have the same day.

2
1 c 2 g 3 b 4 a 5 f 6 d 7 e

3
1 Today, I'd like to talk about an important day.
2 First of all, my country's national day is on 4th July.
3 Since then, people have always celebrated this day.
4 Nowadays, everyone has a day off.
5 Next, families have a big meal together.
6 In conclusion, I really think it's important.

12e (page 140)

1a
Possible answers:
1 Everyone ~~is~~ invited ~~to our~~ New Year's Party!
2 ~~The~~ Annual Party ~~is~~ at ~~the~~ Town Hall on 1st May.
3 ~~There is a~~ huge sale at ~~the~~ Big Bed Shop ~~all~~ this week.
4 ~~You can~~ eat delicious sandwiches at Jill's Café.
5 Visit ~~the website~~ www.greenfest.org for details.
6 ~~The~~ entrance to ~~the~~ disco ~~is~~ free.
7 ~~Listen to~~ live music and ~~look at~~ local art at ~~the~~ Mayberry Arts Festival.
8 ~~You are~~ welcome to ~~our~~ Midsummer Party at nine.

b
Possible answer:
You are invited to plant a tree on 7th October for National Tree Planting Day. We will give you free seeds to plant in the local park. There will be lots of people there and lots of entertainment, so bring the whole family. We'll have hot and cold food, and local shops will sell environmentally friendly products. We'll also have presentations about how to help the environment and information about gardening. The event is in Tenant Park, and it starts at two o'clock and it finishes at five o'clock. The entrance is five euros for adults and free for children under 16. You can telephone us on 088 678 4955 for more information.

Wordbuilding / Learning skills (page 141)

1
1 depth 2 height 3 weight 4 length 5 width

2
1 a long b length 2 a height b high 3 a weight b weigh
4 a deep b depth 5 a wide b width

3
Adjectives: long, high, deep, wide
Verb: weigh* (note the adjective for weigh/weight is 'heavy')

6
1 914 trillion litres – the Earth's rainfall every day
2 47 metres – the depth of the Black Hole of Andros
3 2009 – the year James Cameron made the film *Avatar*
4 18 trillion – distance in kilometres between the Earth and Gliese 581g
5 20 million – the number of people at the first Earth Day in 1970

IELTS practice test

Listening

1 C I saw a notice about a photography club
2 B I'm going back to pick up a book I ordered.
3 Tuesday On Tuesday evening there's a storytelling workshop
4 £1.50 and that's only £1.50
5 Internet on Thursday at two p.m there's an Internet club
6 Thursday on Thursday evening there's a film club
7 £8.50 look at the price – £8.50 a week
8 7.45 That's at seven forty-five too
9 Website on Saturday mornings there's a course in website design
10 £2.75 It's cheaper too – only £2.75
11 A your interview is actually on Monday
12 A When you arrive at the college, go to the main reception …
13 B Howard Green … will be interviewing you
14 B/F we do need to check your identity.
15 F/B a photograph … if you could bring one with you, that would be useful
16 photocopying There is some photocopying to do
17 (tele)phone calls and there will be telephone calls to deal with
18 10 / ten ten hours a week
19 £8.00 The basic rate of pay is £8.00 per hour.
20 22 days Twenty-two days a year
21 C most of the world's rabbits … live in North America
22 B but ten to twelve years is more normal
23 one hour it's going to take one hour every day
24 clean It is necessary to clean the place where they live
25 health you need to check their basic health every single day
26 £50 Having microchips fitted will cost another £50
27 £250 A good rabbit house costs £250 to buy
28 Equipment Then you need to buy equipment to go inside the house.
29 £12 one for food costs £12
30 month £10 per month
31 C what is important is to spend a fixed period of time each day
32 B a relaxed type of activity
33 A you don't have to give up the football training
34 B The local park is fine and jogging on grass is much better for your feet.
35 eight weeks the programme lasts for eight weeks
36 cyclists the type that you see cyclists wearing
37 socks You should buy … special socks.
38 cotton don't wear clothes made out of cotton as they will make you feel too hot
39 drink this probably means that you need something to drink …
40 cold If … you've caught a cold, then you should stop training until you feel better.

Reading

1 C six days a week
2 C £5.50 per hour
3 E weekly bus ticket to the city centre provided
4 B free meals when on duty
5 B uniform provided
6 A supermarket cashier
7 C ability to speak French or Spanish an advantage
8 F temporary contract (six weeks)
9 D possibility of extra hours next month
10 C you have to work in a team
11 TRUE carried out a survey … as part of their course
12 TRUE city residents … a sample of local inhabitants
13 FALSE asked them all the same questions
14 NOT GIVEN
15 FALSE About 12% of the people they asked
16 TRUE In second place in the list was swimming … and in third place came keep-fit exercises
17 FALSE a few very keen walkers who go for long walks in the countryside
18 TRUE walking holidays are the most popular of all
19 FALSE There were an equal number of men and women going on walking holidays
20 FALSE Boating holidays … are the ones where you find the largest number of single people.
21 viii Cycling holidays are much greener than holidays by car, train or plane
22 ix a company which makes all the arrangements in advance
23 v It's up to you what distance you want to cover every day
24 i It isn't necessary to be very strong to ride a bike, but you should be in good health.
25 ii a range of options when it comes to how long to stay away and how to make sure you have a bed for the night
26 iv Holiday companies sometimes arrange for your suitcases to be sent on … This means that you only need to carry a few things
27 iii How much your holiday costs will depend on which type you choose.
28 Scotland Cycling in Scotland, for instance, where there are lots of hills, will give you a good physical workout. But if that sounds too much like hard work
29 centre-based where you return to the same hotel every evening and can have a good meal and a shower
30 March March is the typical month for the birds to arrive.
31 July back again … normally in July
32 C The young cuckoos are born in England.
33 C all spent the winter in the Congo region of central Africa
34 A Lyster flew across France, Spain and Morocco before crossing the Sahara desert
35 B Lyster flew back to England via Algeria … Chris also crossed the Algerian desert
36 C They put a tiny satellite tag on each bird's back to see where they went when they left England.
37 B The three other birds did not return to England and the scientists think they died on their return journey.
38 C the five tagged birds all travelled about 10,000 miles that summer.
39 C Algeria were countries that the other three birds flew over … Chris/Lyster flew back … via Algeria
40 A Lyster flew across Spain … flew back via Algeria … but this time didn't fly over Spain

CREDITS

Text:
The publisher would like to thank the following sources for permission to reproduce their copyright protected text:

Reproduced with kind permission; Dr Adrian Seymour for details on pages 36 and 37, and interview on page 91. Reproduced with kind permission; and Telegraph Media Group Limited for material on page 46 from '50 things killed by technology', *The Telegraph*, 12 December 2011, © Telegraph Media Group Limited 2011; and Telegraph Media Group Limited for an extract from "Landmark cuckoo project reveals bird's migration mystery" by Roya Nikkhah in *The Sunday Telegraph* 6 May 2012, copyright © Telegraph Media Group Limited, 2012.

In some instances we have been unable to trace the owners of copyright material and we would appreciate any information that would enable us to do so.

Photos:
The publisher would like to thank the following sources for permission to reproduce their copyright protected photos:

Cover: Simon Wong/Getty Images

Inside: pp 9 (B. Anthony Stewart/National Geographic Image Collection), 10 (Peter McBride), 12 (Shutterstock), 13 tl (RIA Novosti/Alamy), 13 tm (Shutterstock), 13 tr (Shutterstock), 14 (Shutterstock), 15 t (NASA), 15 b (NASA), 17 Digital Nomad logo (National Geographic Image Collection), 17 Andrew Evans (Andrew Evans), 17 br (Truck stop/Alamy), 18 (Nasa/dpa/Corbis), 20 (North Wind Picture Archives/Alamy), 21 (Mario Babiera/Alamy), 22 (Tino Soriano/National Geographic Image Collection), 23 (Roy Toft/National Geographic Image Collection), 24 tr (Joel Sartore/National Geographic Image Collection), 24 b (J Carrier/Redux/eyevine), 26 (Shutterstock), 27 (Mike Powell/Getty Images), 28 (Reinier Gerritsen), 30 (Travel Pictures/Alamy), 32 (Sir Juan Pablo), 33 (Annie Griffiths/National Geographic Image Collection), 106 tr (South Pacific Pictures Limited; Photographer: Jae Frew), 34 bl (Aleksei Vakhrushev), 34 br (Courtesy of Merva Faddoul), 108 (Courtesy of Adrian Seymour), 37 (Courtesy of Adrian Seymour), 38 (Art Directors & TRIP/Alamy), 39 tl (Agra Art, Warsaw, Poland/The Bridgeman Art Library), 39 ul (Bight River Country, 1992, by Ginger Riley Munduwalawala/Art Gallery of New South Wales, Sydney, Australia/Mollie Gowing Acquisition Fund for Contemporary Aboriginal/Art 1992/The Bridgeman Art Library), 39 ml (V&A Images/Alamy), 39 br (Oli Scarff/Getty Images), 40 (Kike Caho/National Geographic Image Collection), 41 (Ambient Images Inc./Alamy), 42 (Frans Lanting Studio/Alamy), 115 (Mark Carwardine/Peter Arnold/Getty Images), 117 (Harry Sieplinga/HMS Images/Getty Images), 46 (Raul Touzon/National Geographic Image Collection), 48 (Maggie Steber/National Geographic Image Collection), 49 tl (AFP/Getty Images), 49 bl (Nicole Glass), 51 t (Jung von Matt/Alster/Mercedez-Benz), 52 (Oliver Eltinger/Corbis), 54 (Randy Olson/National Geographic Image Collection), 55 all photos (Tom, Dick and Debbie Ltd), 56 (Shutterstock), 57 (Gary Arndt/National Geographic Image Collection), 59 tl (Rolf Nussbaumer Photography/Alamy), 59 ml (Borge Ousland/National Geographic Image Collection), 59 bl (Nigel Hicks/National Geographic Image Collection), 60 mr (Shutterstock), 60 bl (Panoramic Images/National Geographic Image Collection), 62 (Shutterstock), 63 (Keenpress/National Geographic Image Collection), 64 (Edward Parker/Alamy), 66 (Kazuyoshi Nomachi/Corbis), 67 (Raul Touzon/National Geographic Image Collection), 68 (Gagarin Cosmonaut Training Center/CNP/Corbis), 69 (Ira Block/National Geographic Image Collection), 73 (epa european pressphoto agency b.v./Alamy), 73 (Picture Perfect/Rex Features), 75 tl (Shutterstock), 75 tr (Shutterstock), 75 b (Stocktrek Images, Inc./Alamy), 76 (Todd Gipstein/National Geographic Image Collection), 77 (Shutterstock), 78 (Jorge Santos/AGE Fotostock/Getty Images), 79 (Shutterstock), 80 (Thomas J. Abercrombie/National Geographic Image Collection), 81 tl (Eye-Stock/Alamy), 81 mr (imagebroker/Alamy), 82 (Reinier Gerritsen), 94 tr (ClassicStock/Alamy), mr (Alberto Lowe/Reuters/Corbis), 95 (ITAR-TASS Photo Agency/Alamy), 96 tr (Frans Lanting/National Geographic Image Collection), mr (Shutterstock), br (James Forte/National Geographic Image Collection), 98 (Brian J. Skerry/National Geographic Image Collection), 99 (JurgaR/E+/Getty Images), 102 (Kenneth Garrett/National Geographic Image Collection), 103 l (20th Century Fox/The Kobal Collection), r (Carmen Morosan /National Geographic Image Collection), 104 a (Martin Gray/National Geographic Image Collection), b (Steve Raymer/National Geographic Image Collection), c (Bildagentur-online/McPhoto/Alamy), d (David Evans/National Geographic Image Collection), e (Bruce Dale/National Geographic Image Collection), 106 deer (Shutterstock), squirrel (Shutterstock), zebra (Shutterstock), elephant (Shutterstock), lion (Shutterstock), butterfly (Shutterstock), chameleon (Shutterstock), polar bear (Shutterstock), Arctic fox (Shutterstock), giraffe (Shutterstock), 107 (George F. Mobley/National Geographic Image Collection), 113 (Bryan Smith/National Geographic Image Collection), 114 ml (Geraint Lewis/Alamy), bl (Dreamworks SKG/The Kobal Collection), r (Egmont Publishing), 116 tl (Shutterstock), tr (Shutterstock), ml (Shutterstock), mr (Shutterstock), bl (Shutterstock), br (Shutterstock), 120 br (tony french/Alamy), b (Kevin Wheal/Alamy), 122 iPod (Neil Fraser/Alamy), vacuum cleaner (Shutterstock), wheel (Shutterstock), knife (Shutterstock), electrical circuit (Shutterstock), Sellotape (Shutterstock), fire (Shutterstock), internet (Dinodia Photos/Alamy), Morse code (Shutterstock), compass (Shutterstock), Marconi (World History

Archive/Alamy), 123 (Cultura Creative/Alamy), 126 b (Signe Lansky),mr (Doug Lansky), 129 (Emory Kristof/National Geographic Image Collection), 130 tl (Terry Harris/Alamy), ml (Alex Zuccarelli/Alamy), 131 (Rachel Carbonell/Alamy), 133 (Shutterstock), 134 (NASA Archive/Alamy), 136 tl (Stocktrek Images/Getty Images), tr (Shutterstock), ul (Frans Lanting/National Geographic Image Collection), ur (Beverly Joubert/National Geographic Image Collection), ll (NASA/Corbis), lr (Shutterstock), bl (Hemis/Alamy), br (Dean Conger /National Geographic Image Collection), 137 bl (© Red Bull Media House), b (Red Bull Media House), 138 (Antonio M. Rosario/The Image Bank/Getty Images), 139 (Paul Barton/Corbis)

DVD photos: Shutterstock (unit 8)

DVD videos: National Geographic Video Collection (units 7, 9, 11, 12)

Illustrations by Peter Cornwell pp 105, 111; James Gilleard (Folio Illustration) pp 16, 26, 58, 81, 96, 100, 127; Matthew Hams pp 25, 34, 101, 119, 140; Alex Hedworth (Eye Candy Illustration) pp 105, 111; Bob Lea pp 51, 72, 74; David Russell pp 11, 71, 117, 134; Martin Sanders p 61; Laszlo Veres (Beehive Illustration) pp 31, 109, 118, 120, 141